ONLY IN AMERICA

From Immigrant to CEO

**by Paul Oreffice
with Tom Hanlon**

Stroud & Hall Publishers
P.O. Box 27210
Macon, GA 31221
www.stroudhall.com

The paper used in this publication meets the minimum requirements
of American National Standard for Information Sciences—
Permanence of Paper for Printed Library Materials.
ANSI Z39.48–1984. (alk. paper)

Library of Congress Cataloging-in-Publication Data

Oreffice, Paul, 1927-
Only in America / by Paul Oreffice.
p. cm.
ISBN 0-9745376-7-5 (hardcover : alk. paper)
1. Oreffice, Paul, 1927
2. Italian Americans—Biography.
I. Title.

E184.I8O74 2006
973'.04924045092--dc22

2006005153

TABLE OF CONTENTS

Dedication

I dedicate this book to all young people to let them know that in America you can overcome obstacles, you can achieve and even exceed your goals.

I dedicate this book to all immigrants to let them know that if they learn English and become part of our society anything can happen.

The USA is the land of opportunity and it is a society unique in the history of the world. Only in America could someone like me arrive as an immigrant speaking almost no English and become the CEO of a major company. Only in America.

I also dedicate this book to my wonderful wife JoAnn who inspired me and pushed me to write it. My hope is that the book will inspire others to reach for the sky, knowing that it can be done.

Acknowledgments

I need to thank many people who helped me with this book but three in particular stand out.

My wife JoAnn who conceived the idea and then made sure that I kept to the task.

My agent Kathy Lubbers who first said to me "You should write a book and I can help you with it." She was my guide, the voice of experience in a business that I don't really understand, a friend always ready to help me and lead me over the hurdles.

My coauthor Tom Hanlon who not only organized and greatly improved my original material but also guided me all the way through the project. Tom was outstanding at asking the right questions to prod my memory so that I could visualize what it was really like even when I was ten or twelve years old.

This book would not have happened without these three great people.

PART I
A CHILDHOOD INTERRUPTED

∝

CHAPTER ONE

Black Shirts

In some ways it all seems so long ago; in other ways I can remember it as if it happened yesterday.

Venice, Italy, September 29, 1939. I had gotten ready for bed and trudged into the living room to say good night to my parents. I found only my mother there, standing at the second-story window, peering into the darkness below. The flagstones of Calle Scaletta were bathed in yellow street lamps; beyond the calle moonlight bounced off the water of the canal.

"Where's Papá?" I asked. My sister, Sandra, had come in behind me, hurried along by our nursemaid, Fraulein Grete Grossman, who stood in the doorway. We all looked questioningly at my mother, who turned to face us. She forced a smile.

"He'll be home soon," she said. "He probably got a good hand tonight. Come give me a kiss."

We gave her a kiss and went off to bed. It was true that my father played cards in the evening, before coming home for supper, but it was also true he was never late—no matter how good his hand was. I was eleven years old, old enough to see my mother try to mask her concern. Sandra, four years older than me, looked doubtful too, but she didn't say anything.

He wasn't home when we got up the next morning. "Where is he?" I asked again, this time a little more insistent. Our cook, Maria Baraga, was setting breakfast in front of us: breads and pastries with butter and homemade jams, bananas imported from Africa. I watched her face as she set the food on the table; she avoided looking at me, perhaps because she didn't want me to see the worry in her eyes. Maria had a rough exterior and a heart of gold. She would often make treats for Sandra and me without my mother's approval.

"He's on a business trip," my mother said.

"He left already? Without saying goodbye?"

"He . . . he never came home last night. He called after you were in bed."

I watched my mother for a few moments before turning to my food. It was odd that he wouldn't have come home—that he would rush off on a trip like that—but my mother's behavior was odder still.

She was calm, unperturbed on the outside. But she looked away from me when she told me about his not coming home. And she wasn't eating. She had some bread and jam on her plate, and she moved it around a bit, but she didn't bring it to her mouth.

"Eat, children," Grete said. And we ate. We did what we were told. And, of course, we believed our parents. We had no reason not to.

This pattern continued for several days. My mother picked at her food; she had no appetite. We thought she was coming down with something, a mild flu. Faint circles grew under her eyes. She found it harder to smile. She spent a lot of time looking out the window, unless she was aware that Sandra or I were around. We'd ask her when he was coming home and she'd say he wasn't sure. You know him, she'd say. When he's got a deal going he's not going to stop until it's time to stop.

This was true. My father was an entrepreneur extraordinaire. He was a man of the land, a visionary; he could take marshland, land that hadn't yielded a crop in centuries, and he could drain the land, build dams and sluiceways to control and redirect the water, and coax life out of the land. He was like a midwife for the earth, expertly and gently drawing life from it, producing crops on thousands of acres that had heretofore been home only to bog, bug, and peat moss. Perhaps he was surveying the land near Grosseto or Massa Marittima in Tuscany, or Fermo or Jesi in Marche.

It was hard to say, my mother told us. Her tone was, *And don't pry further.* We children had our bounds. We were given glimpses into the adult world, but glimpses only.

∞

A week went by, then ten days. Still no father, still no word. My mother continued to hide her worry, but it was reflected in the eyes of Grete, of Maria, of our maid, Angela.

On the twelfth day, when Sandra and I got home from school, Grete was there to meet us, but Mom was gone. She was typically home when we got home from school, but I wouldn't have been so worried had it not been for my father's hazily-explained "business trip." Grete was many things, all of them wonderful, but she was not an actress. The worry that my mother had managed to suppress fairly well in front of her children came popping out on Grete's brow.

Reading this worry caused a panic to rise in my throat. "Where's Mamma?"

"She was called away. She'll be back soon."

I looked doubtfully at Grete, who loved me as her own child. She shooed me into the kitchen where Maria had some fresh-baked cookies and orange juice ready for Sandra and me. Sandra and I asked a few more questions, but we knew the answers already. Sometimes communicating with adults was like my father's work with the land: adults built dams to control the flow of information, sluices for the words to all flow in a certain direction, to connote just the meaning intended, and nothing more. *She'll be back soon* was all we would get out of Grete. We simply had to wait—and hope Grete was right.

She was. Mom returned late in the afternoon. When we heard her walk in, we ran to greet her, relieved to see her. She smiled, though it appeared to be an effort to do so.

"I have some news for you about your father." She looked first at Sandra, then me. She looked us squarely in the eye; no more avoiding our questioning gazes. This time, the truth—the fuller version—would come out. The sluice-ways were being redirected; we were to be let in on some adult secret.

"Papá is in jail," Mom said. I don't know what I had been expecting; this time of mystery had been a gray fog for me. This pronouncement didn't clear the fog. (Sandra told me, years later, that she was almost happy to hear this news; she had begun to think that Dad had run off with another woman.)

"Jail! Why is he in jail?" I said.

"He is in jail," my mother said evenly, gaining strength from her anger, "because the Fascists see him as a troublemaker."

She went on to tell us about Italy's dictatorial regime, which brooked no dissension, and that my father was in jail because he had dissented, but I couldn't comprehend what she was saying. It was too ludicrous. The racial laws, enacted the previous year by Benito Mussolini, Italy's dictator, had had a negligible effect on our lives to this point. We had been forced to change schools, to go to an all-Jewish school. This didn't bother me. The classes were taught by ousted Jewish university professors; the education was actually better than my old public school.

The effect was no longer negligible. They had yanked my father from our house and thrown him in jail.

❧

Mussolini—who gave himself the title *Il Duce,* meaning, literally, "The Leader"—was a Machiavellian figure in every sense of the term. He used people and issues—for example, early on he was vociferously against Catholicism, but as he gained power he realized the support he could garner from Catholics and shamelessly did an about-face, proposing that Catholicism become the official state religion. He played on public senti-ment according to his immediate desires and needs. He brought fascism to Italy, he consorted with Hitler when he felt it was to his benefit (though he later came to hate and fear the German chancellor), and he, in more suave and charismatic fashion than his German counterpart, demanded the rever-ence of his people. He feasted on the nationalistic fervor that his Fascist regime stirred in conservative, antisocialist Italians; he became bloated on his own power. He had a three-dimensional likeness of his face, twenty feet from forehead to chin, erected on the side of Rome's Fascist headquarters. This face, with furrowed brow and steely gaze, scowled at people passing by in the huge plaza down below. The face was surrounded by one word, repeated over and over again in five-foot-high letters, on the entire side of the building: *Si.* Yes. *Yes, you will support my regime. Yes, you will rally to Fascism. Yes, you will hail me, revere me, honor me, for I am your Il Duce.*

Mussolini changed colors like a chameleon. In 1912, he became editor of *Avantil!,* a Socialist Party newspaper in Milan. He decried World War I as imperialist, but soon reversed himself and called for Italy's entry into the war on the Allied side. The socialists kicked him out of their party, and he became editor of his own newspaper in Milan, called *Il Popolo d'Italia* (The People of Italy). This paper later became the organ for his Fascist movement, which began in 1919, following World War I. Mussolini helped found the *Fasci di Combattimento* in March 1919; this later became the *Partito Nazionale Fascista*, the National Fascist Party. Fascism began as a curious blend of socialism, populism, and nationalism. In postwar Italy, with mothers and wives grieving the loss of sons and husbands, with the country in economic turmoil, and with the five million returning veterans feeling alienated—in fact, the veterans were prohibited from joining the Socialist Party—people were upset, angry, ready for change.

Mussolini sensed this and seized the opportunity. He appealed to the factory workers, the common laborers, the trade unions; he spoke with power and charm of Italy's return to its rightful place among the elite European countries. He stirred the embers of dissent, and he rode the crest of this dissent in the March on Rome on October 28, 1922. About 25,000 Italians took part in this march, which installed Mussolini in power. Fascism was seen by its party members, whose ranks were swelling daily, as the antidote that Italy needed to reverse its downward trend, to revive its economy, to restore its dignity and place in Europe and in the world.

It is telling that Mussolini expressed pride in his coming to power through illegal and violent means. Far from shying away from violence, he revered it, for he found it a useful tool in "convincing" those—like my father—who were not supportive of his dictatorial regime.

⚭

My father, Max Leone Oreffice, never wasted time looking back, bemoaning injustices, second-guessing himself, or plotting revenge on those who had done him wrong. He looked forward, planning and plotting business ventures, seeing opportunities where others saw nothing, cutting boldly through life with an energy that others could get swooped up by, or left far behind. That's why it was somewhat plausible to me that he could be gone at the drop of a hat for twelve days on a business venture.

It's also why he didn't spend a lot of time, in later years, talking about his experience during those twelve days. Years later he was to tell me this:

I received notice from Ludovico Foscari to come and meet with him. Foscari was head of the Fascists in Venice; more than that, he had been my friend. I knew him well, but I also knew that nothing good could come of this visit. It was not as friend that he summoned me, but in his official role as head of the Venetian Fascists. I knew I could not avoid this meeting. And so I went, dressed in a coat and tie, as always. I had nothing to hide.

His tribunal was in downtown Venice. I was escorted into his office by two guards with faces like stone. No light shone from these faces; all the life had been sucked out of them. Despite myself, I became quite nervous. I felt with each passing step that I was entering a place of evil, a place of darkness.

A door slammed shut. I was alone with Foscari. He of course wore the black uniform of the Fascists. He glared at me for several moments. I recognized this as his first attack on me; he was trying to break me down with this glare. A slight sneer curled his lips; he had a terrible secret that I knew he would divulge, in his time.

"Confess."

"Confess to what?"

"Do you say you have nothing to confess to?"

"What are you talking about?"

He kept telling me to confess. He never said what I should confess to. I saw this was a game that I couldn't win. I said with finality, "I have nothing to confess to. Charge me with something or let me go."

He pressed a buzzer on his desk. The two guards who brought me in entered. Foscari nodded to them. They grabbed me and one opened a bottle of castor oil. He poured it down my throat while he and the other guard held me down. I gagged and choked, but much of the oil slid down my throat. I sprayed oil in their faces as I spit out what I could. They began beating me—not for spitting, but because that was next in their routine. They used the santo manganellos, *the "holy cudgels" they used to beat people with. They beat my back, my ribs, my arms, my shoulders, my face. I fell to the ground. This gave them the opportunity to kick me. After a while I blacked out. I was dragged from the room, bloodied, senseless, full of my own excrement because of the castor oil. When I'd regain consciousness they would beat me some more. I was in another room but I don't know where. I only dimly remember being moved.*

This went on for what seemed an eternity, but in all likelihood was a couple of hours. It's hard to say. After a while, I mercifully stayed passed out.

When their enthusiasm flagged because I was no longer conscious to feel the sting of their manganellos, and perhaps because it was time for their dinner, they dragged me to a boat and took me to a jail across the canal. I came groggily to when they dumped me in solitary confinement, left me in a pile of my own blood and excrement.

"Should have confessed," one of them said as they clanged shut the door. I heard their laughter trail down the hallway. I closed my eyes and wished I could lose consciousness again.

✂

My father could read people. He knew when to press an issue, when not to. He could sense vulnerability, leanings, hesitation. This served him well in business, and it served him well in jail.

Several of the guards who brought him his meager food and water had the same stone faces and hard looks of the guards who beat him in Foscari's offices. But one had a look of softness about his eyes, a hesitant and faintly compassionate look. Perhaps he did not agree with imprisoning people for political reasons, when no charges had been brought against them. Perhaps he felt stuck in his role, which had changed significantly since Mussolini came to power.

My father saw this look in the guard's eyes, and he went to work. A smile, a nod of thanks for the stale bread and weak soup. Then casual conversation: the weather, the guard's background. The guard's love of soccer. *Ah, my son, Paul, loves soccer too!* And so my father introduced the concept of family, of a wife and two children who were worried about him, who had no idea of his whereabouts. This idea gnawed at the guard's conscience. My father would inquire about the guard's family. And express concern for my mother, for Sandra and me. *You can get word to them,* my father said. *You can set their minds at ease. Imagine your wife being taken, or one of your children, and you not knowing. They need to know where I am, that I'm alive. Tell them. Will you not tell them?*

∞

My father broke down that jail guard better than most guards break down prisoners—and without, of course, using physical violence. The guard called my mother on the twelfth day of my father's disappearance, told her where my father was being held, told her the words she longed to hear: *he is alive.* Fearing for his own life, he never revealed his name to my mother. That didn't matter. She rushed down to the jail, where she was allowed to briefly see my father, see the bruises on his neck and face. Her initial shock at seeing him in this condition was overcome by her relief that he was, indeed, alive.

"You've got to get me out of here," he said. He told her to be frank with Sandra and me, to tell us the truth. "They need to know." Another veil was to be dropped between our sheltered children's world and the adult world. Sandra and I were to grow up quickly in those years.

My mother, Elena Friedenberg Oreffice, was four-foot-eleven, though when questioned about her height, she would thrust her shoulders back and proudly proclaim that she was five feet tall. And you have to understand this about Italian women back in the 1930s: they were in charge of the house, but Italian families were very patriarchal. Women didn't work outside the home, as a general rule, at least in the middle and upper-middle classes of society. We had a comfortable life, not lacking for anything, up to my father's false imprisonment. A woman's place in Italy was to run the home, more or less in the manner in which her husband was accustomed or desired; she had dominion in certain home matters, but her place was not in political or legal arenas, speaking out on issues, decrying injustices. There was an almost invisible line between the world of men and of women at that time, and most women knew not to cross that line, and indeed didn't care to cross it.

This didn't matter to my mother. Energized by finding my father alive, released from the pressure of having to keep up a false front with Sandra and me, she went to work to free my father from his cell. She worked tirelessly, making phone calls, knocking on doors, tracking down people who could help her. She traveled to Turin, to Milan, to Rome, meeting with influential friends and public officials, pleading her husband's case. Nothing the more reluctant or pessimistic officials could say would deter her from her mission. If they were helpful, she retained them and used their help; if they were unwilling to help, she discarded them and sidestepped them. In our coal furnace at home, she burned any papers that the Fascists might use to show that my father was active in the fight against fascism, should they raid the house.

In the meantime, my father was allowed to write us one letter a week—censored by prison officials—and my mother alone was allowed to visit him, on Sundays. Apparently we kids were seen as too subversive, or perhaps the guards felt threatened at the thought of being approached by a four-foot-eleven (excuse me: five foot tall) woman flanked by two children. It was all ludicrous and in its own warped context it all made sense. Twisted logic had become the norm for Fascist Italy in the 1930s.

In his weekly letter to us, my father would usually include some math problems for me to work out, or some crossword puzzles that he had made up. He often had to write these letters on toilet paper. Perhaps the paper's stiffness made it less than desirable for its intended use, but my father, in his typical way, made creative use of what he had and used it as jail stationary. He wouldn't tell us anything about being imprisoned; instead he would focus on what was going on in our lives. He was, even in jail, looking ahead, keeping positive. "How are the foals coming along?" he'd write. We raised horses; he loved horses and passed that love down to me. "Have you named the two new fillies yet?" He would ask how my tennis was coming along, was I playing soccer, how my studies were going. I had injured my finger while he was in jail, and he wrote, "It's an awful long time that we don't see each other, but I know from your mother your finger's doing better and soon you can be riding your bike and playing tennis." Rather than bemoan his fate and burden us with worry about him, he focused on the good things in our lives.

Because of this response, we became used to him being gone; we didn't like it, but we adapted to it. Mom was a picture of calmness, strength, and resolve through the ordeal, and Sandra and I took our cues from our parents. We looked forward; we tended to our daily lives; we were strong and positive. We carried on.

That's not to say I didn't miss my father; I did, terribly. At times, at night, I would lie in my bed, tears streaming down my cheeks as I wondered when he would get out, when we could ride our horses together again, when we would play checkers again, when we'd work on puzzles together. The days turned into weeks and the weeks began adding up with still no end in sight. We had no idea when he would be released. We tried to hold to a vague sense of fairness and justice, though that grasp was slipperier than it used to be. The logic, of course, went like this: *They can't hold him forever. He hasn't done anything wrong. They must be reasonable and release him soon.* That, plus my mother's relentless campaign to get him out, would surely do the trick— or at least in a fair and just world it would. But as the weeks passed, without us knowing whether he was any closer to being released than he was on Day One, my understanding of the fairness and justice in Fascist Italy began to change, and my worry began to grow.

In the end, my mother got the help she needed from a most surprising source: Galeazzo Ciano, Mussolini's son-in-law. Ciano was one of the highest-ranking Fascists in Italy; when my mother met with him, he was minister of foreign affairs. I still marvel at the thought of this diminutive woman visiting Mussolini's son-in-law and demanding that her husband be released. Whether Ciano was amused or impressed, or both, I don't know. But I do know my mother got his attention, because Ciano looked into my father's case. He met with Foscari, my father's erstwhile friend who had ordered him beaten and imprisoned. Foscari did not want to release my father, saying he was a traitor to his country, a political insurgent who was outspoken in his contempt for Mussolini and his Fascist regime.

"On what charges is he being held?" Ciano asked.

Foscari had not been idle in preparation for this meeting. "There are twenty-five charges against Max Oreffice, including one of defamation against *Il Duce* himself."

"And what is the charge of defamation?"

"He said that one of his horses was smarter than Mussolini."

"Release him. Bring him to trial, if you want, but in the meantime release him."

I wasn't there, of course, but I like to think that a small smile crossed Ciano's face when he heard that this "political insurgent" was being held on charges that included a horse being smarter than his father-in-law. It's significant to note that Ciano was relieved in February 1943 of his post by his father-in-law because Ciano was strongly opposed to making Italy subservient to Germany. Later that year Ciano led a group who voted to overthrow Mussolini. In January 1944, German troops captured Ciano and he was handed over as a trophy to Mussolini's Italian supporters, who executed him.

∞

Sandra and I came home from school one day in mid-November 1939; Grete, who had been watching for us, opened the front door to let us in. She had a strange look on her face—one of excitement and of worry. "Go into the living room," she said, and we dropped our books on a table in the entryway and rushed into the living room.

My father's grim face broke into a broad smile when he saw us; he was sitting on the divan with my mother. We cried out and ran to him and gave him hugs. I felt his bristly whiskers against my face. I pulled back to look at him again and hoped my worry was hidden. I was extremely happy to see him, of course, but I understood the worry in Grete's eyes: the six weeks in jail had not helped his appearance any. Here was a man who, even when riding horses, dressed in a pressed shirt, a tie, a sharply-tailored coat, and a hat; he had always been trim and athletic with a clean, healthy sheen to him and a sharp eye. Now his face was gray, with that scraggly growth of beard, and his eyes were sunken; he looked emaciated. His clothes were dirty rags. He looked like a beggar Grete had taken in.

But he was home. He was home, he was alive, and that was all that mattered.

He saw the questions and concern in our eyes. "I'm fine," he said. "I'm home, thanks to your mother. I'm home, and in a few moments I'm going to clean the filth of the prison off me and throw these rags out. But first, tell me," he said, looking at me, "How's your riding coming?"

"Very well."

"And how many boyfriends do you have?" he asked Sandra, a twinkle in his eye.

"None right now."

"You watch, they'll be at the door in no time."

I had a hundred questions for him, but none could find their way through the tangled maze of my mind. I was too choked with emotion at seeing my father—and at seeing how different he looked. All I could think was how horrid his time must have been in that tiny cell. A grimness hung on him like fine soot. I had never seen that before. I also saw the familiar, positive side of him. I felt I was seeing him through a kaleidoscope. I was having trouble piecing the images together, drawing, as it were, a new composite of my father, a composite that had partly been etched by the Fascist regime.

I quickly learned that he was released, but not freed: he was under house arrest. Upon his release earlier that morning, he had been given orders: return to his home at Calle Scaletta 6039, straying neither left nor right. This direct path had brought him by Piazza San Marco during midday; as he made his way past the Piazza on the side of the basilica, he heard someone shouting, "Max! Max!" He turned to see his old friend Vilfrido Casellati, the mayor of Venice. As Casellati approached him, my father motioned to keep away, explaining that the mayor was endangering himself, because he, my father, was a political prisoner. To be seen consorting with a political prisoner—especially a Jew—was risky business in 1939 Italy. Casellati waved that off and gave my father a big hug, telling him how great it was that he had gotten out of jail.

"Great to be out, greater yet to stay out," my father said. He told Casellati of the trumped-up charges brought against him, of his impending trial, of the conditions of his release.

"They have nothing on you, Max. You'll find justice still resides in our courts."

"We'll see, Vilfrido. That's my hope and my belief." My father had not run much into justice in recent days, so his uncertainty was understandable. He looked over his shoulder. "Better go. You don't want to be seen hanging around with undesirables."

Casellati took hold of my father's shoulders and looked him in the eye. "Don't give in to fear. That's what they want."

❧

My father explained to us briefly what house arrest meant: he could not leave Venice unless he was given approval to do so, and was escorted by Fascist officials. He could not leave the house until it was light in the morning and he had to return before it became dark. Once it was dark he could not leave.

And the Fascist police would be checking on him every night, several times a night, to make sure that he was in the house, that he had not slipped out to meet with other subversives to plot the overthrow of the government. I suspect the Fascists were not so concerned about my father slipping out, but enjoyed the thought of disrupting our sleep and imposing their ugly presence in our lives.

"You mean they'll be coming here?" I asked. He nodded, and then changed the subject, because he didn't want to give the Fascists any more power in his house than they already had. A chill ran down my spine as I thought of seeing Fascist police, of seeing the faces of some of the people who were at least indirectly responsible for the beating and imprisonment of my father. To put a face on these criminals made it that much more personal for me.

Sure enough, at about 8 P.M. that evening, a sharp rap resounded on the door. Angela went to answer it, but my father—clean-shaven now, washed and dressed in freshly-laundered and pressed clothes that hung on him a bit with his lost weight—was not far behind; he knew who it was. I walked to the hallway, well behind my father but in view of the door. My mother came scurrying up and I stood behind her. My blood raced as Angela extended her hand to open the door; I knew in a few seconds I would be able to put a face to the people that had taken my father from me.

Angela opened the door to two Black Shirts—the name given to Mussolini's paramilitary squads, the Fascist police who used violence and terror as weapons against those who had the gall to oppose fascism. These Black Shirts had a menacing look about them—they were swarthy, which was more common of southern Italians; they were squat and powerful, with stubbly growths of beards. One had a thick mustache hanging over his lip. Everything about them—even the watery redness of their dark eyes—seemed menacing. Including the way they stomped loudly into the hallway, slamming down their dark boots as they stepped inside. My jaw dropped open as I saw them.

"Max Oreffice!" the one with the mustache barked.

"I am here." My father appeared unruffled, pleasant, smooth. With his reply, an electric surge of confidence shot through me; this was our house they had so rudely entered! This was my father they were speaking so rudely to! That my father replied so calmly made me almost want to laugh in glee. These Fascists were in our house, but they did not rule in it.

Angela skittered away, glad to get away from these Black Shirts, who proceeded to read my father a long list of rules that he had to abide by unless he wanted to be thrown in jail again. They told him the areas he could be in and when he could be in them. He could never leave the house after dark. My father nodded, smiled, assured them he would abide by the rules. The Black Shirts scowled; perhaps they hoped he would argue with them, give them something to tear into. They left, having completed their initial duty. My father closed the door and looked at my mother and me. Despite that surge of confidence I had felt earlier, my father saw the look of fear in my eyes.

"We cannot live in fear. That's what they want."

I nodded, but, try as I might, for a time I really dreaded the Black Shirts. They had taken my father, beaten him, thrown him in jail, and now put him under house arrest. I couldn't tell anyone my feelings about the Black Shirts; I felt I could no longer trust anyone outside my family, not even my closest friends.

∞

My father eventually had a bell installed by his bed. When the Black Shirts came in the middle of the night, they'd ring the bell, and he could respond directly, rather than having them wake the whole house.

The Black Shirts made these visits every two or three hours during the initial part of my father's house arrest. They would always come in pairs, whoever was on duty in that part of Venice at that time of night. Several pairs eventually made their way to our house—and more than a few made their way to our table, too. Ostensibly they were fulfilling their duty, making sure my father was there; but a sandwich of cold cuts and a glass of wine wouldn't hurt while they were there, would it?

While I didn't see these middle-of-the-night visits, I learned of them, and what I learned helped me to realize that not all Black Shirts were alike. Not all were stone-faced, hateful, unfeeling instruments of violence, unthinkingly bent on carrying out Mussolini's destructive methods in championing his regime. Some were pleasant, some were grateful for the food my mother prepared for them, some had a sense of humor, some were perhaps a bit afraid themselves—afraid of somehow stepping out of line with the Fascist party, afraid of raising the ire of *Il Duce*. Some were bored, some were sullen, some were, no doubt, depressed and melancholic. Perhaps some loved soccer, and horse racing, and playing checkers; perhaps they loved playing with their children, reading to them, taking them out for *gelato*.

It made me wonder even about the first two Black Shirts I saw: perhaps in another light (and out of those black uniforms that succeeded in their intent of helping them look so imposing) they were not so evil, so rude, so menacing. Perhaps, perhaps not.

The thought that they were caught up in something that was much larger than them, that they were pawns in a deadly game, entered my mind. This didn't absolve them of being responsible for their actions; I wasn't filled with compassion for them. But I began to see them, and the whole political situation, in a new light.

∞

It was Mussolini who first used the term *Fascism*. He did so in 1919, seizing on the social and political unrest after World War I and the Russian Revolution of 1917. *Fasci* means *union* or *league*. Its symbol—the fasces, a bundle of sticks bound to an ax—represents civic unity; it originated with the ancient Romans, and was a graphic reminder that Roman officials were free to punish those who were not in step with their state.

When Mussolini formed the *Fasci Italiani di Combattimento* in 1919, he assembled returning war veterans, revolutionary socialists, and futurists whose vision of a new Italy included a dramatic break from its past. The Fascist platform was crafted with leftist ideology, calling for government reform, increased workers' rights, and a redistribution of wealth. The shadow of fear and uncertainty that swept over postwar Italy proved to be the veil that Mussolini needed to rise to power.

He and the National Fascist Party presented fascism, of course, as the remedy Italy needed to be restored to health and power. When the Socialist Party orchestrated militant strikes in Turin and other industrial cities in the north, fascism was looked on in favor by greater numbers of Italians. Fearing that socialism would further damage their already weak economy, more and more Italians turned to fascism, swayed in part by Mussolini's rhetoric and promises.

Mussolini promised, in essence, the delivery of a revolutionary, modern state for Italy, through fascism; he promised health and prosperity for Italy; he promised harmony among workers, managers, and the state; he promised a glorious new state that would be the envy of the world, and a model which other countries would follow. In his "The Doctrine of Fascism," published in the *Italian Encyclopedia* of 1932, Mussolini states, "Fascism reaffirms the State as the true identity of the individual. . . . Outside the State there can be neither individuals nor groups (political parties, associations, syndicates, classes). . . . The nation is created by the State, which gives to the people, conscious of its own moral unity, a will and therefore an effective existence . . . . The Fascist State . . . is the form, the inner standard and the discipline of the whole person; it saturates the will as well as the intelligence. . . . It is the soul of the soul."

Looking back, it's amazing that people bought into his rhetoric and his fascist ideals; but Italians were unhappy with the present system, with the direction the country was headed, and the fascist ideals, the creation of a single-party state, the lure of a unified national identity and will, the promise of an end to political instability, economic woes, and worker struggles, soothed the minds of many Italians. Indeed, *Il Duce* presented fascism as divine intervention: "Fascism is a religious conception in which man is seen in his immanent relationship with a superior law and with an objective Will that transcends the particular individual and raises him to conscious membership of a spiritual society. . . . The man of Fascism . . . through the denial of himself, through the sacrifice of his own private interests, through death itself, realizes that completely spiritual existence in which his value as a man lies."

Mussolini stopped just short of saying he had personally been anointed by God to restore a purified Italy to its rightful place in the world.

Il Duce was true to his word: death did not stand in the way of his pursuit of a Fascist state. He effectively used violence in controlling the Socialists, and in 1925, he seized dictatorial powers after his Black Shirts murdered the socialist Giacomo Matteotti, an outspoken critic of his. Three years earlier, in the March on Rome where Mussolini threatened to stage a coup against King Victor Emmanuel III, the king had a chance to impose martial law and destroy the Fascists through military force. Instead, he offered Mussolini a position in the government, and Mussolini accepted. The rest, as they say, is history—and a sad portion of Italian history it is.

Those who did not live in those times, and especially those who did not live in Italy in the 1920s and '30s, reduce history to simple terms and wonder how Mussolini was able to come into power. You had to live through it, you had to be immersed in the political and social and economic turmoil, to be placed in the labyrinth of lies and empty promises, to understand why people could be swayed by this man and by fascism. And, for those of you who are quick to judge, remember this: the United States, Great Britain, and a great number of Italian Jews all found fascism, in its early stages, to be just what Italy needed. Mussolini enjoyed early successes; under him, the government built new stadiums and huge new buildings and monuments. It hosted large sporting events, it held grand parades and celebrations and rallies that were attended by hundreds of thousands of Italians; it created a new calendar of holidays that celebrated key events in Fascist history. The economy did begin to revive, and fascism was seen by many as the catalyst. *Il Duce* had duped Italy, and the rest of the world, and his Black Shirts were like the nails in the coffin of people who wanted to return to life without fascism. For Mussolini, there was no escaping, no turning back. Everyone was to get on board, or be thrown overboard.

∞

Il Duce may have duped Italy, but he had not duped my father. The Fascists boasted about the new roads they had built as a sign of improvement for the country; my father scoffed at this and told me, "If you want to see true improvement in roads, look at what they're building in America. In Italy, we are improving the roads by using slave labor from Libya and Somalia, and the ends do not justify the means. The United States has some roads with eight lanes and we keep strutting around saying we are the best because we have a few four-lane roads."

My father had a deep respect for America, even in the '30s, before he had visited the country himself. This respect tied in with American idealism and with capitalism, including the notion that hard work should be rewarded. He was a true Liberal—one who believed in liberty, in individual responsibility, and in free enterprise. In Italy he belonged to the Liberal Party, which was grounded in those ideals. (Today, the term "liberal" has been prostituted, especially in the US; what we call liberals today are people who *don't* believe in personal responsibility and who think that government should do everything for the citizens. What we now call "liberals" are really Socialists who don't want that term applied to them because of the implications of Soviet Socialism.)

Mussolini, of course, abolished many civil liberties through Fascism, ran a controlling, strong-armed government that leaned heavily on its people and closely watched their activities, and preached on the need to replace individual responsibility with the subjugation of the individual to the state. All this was in direct opposition to what my dad believed in, and was ready to fight for. Had King Victor Emmanuel been willing to stand up against Mussolini and his Black Shirts in the March on Rome in 1922, Max Oreffice would have been first in line to defend king and country. But Emmanuel sold out Italy for promises of added territories and titles, and this treason grated on my dad until the day he died.

As my father would see or hear of Mussolini speaking from yet another of his new palaces, his face would become grim and set and his eyes would harden. He always maintained control of his emotions, but it was not difficult to see when something upset him. "How can you justify spending so much money on *girigori* when people are starving?" he would growl. *Girigori* refers to excessive and frivolous thrills spent on anything. It essentially means opulent waste, and that is one way my father would describe Mussolini's reign.

My father could have despised Mussolini but played it safe and kept his mouth shut. That, however, was not his style. He refused to be muzzled, to be stripped of the freedom of expressing his own thoughts. He refused to be subjugated, as Mussolini demanded, to the will of the state—not when the will was so warped by such a madman.

And so he expressed his opinions. He expressed them without fear to the people around him: those who worked on his farm, and to his business partner, a silk baron from Como named Cugnasca. He expressed them because he refused to be bought out. To accept Mussolini's edicts, to acquiesce to his fascist ideals, was, in my father's view, to walk willingly into an open prison and swing shut the door behind you.

I am certain, if he had it to do over again, he would not remain silent. Through his silence he would have betrayed himself and lost self-respect. Instead, through his spoken words, he opened the door for others to betray him.

∞

My father's big farm project of the 1930s was *Prati Nuovi*, "The New Grass Fields" or "The New Lawns." *Prati Nuovi* was located on 2,800 acres about halfway between Venice and Trieste on the Adriatic Sea. When he took it over you could see large areas of marshland where the sea had seeped in, then receded, leaving behind a pale cloak of salt. Only about 250 acres were productive.

My father knew how to separate land from sea and withdraw the cloak of salt, but he needed financial backing. Enter Signore Cugnasca, who became my father's "silent partner," meaning he put up most of the money in return for 50 percent of the income. Cugnasca had been known to my mother's family for quite some time, and for seven or eight years was a good partner to my father.

Prati Nuovi, like other Italian farms, was run under the *mezzadria* system, in which the owner provided the land, a house for each family who worked the fields, the seed and fertilizer, and all the tools, equipment, and machinery. Each working family had property assigned to them, and the proceeds from the crops were divided evenly between the owner and the *mezzadros*, or the laborers. In many cases the *mezzadros* lived and worked on their farm for their entire lives. About a dozen such families lived on *Prati Nuovi*. Each family also had their own vegetable garden by their house.

Luigi Ghirardelli was the *fattore*, or supervisor, of *Prati Nuovi*. He lived with his wife and several children in a house my father had built for him on the farm. My father had given him more money in the ten years they had worked together than Ghirardelli had ever seen before. He also gave Ghirardelli the power to make many decisions when my dad wasn't around.

Ghirardelli came from the South of Italy, from poor people, and he was squat and strong. He had a swarthy complexion and, in retrospect, it appeared that he was trying to look like *Il Duce*, with his jutting jaw, stern visage, and short-cropped hair. But of course this in itself meant nothing at the time, and my father and Ghirardelli enjoyed a good working relationship for a decade before my father's troubles began. For his part, Ghirardelli had performed well as *fattore* of *Prati Nuovi*. Working together, my father and Ghirardelli had managed to increase the production from 250 acres to about 2,000 acres. *Prati Nuovi* was transformed from dead marshland to productive farmland, each year yielding bountiful crops of wheat, corn, rye, oats, beets, with smaller areas dedicated to beans, white asparagus, peas, potatoes, and grapes. The latter were grown in quantities sufficient for our needs and for those of the families living and working there. We just ate the grapes, but the other families made wine from them.

For a long time, my father didn't know who betrayed him, why Ludovico Foscari had summoned him, had him beaten and imprisoned. He had not been as careful as perhaps he ought to have been, given the political climate. He had expressed his antifascist views to Cugnasca and to Ghirardelli, to his neighboring farmer, Bastianello, who, along with his wife, were friends, and used to play cards with my parents, and to others. He had expressed his views whenever he felt like it, and he probably couldn't recount all the people to which he had he spoken about his disdain for fascism and for Mussolini. Regardless, it was apparent he had spoken to at least one too many. His views had landed him first in jail, and then, after my mother had been able to obtain his release, it landed him in court in February of 1940, where the prosecuting attorney asked for the death sentence. At the time, Sandra and I knew nothing of this; fearing for our psychological and physical well-being, our parents had sent us to a boarding school in Switzerland, keeping us clear of the tumult below. Only later did we learn of the proceedings.

At the trial, Bastianello was brought forth as a character witness for my father. As he took the stand, he refused to make eye contact with my dad. Bastianello placed his hands in his lap to keep them from shaking. He kept sucking on the ends of his bristly gray mustache; my father said he had a miserable, nervous look on his face. He blinked nearly nonstop, and would not look the defense attorney in the eye when the attorney asked him, "Do you know Mr. Oreffice?"

Bastianello licked his mustache some more and looked down at his hands before lifting his head and looking at no one as he said, "No sir."

The defense attorney was stunned. "You do not know Max Oreffice? You do not know this man right here?" the attorney said, pointing to my father.

Bastianello looked vaguely in my father's direction, still avoiding eye contact. "No sir. Not really."

"*Not really?* What does *not really* mean? You either know the man or you don't."

"Well, sir, my farm borders his, and I've seen him on occasion, but I can't say as I know the man."

It was my father's turn to be stunned. He had, after all, spent many evenings playing cards with this man and his wife! My father's head began to swirl. If the Fascists could beat him, lock him up for twelve days, conjure up charges against him, and his own friends could either turn him in or not stand up for him, then who was to say that the death sentence—as ludicrous as it seemed—could not be passed?

Not far into the trial, Luigi Ghirardelli was called to the stand. After the *fattore* of *Prati Nuovi* was sworn in, he sat fidgeting as he waited for the prosecuting attorney to question him. His eyes darted around the courtroom; he appeared greatly agitated and excited. My father was confused. If the *fattore* had been called as a character witness, why had the prosecuting attorney called him? Ghirardelli seemed impatient to speak, as if he had something of great importance to say. Even with the ten years of friendship, something about Ghirardelli's demeanor made my father brace himself.

After identifying himself and his relationship with my father, the *fattore* said, "Max Oreffice has spoken to me on numerous occasions about his disdain for Mr. Mussolini and for fascism."

"And how did he put it to you?" the prosecuting attorney said.

"He said that Mr. Mussolini was ruining the country, that fascism was Italy's shame, and he questioned Mr. Mussolini's intelligence."

"How did he question Mr. Mussolini's intelligence?"

"He said that one of his horses was smarter than Mr. Mussolini."

A murmur went through the courtroom. The prosecuting attorney smiled in satisfaction; Ghirardelli looked indignant and self-righteous. The judge released a weary sigh from his bench. My father stared incredulously at the *fattore*.

The prosecutor pressed on. "Do you have reason to believe Max Oreffice was conspiring against the state?"

"Max Oreffice is an intelligent man, and he knows a lot of people throughout the country," Ghirardelli said. "He is capable of trying to subvert the efforts of our government, to sway people to his antigovernmental stance, to undermine the efforts of Mr. Mussolini to restore the economy and rebuild Italy into a power once again. Why anyone would want to do this, I don't know. But if you are asking me is he capable of doing this, I would have to say yes, he is. Max Oreffice is capable of many treasonous acts, and is outspoken in his opposition to Mr. Mussolini and Fascism."

And so it was Luigi Ghirardelli who turned my father in, who alerted the head of the Fascists in Venice, Ludovico Foscari, that my father was a "menace to society," a rebel who refused to subjugate himself to the will of the state, who refused to bow to the dictator, who unfavorably compared the dictator's intelligence with that of a horse.

Ghirardelli was a big shot—or at least he considered himself so—in the fascist system of a small community. By turning in my father, Ghirardelli no doubt thought he would rise in the system. My dad had underestimated Ghirardelli's commitment to and passion for the Fascists and had overestimated their own relationship in working together for ten years. To work the land together, to take 250 acres of producible land and turn it into almost 2,000 acres of productive land, that meant something to my father. And he showed it in how he compensated Ghirardelli. But evidently, ten years of kindness, good treatment, and respect meant nothing to the *fattore*. Such was the zeal of Fascism in those days. It swept through Italy like the Plague, and Ghirardelli was one of those infected.

Ghirardelli's betrayal blindsided my father. All twenty-five charges that the *fattore* had helped conjure up were intended to build the airtight case that my father was a traitor to his country, that he was conspiring against Mussolini, and that he was a threat and a danger to Italy and perhaps even to Mussolini himself. There was no telling what a madman such as my father would do, given half a chance. Thus, better to kill him before he grabbed that chance.

The trial lasted two weeks. The twenty-five charges were all vague fabrications, like wisps of smoke that were blown in the judge's eyes. Rather than veil the judge from the truth, however, the smoke merely irritated him: he saw that the case was wasting the court's time. The judge dismissed all the charges. He castigated the prosecutor for clogging up the court system with such a flimsy case. Mayor Caselatti's words to my father proved to be true: justice did still reside in Italian courts. My father, breathing a sigh of relief, walked out of the courthouse a free man.

But free as an antifascist did not mean truly free. The Fascists had no real concerns about what the court said. My dad was met at the bottom of the courthouse steps by a man he did not know. The man blocked my father's path. "Oreffice?" he growled, with what seemed like a throat full of gravel. "Mr. Foscari has a message for you." The man turned his head and spat on the sidewalk, never shifting his eyes from my father's. "You are still under house arrest. Nothing has changed. You understand? Go home. We'll be watching you."

My father stared at this henchman for a long time. Then he slowly nodded.

"Mr. Foscari doesn't like you, Oreffice. Don't do anything to make him mad. He won't sit idly by next time. *Capisce bene*?"

My father gave a brief nod. Only then did the man take a half step to the side, allowing my father to pass.

"We have eyes everywhere, Oreffice."

∽

Not long after he was acquitted, my father had two interesting meetings. The first was with his business partner, Cugnasca. "I want to buy you out of *Prati*

Nuovi, Max," Cugnasca said. What Cugnasca offered to pay was an insult, not even worth ten cents on the dollar of my father's portion.

"You can't be serious," my father said.

"Take it or leave it. If you leave it, you'll be sorry."

"And why would I be sorry?"

"Because I know some people."

"What does that mean?"

"These people work outside the courts, Max. And it's dangerous for me to be associated with you. These people don't like people like you. You understand, I need to distance myself from you. The things you say, they can get you in trouble. And me too, because I am your partner. And I don't like to be in trouble."

"Then offer me a fair price for my portion."

"Considering your predicament, I'd say any price at all is fair."

"So you're in with them too?"

"I'm simply saying, Max, for your own good, you need to take this offer. You're a smart man. Surely you see the wisdom in this."

My father saw only greed and betrayal in Cugnasca's "offer." But he was convinced that the vague threat behind Cugnasca's words was real enough. My dad wanted no more trouble. And so he sold his stake in *Prati Nuovi* for a sliver of its worth.

A few months later my father's friend, Marcello Vaccari, the *prefetto,* who is the federal repesentative of the province of Venice, called my father to his office. Vaccari shut the door and offered my father a seat. My dad—who had regained most of his weight and looked healthy again, and as finely-tailored as ever—asked if there was a problem.

The *prefetto* slid open a desk drawer and pulled out some papers, placing them on the desk between himself and my father. "Max, these are papers ordering your *confino.* You are to be sent away for five years." *Confino* meant you were shipped to a town or an island in the southern part of the country, where you were confined by the Black Shirts, where every move was watched, where no family members could visit. It was a milder form of concentration camps—and indeed, most Italians placed in *confino* later died in German concentration camps.

My father looked into his friend's eyes, wondering if Vaccari would betray him as Ludovico Foscari had.

"I will hold on to these as long as I can, Max, but you must leave. Don't delay. Do you understand?"

∽

CHAPTER TWO

Life on *Calle Scaletta*

My father had no intention of delaying our departure from Italy. He had been through enough to know that his acquittal meant next to nothing, that he—and much more importantly to him, his family—was in greater danger as each day passed. He had been targeted once, and the Fascists had keen memories.

Still, it was anathema to him to flee; Max Oreffice was not accustomed to fleeing. Indeed, when Italy entered World War I on the Allied side in May of 1915, Max cut short his studies at the University of Wales Institute of Science and Technology in Cardiff to return to Italy and enlist. As a student, he was exempt from military duty, but he had no intention of staying out of the war. After a harrowing trip through a Europe already at war, he eagerly joined the Italian Army at the age of 23. It was a war, he wrote to me in a long letter many years later, "that we fought feeling sure that once we stomped the Germans we could go back to normalcy. . . . With the certainty that the triumph of our armed forces would bring the world freedom, tolerance, goodness, and prosperity, I fought the whole war with serene tranquility, a sporting spirit, and with extremely high morale even when the sacrifices of the moment didn't really paint a rosy picture."

Max became a captain in the Italian Field Artillery and was immediately sent to the alpine front. The mountainous terrain limited fighting between the Italian forces and the Austro-Hungarian and German forces to the Isonzo

River front near the Austrian town of Gorizia, which is on the Italian border. Max was in charge of a small group of Allies fighting several battles in the Isonzo Valley. After a patrol mission, Max's unit was returning to its base with some other Allied troops when he and four of his men, who made up the tail end of the patrol, were caught not by enemy troops but by Mother Nature in the form of an alpine avalanche. All five men were buried in the snow; one was immediately crushed and killed. Max had the presence of mind to remove his pistol from his holster—he was barely able to do so— and fire off several shots. This did two things: it provided holes for air to enter, and it alerted Allied troops that they had encountered trouble. They were dug out, and Max and the other three who survived suffered no severe injuries. Later Max received several medals, including one for bravery, and one similar to the Purple Heart. (After the war, the Isonzo Valley was included within Austrian territory ceded to Italy. Italy kept that territory along the river north of Gorizia for less than 30 years before ceding it, through the Treaty of Paris in 1947, to Yugoslavia. In 1991, the territory became part of independent Slovenia. Such are the spoils of war.)

So, no, my father was not used to running. He had no fear in him. But he knew when enough was enough. He and my mother began to make plans for us to leave Italy shortly after he was acquitted, and while he was still under house arrest.

It must have been strange for them to prepare to leave their native country, one that they loved and that my father had served in World War I. But then, many strange and surprising things were happening in Italy in the 1920s and '30s. And one of those surprising events was Max's courtship of the woman who would become my mother.

∾

When the war was over, Max, who spoke several languages, including German, was asked to serve on the Armistice Commission in Vienna. "In the chaos after the war," he wrote in that same long letter written many years after the war, "I lived some of the most relaxed and wonderful times of my life, first as an officer in Vienna, then in Vienna representing my pre-war boss, then in Paris suing that same boss. They were years without worries, with little money but lots of dancing, lots of women, and lots of bridge playing."

He returned to Venice in late 1919 after serving on the commission for about a year; he never finished his university degree. He was never enthralled with being a student. He was intelligent and quick, but book learning didn't hold him. He wanted to be out experiencing things, doing things, making things happen, and after the war he lost all interest in pursuing a university degree. He just wanted to get on with life.

And after the war he gained a reputation for being a playboy. He attended lots of social events and parties in Venice, he knew everyone, and he was a decorated war hero with a trim, athletic build and sleek, good looks. He took pride in his appearance, and more than one young lady swooned when he asked her to dance or to go out with him. Despite being a teetotaler, he was the life of whatever party he was at, and the object of more than one young woman's desire. He certainly did not appear to be someone who was looking to settle down.

Elena Friedenberg was five years younger than Max Oreffice, and when she met Max in 1920 after he had returned to Venice, she was not as impressed with Max as most women were. She knew of his reputation, and that didn't fit her style. She was more serious, and a little shy; she was more interested in substance than in charm and élan. So when Max and Elena first met on social occasions, no sparks flew. Yet, as all the other young women preened themselves in hopes of attracting Max's attention, it was the 23-year-old Elena Friedenberg, standing off to the side and talking with her girlfriends, paying the dashing military hero no heed, who captured Max's attention. Having his pick of the young ladies in Venetian social circles, Max slowly gravitated toward the one who seemed *least* available.

And so Max Oreffice and Elena Friedenberg began dating—to everyone's great surprise. They seemed mismatched, and not just because Max was a foot taller and five years older. Elena herself thought nothing would come of it, and she was not so sure that she wanted to be going out with him at all, but she gave him a chance. (And I must say I'm glad she did!)

Max's playboy reputation began to fade as he dated Elena more and more seriously. The young ladies who preened themselves for him, who placed themselves in his path or line of vision at parties, no longer attracted his attention; he was too busy talking with that Friedenberg girl. After a while, as Elena warmed up to him, he was nowhere to be found at the parties; he was alone with Elena, at the theatre or at a restaurant or strolling along the Piazza San Marco. There was something about Elena that made Max all too happy to shed his playboy image and to slowly but surely open his heart to this beautiful young woman.

Max had known of Elena; the Friedenbergs and the Oreffices had known each other for a long time. And Elena's father, Vittorio, took immediately to

Max. Vittorio was a highly successful entrepreneur, and he saw in Max the entrepreneur's spirit. As Max called on Elena at the Friedenberg home, Vittorio would often draw Max into long conversations about business opportunities, Vittorio's own enterprises, and Max's aspirations—trying Elena's patience as she waited for her father to release Max to her for the evening.

"Yes, yes, you two go enjoy the fresh air," Vittorio would say, and Max would give Vittorio a warm smile and a wink as he took Elena's arm and led her to the door.

"Sometimes I don't know if you're dating him or me," Elena would grouse, though she secretly was pleased that Max and her father had hit it off so well.

Vittorio Friedenberg had started out at age 13 as a clerk for a Venetian company that traded in cereal grains. He was still going to school, of course, but after he finished school he rose quickly through the ranks and ended up owning the company when he was still in his twenties. He was very progressive; he was not satisfied with the status quo. He questioned things, he continually looked to improve operations, to expand the company, to make it more profitable. For example, until he became owner, the company had shipped everything in bags. They'd bring in wheat from Argentina or the US or Australia, and other grains, too; it was all shipped in bags, thousands of bags. Vittorio wanted to ship the grains in bulk, but there were no facilities, so he built grain elevators and silos at the Venice port and started bringing in grains in bulk. At the time, this was unknown in Italy. Of course, shipping in bulk was much more economical, and his company became very profitable. In building the silos and elevators, he captured the imported grain market for all of northern Italy, and essentially for all of Italy. He began to amass quite a fortune, one that was later decimated, in part, by World War II. His sons Mario and Alberto began working with him when they were old enough.

"And what are your plans?" Vittorio asked Max when he recognized Elena was becoming serious about him. "Do you want to follow your father, go into medicine?" Max's father, Fausto Oreffice, had pioneered the use of X-rays in southern Europe. Unfortunately, he paid the price for this; he died from overexposure to X-rays a year before I was born. The risks of exposure were not known back then.

"No sir," Max replied. "My interest lies in the land. I want to develop land."

Vittorio studied Max for a moment and then smiled. "A wise choice," he said. "Land. Real estate holds it value. Yes. Tell me your plans, then."

"There's a lot of undeveloped land in Tuscany, near Grossetto. It's all marshland, but it can be improved."

Vittorio narrowed his eyes and waited for Max to continue.

"This land is cheap, in relative terms," Max continued. "Of course, who would want to buy it? It's unproductive. You can't grow anything on it."

"But you are interested in it?"

Max's eyes gleamed. "You build huge pumps to drain the land. You build sluiceways to reroute the water and dams to keep the water from returning. And you turn marshland into productive land. You take nearly 3,000 acres of nothing and you make it into something that produces excellent crops, year after year. It can be done, and I can do it."

Vittorio liked the way this young entrepreneur thought. "And you have inquired into the price of this land?"

"I've made some initial inquiries. Enough to know it's worth pursuing."

Vittorio strolled over to the window in his living room and looked out. It was early evening and the sun was setting; the clouds were streaks of brilliant purples and pinks. "We'll talk some more," is all he said.

Those talks led to the deepening of an already good relationship. Vittorio was well off by that time, and he liked Max's ideas, his ideals, his enthusiasm and passion. This would be a good son-in-law, a good man for his daughter. Vittorio and Max were two peas in a pod.

A few months later, in late 1921, Max asked Elena to marry him. A few short years ago, this idea would have been preposterous to Elena, but now it made her extremely happy. One of the more unlikely courtships in Venice had not only been undertaken; it had held. While they were engaged, and as Elena and her mother, Emma, planned the wedding, Vittorio and Max had another conversation.

"Tell me more about Grossetto," Vittorio said.

Max told him about further negotiations for the land, and more detailed plans for developing it, including working with engineering consultants to help him drain the land and build the dams and sluiceways.

"And what do the banks say?" Vittorio asked.

"They are a bit reluctant to back this project," Max admitted. The truth is, more than one banker had laughed in his face.

Vittorio snorted. "Many bankers are too wise for their own good. They have no vision, but to hear it from them, they have a crystal ball that tells all. They would do better to assess the person, not the project."

"Maybe I haven't found the right banker yet."

"I look at the person, Max. When a capable, enterprising, bright young man puts his mind to something, then it's time for old men like me to take heed. Do you like horses, Max?"

"I have a great love for horses."

"Tell me, what makes a great horse?"

Max considered for a moment. "Well, you have to have the lineage, the innate ability. But many horses have great ability yet rarely win. In my estimation, what sets the winners apart is their passion and undying desire to win. Nothing stops them. I've seen horses so tired that they stagger in the homestretch, and they win on guts and character. They simply will not allow themselves to be beaten. They know, walking to the gate, that the race is theirs."

Vittorio smiled. "Your father is one of the best doctors in Italy, a true pioneer. He is a man of great vision in his field, a man with great passion for his work. You are passionate as well: you came back from your studies to enter the war when you weren't required to, because you felt strongly about it. And you are gifted: in your military service you rose to the fore. You are quick on your feet, quicker with your mind. You have inherited your father's intelligence and passion, and you have presented a well-researched plan to a group of stodgy bankers who underestimate your vision and your drive. They are fools." Vittorio paused. "But I am not."

"Perhaps if I presented my plan a bit differently."

"Pah! To some of these bankers you could present how to eat with a fork and spoon, and they'd look suspiciously at you and say that will never work. No. You need someone who believes in you, someone who recognizes your passion and what it takes to be a successful entrepreneur. I would like to help you get started. I want to finance your Grossetto project."

Max's jaw dropped; as quick as he was, he found no immediate words.

"And, if I understand correctly, you currently have no office. It will not do for a businessman such as yourself to have no office. I will provide you office space in my building." Vittorio owned a building in downtown Venice, the entire city block; on the first floor were the offices, on the second, Vittorio and his family lived, and on the third, Vittorio's son, Mario, lived with his family. Elena's father raised a sly eyebrow. "I'll put you on the same floor as me, so I can make sure you're spending my money wisely," he added, chuckling.

"I . . . I don't know what to say." Max's eyes became moist. The two men shook hands. "Thank you," Max said. "You don't know what this means to me."

Vittorio winked. "I think I might," he said. "I was a young entrepreneur once, looking for someone to believe in me. Besides, if you are to marry my daughter, you need to keep her in good stead, no?"

Max grinned. "I intend to, sir. I intend to."

∽

Max and Elena were married on October 17, 1922, at her parents' home in Venice. It was only 11 days later that Mussolini and his Black Shirts undertook their March on Rome, though no one realized at the time how black that day would be in Italy's history. More important to my own family history was Sandra's birth in 1924, and my own in 1927. By this time my father was doing well in his land development business (though if you were to ask him what he did for a living, he'd shrug and say, "I'm a farmer"). The Grossetto project had been a success, and he sold Grossetto before taking on another project halfway between Venice and Trieste, near the village of Latisana, where the lowlands were overrun by the Adriatic. (This was the *Prati Nuovi* project, for which my father partnered with Signor Cugnasca, who proved to be a very good silent partner until my father's trial occurred many years later.)

Prati Nuovi took on great significance for our family, because we ended up spending much of our summers on this land. Backed in part by the money that Cugnasca put up, my father purchased about 2,800 acres and built a house on the land when I was three or four years old. The house was one storey, and very modern for a farmhouse—each bedroom had its own bathroom. Even in our house in Venice, Sandra and I had to share a bathroom.

My father immediately went to work, building dikes and levies to salvage the land. But of much greater interest to me was the half-mile track that encircled our house. Dad bred horses, Percherons and harness horses, more as a hobby than a business. Percherons are big Belgian horses, strong work horses. The harness horses were trotters, and my dad would run them on the track around the house. I would come outside and watch the horses go around and around, and each time they passed my heart soared.

I looked forward eagerly to the summers on the farm because I loved the horses. Some kids had dogs for pets; I had horses. By the time I was five or six years old, I would regularly sneak out of my bedroom window shortly after dawn to go "help" Bepi Rosini, who was in charge of the stables, to take care of the horses. Bepi was a rough-hewn character, rangy and strong, not well educated, but smart. He lived on the farm with his family; some of his kids were old enough to help plant and harvest. Bepi would smile when he'd see me walking into the stables.

"Hey, Paolo, it's about time you got up," he'd say. "I can't feed these horses all by myself." And I'd help Bepi distribute oats or hay, and then he'd hand me a rake to muck out the stalls with, and I was the happiest boy on earth. Bepi showed me how to brush the horses, how to check them for injury, how to inspect their hooves and remove any stones that might have gotten lodged. I loved the rich, earthy smell of the horses and their stables, the hay, the sweat, the wildflowers and clover whose scents wafted into the stables. I loved the feel of horses, their shiny coats and long manes, their long, muscular necks. Horses are intelligent creatures. Their large eyes seem to take in everything, and the bond between a horse and its owner or trainer becomes strong and special. Everything about horses was wonderful, including even the pungent smell of the manure I mucked out in the morning. Heaven, as far as I was concerned, was just a stone's throw away from my bedroom window.

∞

Chirignago was another special place for me and for my whole family. Chirignago is a picturesque little town about a twenty-minute drive north-west of Venice. Nonno (Grandfather) Vittorio owned a villa about a kilometer from Chirignago, a large country estate with farm and residential buildings, including a principal residence in which several families were easily housed. Nonno Vittorio and Nonna Emma would be there, and their sons Mario and Alberto and their families, and their four daughters (including my mother) and their families. We would gather at Chirignago in late summer, and the cousins would play in the villa's park, and in the fields, and ride our bikes into the village of Mestre to get *gelato*. My cousin, also named Paolo, was a year younger than me, but we were together from start to end at Chirignago, exploring the park—which was about 20 acres but seemed about 5,000 to our young minds—and riding our bikes to the lake in the park. One afternoon, shortly after I had fallen into a cactus after losing my balance on a plank in the park, Paolo dared me to ride my bike as fast as I could down the hill that overlooked the lake; he said I was too chicken to ride it fast. My rear end was sore enough, and I figured it was time for him to risk something, so I dared him back. He shrugged cockily and said, "No problem." He rode his bike as fast as he could down the hill, his legs pumping furiously as his speed increased and the wind blew his hair back. It looked like great fun until he lost control at the bottom of the hill and ended in the lake, his bike tires still spinning by the shore. I doubled over in laughter at the top of the hill; my rear end didn't hurt quite so badly after that.

The culmination every year at Chirignago was Nonno Vittorio's birthday celebration on September 20th. These were grand occasions in which a sumptuous feast was prepared, an elegant table set outside to enjoy the fresh air, and all Nonno Vittorio's six children and their families gathered to celebrate for the entire day. Mario, Nonno Vittorio's eldest son, would toast his father, and pastas and vegetables and meat dishes and fresh-baked breads and pastries and fruits would magically appear, and I would eat until my stomach hurt. Half an hour later, Paolo and I would be chasing each other again. The summer nights were long, but they were never long enough at Chirignago.

As can happen with young boys, Paolo and I were sometimes so caught up in our playing that we would lose track of time. Nonno Vittorio was kind and loving, and he was also an Old World gentleman who could be very demanding. One thing he believed in was punctuality. If dinner was served at 8 P.M., and you arrived at 8:01, you did not get dinner. Paolo and I found this out at Chirignago one summer, and it made an indelible impression on me. To this day I am punctual. I believe in being on time, and when I ran meetings later in life I expected others to be on time, too. I think one reason I believe in this so strongly is that punctuality is tied to your word. If you say you are going to be someplace at a certain time, you should follow through. If you can't be trusted with small things—such as being on time—then perhaps you can't be trusted with larger things, either. At any rate, Nonno Vittorio taught me about punctuality, and it was a lesson I never forgot.

He taught me something else, too. When I was ten years old, he watched me play a game of checkers with my dad at Chirignago. After a particular move, in which I was setting up an exchange, Nonno Vittorio said, "Paolo, why did you do that?"

"To capture one of his pieces."

"Yes, but you gave up one of your own."

I shrugged. "That's just the way it's done, Nonno."

He smiled. "Yes, but if you had moved here, instead of there, then do you see what would have happened?" He showed me the move. I would have captured one of Dad's pieces without losing one of my own. I looked up in surprise at Nonno.

"Conventional wisdom is not always the best route," he said. "If you want to do well in checkers, or in anything else, don't think conventionally. Think ahead. Think of *new* things."

"Hey, Nonno, quit helping him beat me," my father said.

"Soon enough he won't need my help," Nonno replied.

I don't remember who won that checkers game. But that conversation stayed with me. He repeated that idea to me several times over the next few years, and he practiced what he preached. When he built the grain elevators and silos for his company, it was certainly against the conventional wisdom of the day. Nonno was, as usual, thinking ahead, quite happy to go against the conventional wisdom. "When everybody knows how to do something, and they all do it the same way without thinking, then there's usually a better way to do it," he told me. "Don't take things for granted. If you want to get ahead, you have to think ahead."

As a child, my thinking ahead usually consisted of thinking of summers at the farm, and at Chirignago, and of going to Cortina d'Ampezzo, in the Alps in northern Italy. There we'd hike in the Dolomite Mountains, which are part of the Alps, and we'd go to one of the beautiful lakes. And I was always excited to go to Lido, which is an island reef on the Adriatic that separates the Lagoon of Venice from the Gulf of Venice. Lido is, in my estimation, the best organized beach in the world, with well-equipped cabanas with attendants, where they served a variety of very good foods, not just hot dogs and snow cones and pretzels. We would rent a house at Lido for a month or so, spend the whole day at the beach, play soccer, and build huge tracks in the sand with banked curves on which we'd race marbles. Of course someone would destroy the tracks after we'd leave for the day and we'd have to rebuild them the next day.

I looked forward to winters, too. We spent many winter vacations at the Hotel Cristallo in Cortina. The roads to the resort were winding, and the surrounding countryside was beautiful, and I loved the three-hour drive there because Dad would take it fast. Leo Menardi was the owner of the Cristallo, and he had been a great skier. I took ski lessons there, starting out at 4 years old at the lowest level—C level—and by the time I was 12 years old, I had worked up to the A level and was skiing down the slope that had been used for the Olympic course.

On January 6th each year at the hotel we would celebrate the Epiphany, which was like our Christmas in terms of receiving presents. We called it *Befana,* and the name is believed to derive from the word *Epiphany,* which of course commemorates the manifestation of the baby Jesus to the three Magi. According to legend, "Befana" is a kind, old woman who flies through the skies on a broom, carrying over her shoulder a sack full of presents, leaving sweets and gifts in the stockings of good children and lumps of coal for children who have been bad. We celebrated the holiday on the 6th, like all other Italian children, and then we'd return to Venice and start school.

My father was against organized religion. In Italy, "religion" meant mainly Catholicism, of course, and if you weren't Catholic, you were Jewish. Of course, there were many more Catholics than Jews—of a nation of 45 million, there were fewer than 50,000 Jews. But I need to explain something here about the relationship between Catholics and Jews in Italy back in the 1920s and '30s. It was a different climate then; it wasn't that big a deal whether you were Jewish or Catholic or anything else. What you were was Italian. Many Jews married Catholics, and some Jews became Catholic, and some Catholics became Jewish, and they all remained Italian. There was no big separation or distinction, no dividing line. My own family is a prime example: five of my ten aunts and uncles—Jewish by heritage—married Catholics, and the other five married Jews. My first wife was Catholic, and I raised my two children as Catholics, though I never joined the Catholic Church or any other church. Religion just wasn't a big part of my life growing up in Venice, and it still isn't.

That didn't mean my father held no strong views on organized religion. He held Catholicism in disdain. "Why go to priests and nuns for wisdom or guidance in relationships?" he would say. "What would they know about marital relationships?" He believed in God, but he also believed that religion was a detriment to the family and that he didn't need help from a rabbi or a priest or nun to tell him what to believe and what to do. So I had no religious upbringing to speak of, and I didn't think in terms of "This person's Jewish, that person's Catholic."

Family, on the other hand, was everything. We had a very close-knit family. Venice itself was not a huge city in the 1930s, and because there were no yards or fields to speak of, everything was packed in, everyone lived close together. We lived within walking distance of many of our aunts and uncles, and saw Nonno Vittorio and Nonna Emma almost every day. My paternal grandmother, Nonna Alice, lived nearby as well. She had severe diabetes and we had to continually watch her, because she'd sneak out and buy sweets.

There's an interesting side story involving her husband, Fausto, who died shortly before my birth. My father evidently felt obligated to carry on his father's name, but Dad didn't really like the name Fausto. He finally decided to put "Fausto *detto Paolo*" on my birth certificate, which means my legal name was Fausto but I would go by Paolo, and I always went by Paolo Oreffice. Many years later, when it came time to register as a citizen of the United States, I declared my name as Paul Fausto Oreffice. A few weeks after this declaration, my birth certificate arrived from Italy, and I was shocked to find that *Fausto* didn't appear anywhere on it. My father had an impish streak in him, and he always told people he had named me Fausto, but he couldn't bring himself to put that name on me. Because I had already declared Fausto as my middle name, in essence I stuck that name on myself.

As for Sandra, we got along as well as any brother and sister, I suppose. She was nearly four years older, and as kids that's a huge difference, so we didn't do a lot together when I was growing up. We each had our own sets of friends and went our own ways (oddly enough, many of my friends were named Paolo too—though none had a false "Fausto" in front of his name!). And I must say, I was my mother's favorite, and both Sandra and I knew this; Sandra was always a little jealous of this. It was later in life, as adults, that we became close friends. Not that Sandra and Mom weren't close; they were. They used to drive Dad and me crazy in the car sometimes. Sandra was a voracious reader, and loved poetry, as did my mother. On vacation trips, with a captive audience of Dad and myself, Sandra would start reeling off verses of poems she had memorized, and my mother would join in, much to the chagrin of the males in the car: *I cipressi che da Bolgari alti e schietti / Vanno a San Guido in duplice filar* ("The cypress trees that go from Bolgari to San Guido in a tall and lean double line")

These were just a few of the lines they would recite as we drove by Bolgari on our trips south. I suggested to Dad that we take another route, but he told me I'd just have to put up with it.

∞

Our life at home was very comfortable. We had a huge condo in the building my grandfather owned, 6,000 square feet of living space with wide rooms and 15- to 20-feet ceilings. The hallway was about 30 feet by 18 feet, and we had a formal living room, an informal one, servants' quarters where the cook and maid lived, a large kitchen, and a nice bathroom. There were 52 steps to get up to the second floor. One side of the condo looked out on a canal; from my parents' bedroom I could see, across the canal, a plaque that read, "Marco Polo was born here." The other side—the side my room was on—looked over a courtyard. I was born in this house, and lived there the whole time we were in Venice.

The only complaint I had was that Venice was a lousy place for a kid to grow up. It's a beautiful city to visit, but it has very few parks and fields, very few places where kids can gather and play soccer or any other game requiring grass. There also were no gyms to speak of, no facilities to play sports, and no organized sports for children, when I was growing up. That's one reason one of my dreams as a child was to play on an organized soccer team. Organized teams didn't start until the upper teen years. These teams were used as feeder teams for the professional teams, so only the best players made it.

The houses didn't have yards. It was very frustrating as a kid. My friends and I walked almost everywhere—Venice is a city where you walk a lot, or take boats. There are boats that run like buses with regular stops. But finding a green patch of grass to play on was like finding an oasis in the desert. Maybe it was real, or maybe it was a mirage (or it might be claimed before you arrived). That was one more reason I loved going to the farm and to Chirignago in the summer—to feel grass and sod under my feet, to get away from the concrete, flagstone, and canals.

I had lots of colds and ear and throat infections as a child, so I was home schooled until fourth grade (I had my tonsils out the previous year, and my health improved dramatically). Many teachers taught half days back then, and they or substitute teachers would come to the house in the afternoons, four days a week, teaching me the same curriculum that was taught in the public schools, and when I entered the public school in fourth grade, I hadn't missed a beat. Grete, our nursemaid, started teaching me math and reading when I was four years old.

Still, it was a bit difficult to enter school for the first time in fourth grade. Making matters worse, I was two years younger than my classmates, because my parents had started my home schooling when I was four. I was always small for my age as it was, and that plus the two-year difference—and the fact that I had never been in school before—really set me apart from my classmates. To top it off, I had inherited some of my mother's shyness. All in all, I was pretty miserable in fourth and fifth grade.

Except for math class. I loved math class, and I attribute that to Maestro Fazzini's expert teaching. He made math fun. He connected the problems to the real world—you know, "If your soccer team leads 3-0 at the half, but the other team scores a goal every 20 minutes in the second half, who will win the game and by what score?" I suppose it helped that I loved numbers in the first place. I used to keep detailed statistics on marble races I'd have in my bedroom—most floors in Venice have some slant to them. I kept tabs on head-to-head competition among the marbles, on total number of wins, on winning streaks, you name it. I could handicap my marbles just like horses are handicapped. I don't race marbles anymore, but I do keep all kinds of statistics on the horses I have part ownership of—what they cost, where they've run, how they performed, what money they've earned, and so on. All this comes from my early love for math and for statistics, fueled by Maestro Fazzini in fourth and fifth grades.

What Venice lacked in fields and facilities, it made up for in cuisine. The food in Venice is outstanding: shrimp, fish, all kinds of wonderful seafood. Maria Baraga was a great cook and she took it as a challenge, if not a personal affront, that I was so small and thin. "Look at you Paolo, when you turn sideways you disappear!" Maria would say as she served me seconds of pasta dishes, meat dishes, or heaped more mashed potatoes on my plate. She cooked for the entire family, of course, but I became her special project, a mystery that she determined she would solve through her myriad of delicious recipes, dishes, and desserts. "You need some meat on your bones, Paolo," she'd say. "A strong wind might blow you away." I would happily adhere to her ample diet, but it would be years before I would shoot up in height and fill out some. I wanted to grow, too, in part because I loved sports, and I knew greater size and strength would help me succeed.

In later years I did have success in a number of sports, from horse jumping to tennis to ping pong to cross country to soccer, leading people to believe that I was a natural athlete. However, as a child I was not well coordinated, I was small for my age, and I was often near the last to be chosen in pick-up games. But this didn't dim my enthusiasm for sports, and I especially enjoyed the times my father took me to professional soccer games in Venice and in Rome.

∞

When I was ten years old, my family took a trip to Rome over Easter—something we often did when I was a child. My Uncle Giorgio Casoni and two of his sons, Cin and Gian, stopped by our hotel rooms unannounced one morning. Cin was about six months older than me, and Gian was three years younger, and we got along well. I was delighted to see them, because I loved my cousins and especially Uncle Giorgio. He was CEO of the Banco di Roma, one of the largest banks in Italy, but to me he was fun-loving Uncle Giorgio who always brought treats for Sandra and me and who brightened any room he walked in.

"Hey Paolo, you sleepyhead, what are you doing inside on a beautiful day like this?" Uncle Giorgio said. "You should be outside, running around, playing soccer." He winked at my father, who was having a cup of coffee and reading *Il Messaggero*, a daily Rome newspaper.

"But Uncle Giorgio, there's no place to play soccer around the hotel."

"No place to play? That's a crime. Someone should be arrested. Max, how could you allow this to happen? You're a land developer. Why don't you develop some land around here for your son to play soccer on?"

Max just smiled. I had the feeling he was in on a secret of Uncle Giorgio's.

"I'll tell you what," said Uncle Giorgio. "Paolo, you come with me— Max, you too—and we'll learn a little something about soccer today."

"But Uncle Giorgio, I know how to play," I said. "I just don't have a *place* to play."

"I know of a place where soccer is played. But young boys who talk all morning long might make us late to this place."

"To *what* place?" I asked, my heart beginning to pound with excitement.

"See? There you go again, delaying us. Come on, let's go! The day is wasting away!" Uncle Giorgio said, and he ushered me outside. My father put down his coffee cup, kissed my mother, who had come into the room to greet Uncle Giorgio, and picked up his hat. I gave my mother a hurried kiss and off I went, trailing after Uncle Giorgio.

Cin and Gian were in on the secret and enjoyed keeping it from me. They enjoyed it even more as I begged them to tell me where we were going. In Uncle Giorgio's car, we headed for a destination unknown—at least to me. After about ten minutes, a large stadium loomed into sight. Suddenly it clicked in. "I know where we're going!" I said. "We're going to see your club play!"

Uncle Giorgio was president of Lazio, one of two major league soccer clubs in Rome. The other was Roma, and on that day those two big rivals were playing each other in Stadio Nazionale.

Uncle Giorgio turned to give me a smile. Then he looked over at my father. "You see, I told you!" he said to Dad. "That boy might be small, but his brains are huge!"

I was ecstatic. I loved soccer, and to see Lazio and Roma play in Stadio Nazionale was like an American boy seeing the Yankees and Red Sox play in Yankee Stadium, or the old Brooklyn Dodgers and New York Giants play in Ebbett's Field or the Polo Grounds.

We parked and soon joined the 80,000 other fans entering the stadium, many wearing the red and yellow of the Roma club and just as many others wearing the pale blue of Lazio. We found our way to our seats, the choicest seats in the stadium, thanks to Uncle Giorgio. Pennants of the various league teams ringed the upper reaches of the stadium and flapped briskly in the wind; the sun shone on the field and warmed my face, and an electricity was in the air that I had never felt before. As the players for both sides came out and warmed up, great swelling roars of approval came from fans all around the stadium. The players themselves seemed not to notice; they appeared at ease and yet focused as they went through their warm-up drills. They were like gods, unaffected by the raucous calling and rabid adoration heaped on them by the multitudes of mere mortals like me.

"Now, isn't this better than staying in a hotel?" Uncle Giorgio said, smiling at me.

"A hundred times better!" I replied.

The match got going and it was tightly fought and evenly played. People who don't know soccer probably think a low-scoring game must be boring, but this game, which ended in a 1-1 tie, was the most exciting event I had been to in my life. Every moment was packed with tension, which mounted as the game wore on, and many fans released the tension by heaping verbal abuse on fans of the opposing team. Some of the more drunken fans didn't stop at the verbal abuse, but engaged in fisticuffs; more than a few noses were bloodied that glorious afternoon, though the fighting was nothing like that at matches in England.

After the match ended and the roars of the crowd died down, and as people began filing out of the stadium, Uncle Giorgio looked over at me. "Want to go down on the field and meet a few players?" he said casually, as if he were asking if I'd like a *gelato*.

My eyes grew huge. "Are you kidding?" I said.

Uncle Giorgio smiled. "Would I kid you?" he replied. Truth is, he would, and he did, all the time—but he wasn't kidding now. We went down on the field, and I got to meet several players, including Piola, the great forward for Lazio; he had scored Lazio's lone goal that day. This was a huge thrill, like an American boy getting to meet Joe DiMaggio and his Yankee teammates, or Duke Snyder and other Dodgers. Piola ruffled my hair a bit, and when I recounted this later to Sandra and Mom, with a reverential, far-off tone in my voice, Sandra kidded me for days afterward, saying that I wasn't going to comb my hair because it had been touched by a god.

∞

My dad took me to other games and events too, but I didn't see him as much as I wished, because he was often away on projects. On weekdays Sandra and I would see Dad before we went to school and briefly in the evening. Sometimes we'd be in bed before he arrived home. Sandra and I would eat dinner around 7 P.M., before our parents did—Maria would serve us in a little room off the kitchen, and then at 8 or 8:30 she'd serve our parents in the formal dining room.

I idolized my dad; he was my friend and teacher. Another reason I loved going to the farm was because I got to spend more time with him there. My dad was my best friend when I was a child, and today my son is my best friend.

With that said, I was probably closer to my mother because we were together more. My mother ran the household and ran it very well. She treated the servants kindly and fairly, but she had her rules and she would follow through on them. A maid who brought a young suitor to her quarters—expressly against her agreement with my mother—found this out. Her young suitor was tossed out and the maid was fired. Later in life, I took my cue from my mother in handling personnel. I was very good to my employees unless they crossed me. Then I could be a real SOB.

My parents never raised a hand toward Sandra or me. They didn't have to. Their "No" meant no, and their "Yes" meant yes. We knew better than to argue. Parents who say "No" but then give in, or who talk about consequences but then don't follow through, find themselves in trouble when they raise their kids. The kids keep pushing, and the parents keep giving in, and eventually "No" becomes "All right, go ahead, but just this time."

That never happened when I was growing up. For example, one night I refused to eat my spinach, and I told my mother in unequivocal terms that I would not eat it. "You refuse to eat it?" she said. "I won't eat it. It's gross," I confirmed. "Fine," she said. "You can leave the table. And when you are hungry for a snack later this evening, your spinach will be waiting for you."

I looked at her doubtfully as I left the table, but at least I was getting out of eating it for dinner. Later, when Maria was getting Sandra and me a snack, Mom chimed in, "Paolo would like to finish his spinach, Maria. Why don't you heat that up for him."

A few minutes later I stared—with great repugnance—at the plate of wretched, limp spinach in front of me. My mother stood in the kitchen, talking with Maria, but really keeping an eye on me to make sure I didn't sneak any "real" food. I looked over at her and she raised an eyebrow. "You're not eating, Paolo. Still not hungry?"

"I'm hungry for real food, not for this stuff." I was pushing her, standing up for my rights. I saw this as cruel and inhuman punishment.

My mother was more than up to the challenge. She gave a little shrug and said, "Well, if you're not hungry for it now, maybe you will be in the morning. Because, believe me, Paolo, that spinach is going to be the next thing you eat."

I went to bed enraged—and hungry. In my anger, I vowed that no matter what I would not eat that spinach. Surely she would relent in the morning and see just how cruel and unfair she was being.

Come the morning, nothing had changed. She greeted me with a kiss and then told Maria to get my spinach ready. "Paolo must be starved by now!" Mom said. Maria was torn; she liked me and loved preparing spinach-less breakfasts for me, but the cook in her appreciated Mom's edict. To Mom, it was a matter of obedience and discipline. To Maria, it was a matter of not wasting food. To me, it was a matter of despair—because I saw I was not going to win. I wrestled with the idea of going on a hunger strike, but this lasted for about three minutes. My resolve was not helped by the smell of Maria's fresh-baked muffins that she took out of the oven just about the time she placed the offensive plate of reheated spinach in front of me.

"Mmmm," Sandra said, relishing her little brother's moment of distress. "These muffins sure are good, Maria. They just melt in my mouth." She smiled sweetly at me as she took a big bite.

With a little cry of despair, I caved in and ate the spinach. Then I downed three muffins, glowering at my mother as I did.

"I guess he was hungry for his spinach after all, huh, Mamma," Sandra said.

"Hush now, let him be. He ate it, and nothing more needs to be said."

Nothing more, indeed. I had learned my lesson: I knew who was boss of the house, and I knew whose word was final. And it wasn't mine.

∝

Mom might have been boss of the house, but she had plenty of help. Besides Maria, our cook, and Angela, our maid (not the maid who was fired for sneaking her boyfriend into her living quarters), there was the aforementioned Grete, who was at once gentle and stern. That's probably why my mother liked Grete so well: she knew we would never get anything past Grete, that Grete would brook no nonsense and would not be cajoled into allowing us to do something that we shouldn't be doing. Grete was like an extension of my mother, in some ways; she cared for us fiercely, and would often not go out on her off days, though she would take her annual vacation to her homeland of Czechoslovakia. When Sandra, who was rebellious at times and got into tiffs with my mother, needed a confidante, it was Grete she went to. Grete was my first teacher, teaching me German as well as math, reading, and writing, and she made sure I did my homework. One time when I had a dangerously high fever, Grete stayed by my bedside throughout the night, putting cold compresses on my forehead. She was as dedicated to Sandra and me as if we were her own children. Grete, quite simply, was grafted into our family, and I loved her like a second mother. She would accompany us to *Pravi Nuovi* in the summers, and with her there, with the increased time with my father, and with the wonderful, majestic, equines inhabiting our barns, I felt I was the luckiest kid in Italy.

CHAPTER THREE

A Passion for Horses

By the time I was six, we had more than forty horses on our farm, and each summer several mares would give birth to foals. The gestational period for a mare is eleven months, and I impatiently awaited the impending births. As a mare's time neared, every day I would ask Bepi Rosini, our head of the stables, when the foal would arrive. "The foal will arrive when it is ready to arrive," Bepi would say. "And not a moment sooner." I had heard this answer many times but still had to ask the question. During the summer when I was six, we had two mares whose moment appeared to have arrived almost simultaneously.

So it was with great excitement that I awoke one morning and rushed off to the stalls to find that indeed two foals had been born. However, both foals were in the same stall. It was rare for a mare to give birth to twins, so I was a bit puzzled. Bepi had dark circles under his eyes; he had apparently been up much of the night with the mare who had given birth. One foal was feeding on his mother's milk, standing in the stall on his spindly legs, while the other foal lay in the hay, taking in the sights and sounds and smells of his new world. The other mare, who was apparently still pregnant, was several stalls down. I ran down to her stall. She nickered and moved around, agitated. She even kicked out with her back legs a bit, and I saw that she wasn't pregnant. I thought maybe she was protecting her foal from me, but found it odd that she would kick up, because she was risking injury to her newborn. I peered through the bars of her stall but couldn't see any foal. After a moment I looked questioningly at Bepi. He pointed to the foal that was lying on the ground, waiting his turn to feed. I walked over to the stall where the two foals were.

"I thought Serena was pregnant too," I said.

"She was, and she gave birth. Here's her foal."

"But why isn't he with his mother?"

"Because his mother tried to kill him." Bepi saw the shocked look on my face, and smiled sadly. "Sometimes that happens. I moved him before she could do any damage."

"What was she doing?"

"Kicking at him, butting him. She didn't want him."

The idea of horses being mean to each other—and especially of a mother trying to harm her own child—was hard for me to understand.

"But she just gave birth to him. Why would she want to hurt him?"

"Things are not always fair in this world. But look. Panaro is going to be all right. His new mother likes him." Indeed, Panaro, the foal Bepi had rescued, was now up on its wobbly legs, looking at the mare that had agreed to take him in. She exhaled deeply through her nose, then nodded, and Panaro made his way to her milk while the other foal looked out on his first morning.

I rested my hands on the stall bars and watched Panaro nuzzle up to his new mother. Though the mare was willing, he looked more cautious about the feeding process than the other foal.

"Is he going to be all right?" I asked.

Bepi shrugged. "I think so. But he knows he's been rejected. We'll see how things go with his new mother."

I helped Bepi feed the horses in the other stalls, and I mucked out a few stalls, including the one next to Panaro's real mother. Before I did, I looked at this mother who had tried to harm her own child. She stared defiantly at me, and for a moment I think she wanted me to come in so she could stomp me instead. She nickered loudly and I ran out of the barn.

⚬⚬

Panaro became my special pet. I would go to the paddock with carrots and sugar cubes in my pockets, and I would go first to Panaro. He got to know me quickly, and as I would walk up to him, he would nuzzle my pocket, prodding me to give him his treat. He got to following me around the grounds; he knew where his treats were coming from. He followed me just like any dog would follow a boy. Six or seven foals were born that spring and summer, but Panaro was my favorite. Though he had been taken in by his new mother, there was something about him that made me think he knew he had been rejected. I felt sorry for him.

One day when he had followed me to the yard, I got an idea (a bright one, I thought at the time). Panaro was small, and he was essentially my pet. Why shouldn't he go inside our house? Isn't that where pets belonged?

I clucked at Panaro and said "Come on, boy," and led him to our front steps. He paused there, reluctant to go up the six steps, but I patted my pockets and that reminded him that I was the Candy Man as far as he was concerned, and he followed me, clumsily and falteringly, up the steps, his hooves clopping hard on the cement. But he made it, and I opened the door, peering inside to see if anyone was around. I could hear someone in the kitchen, and I was pretty sure it was my mother, but no one was within view, so I led Panaro into the living room. Then I proudly called out to my mother, who came from the kitchen and stopped in her tracks when she saw Panaro.

"Paolo! What on earth are you doing with a horse in the house?"

I shrugged. "He wanted to see the inside of our house, that's all."

"Horses do not belong in houses! Take him out!"

"But Mamma, he's my pet. I just wanted to show him what it's like in here."

"Yes, and what if he has to do what you do, you know, in the bathroom?"

"You mean brush its teeth?" I said innocently.

"You know what I mean! How do you know he doesn't have to go?"

I shrugged again and looked at Panaro. "Do you want to go to the bathroom, boy? It's right over here." I made as if I were going to lead him to the bathroom, setting my mother into swift and efficient motion.

"No you don't! Get him out of here, Paolo! Now! Go, horse, shoo! Go outside where you belong!" As I led Panaro back outside, Mom said, "Paolo? That was not one of your better ideas." But she had to struggle to keep a smile from crossing her face.

∞

Personally, I thought *all* ideas regarding horses were splendid ideas, including having one in the house. After all, my father had perched me majestically atop a steed when I was less than a year old. I have a picture of this, and all you can see of my father is a pair of legs below the horse's midsection; his hands are supporting my back, invisible to the camera eye. My mother was probably a little leery of this, but not nearly as much as when I began breaking horses at age nine. When I was an infant, my father held me on; when I began breaking horses, I of course had to hold on myself, as best I could. I remember one afternoon in Chirignago when a horse named Vespa—a particularly frisky filly who couldn't stand to have anyone on her—tossed me onto the soft grass a dozen times. (It seems appropriate that Vespa means "Bee.") After the third or fourth time my mother came racing out of the house, pleading with my father, saying, "Stop! You're going to kill my boy!" He assured her that the falls were not hurting me, that there was no great danger in falling from a horse so long as the horse didn't fall along with you, and that the grass was long and soft and that I knew how to fall.

"But Paolo's fallen several times," my mother said. "How many times are you going to let him fall?"

As Bepi brought Vespa back, he and my dad shared a small smile. Bepi shrugged and raised an eyebrow, and my father, looking again at my mother, said, "As many times as it takes, I guess."

"Paolo, are you okay?" she asked me.

"I'm not stopping," I said. "This horse isn't beating me." Vespa nickered and shook her head as Bepi handed me the reins, but she allowed me to get back on. No one else had been able to ride her, either—neither Bepi nor my dad. They had been teaching me how to break horses; Bepi had been my main teacher. It was his idea that I break Vespa. "Do you think he's ready?" my father had asked him.

"I know he is," Bepi replied without hesitation. "Paolo knows horses. He'll handle Vespa. You just watch."

And so I rode, and was bucked off, and rode, and was bucked off some more. I had been riding since I was four, jumping horses since I was seven, racing them—on the farm, against my father, who always gave me the better horse—since I was eight. (My father, as usual, would be impeccably dressed when riding: coat, tie, hat. He never went anywhere, even on the farm, without looking splendid.) When I began riding at four, I rode horses, not ponies. My father would put me on the slimmest horse and he would lead the horse around. But by the time I was five, I rode the horses without his assistance. My father did not shelter me unnecessarily around horses; he let me experience them and groom and feed them and learn their habits and peculiarities and bond with them, and he let me be taught by Bepi, the unschooled and, in my eyes, unequaled master concerning all things equine. My father would listen when Bepi talked to him about horses, whether it was about selling or buying or breeding or training. Bepi was far more than just a hired hand to my father, and he was far more than just a horseman to me.

When I was six, Bepi helped me become a better rider. "Here, Paolo, to be a good rider, you must have your knees tucked in, firm against the saddle, like this," Bepi said, and he showed me on Ravenna, a mare that had been a racehorse. We then cantered together and he watched me carefully as I rode on Stella, a gentle mare.

"Like this?" I said.

"That's not bad, but let's try it like this," he replied, slipping a coin the size of a dime between my knees and Stella's saddle. If the coins slipped out, my knees had been too loose. I cantered for about three hundred yards before the coins slipped out onto the track.

"Keep your knees in," Bepi said as he stopped to pick up and replace the coins. "I'll tell you what. If you can make it all the way around the track twice with the coins still in place, I'll take you into town and you can buy some *gelato* with it."

I loved challenges, especially ones with *gelato* riding on them. And so I rode, focusing on keeping those coins pinched tightly between my knees and Stella's saddle. Around the second turn, I was still going with the coins clamped between Stella and me, as if a bolt had clamped my knees to the saddle. Down the backstretch, I began to think I could do it. I urged Stella on, forgetting for a moment that it wasn't speed, but style, that counted. Her coat glistened in the sun and her mane bounced rhythmically with her cadence. We reached the third turn, and while I wanted to shift my eyes to the left, where I knew I would find Bepi observing me, waiting by the finish, I forced myself to focus on looking straight ahead and on keeping those coins in.

The fourth turn came and went and now I could see Bepi without craning my neck. I was in the homestretch. I glanced at Bepi's face and saw fierce pride. I almost lost the coins right there but managed to keep them in place. I crossed the finish line and pulled Stella to a stop, patting her neck.

"Good girl," I said, and I allowed myself a smile for Bepi.

"No other six-year-old can ride like that, I can guarantee you," he said. "You have earned your *gelato*."

When Bepi took me into town that evening so I could cash in on my reward, he told several people what a great rider I was, that I was riding horses, not ponies, and that I was riding them *correctly.*

Gelato had never tasted so good.

∞

My mother might have been worried about me breaking horses, but she had no need to be, because I was trained by the best. Bepi taught me how to first give the horse a feel for the saddle and the bit, then walk it, leading it by the reins, and then, once the horse began to get accustomed to the bit in its mouth and the saddle on its back, to put weights over the saddle. After the horse got used to the inanimate weights, we'd let go and the horse would run with the weights on its back. When it seemed the horse was ready for animate objects on its back, one of us would get on, grab hold of the reins, and ride. At first it was always Bepi, but as I got the hang of it and Bepi saw that I could handle it, he would let me be the first. Sometimes the process took two weeks, sometimes two months. Vespa, the horse that kept dumping me onto the turf, causing my mother to come out and plead that I stop, was one of those that took longer to break. But we did break her, and we broke Pasquina as well.

It was Pasquina whom my father allegedly referred to when he told the fascists that he had a horse that was smarter than Mussolini. I don't know if Pasquina was smarter than Mussolini (though my inclination is to side with my father here), but she certainly was more trustworthy and easy to train. I broke her as well as Vespa, and then we began training her to jump. We'd start her with low jumps over barriers, and as she got used to the jumps, we'd slowly raise the barriers. The horses learned to clear the barriers by feeling the sting of clipping them with their forelegs.

I watched Bepi train horses to jump for several years, and practiced jumping with them myself, before Bepi approached me at the stables one afternoon in March 1940. "Padua is coming up in six weeks," he said. "*Gran Concorso Ippico di Padova.*"

"Are you going to jump?" I asked, thinking that was where he was leading the conversation. *Gran Concorso Ippico di Padova* was a big competition and the thought of watching Bepi jump with Vespa or Pasquina excited me.

"Me? No. I plan to go, but to watch. I thought you might want to jump."

I knew the competition was for adults; there were no categories for children. "But I'm only twelve," I said. "How can I jump?"

Bepi shrugged. "There's no rule that says a twelve-year-old can't jump."

I grinned. "Which horse?"

Bepi looked at Vespa and then at Pasquina; they were in their respective stalls. Then he smiled. "How can you choose? They're both excellent jumpers. I say you jump with each of them."

I agreed that was the best way. Then I tore off toward the house to find Mom to tell her that her son would be jumping at Padua.

⚮

I spent the next six weeks in earnest training, riding day in and day out with the coins between my knees and the saddle, even when jumping. It was not an effort to practice, because I loved to ride, but now I was riding with a real purpose, to prepare for *Gran Concorso Ippico di Padova*. I would practice in the mornings and afternoons, and at night I'd lie in my bed, seeing myself sometimes on Vespa, sometimes on Pasquina, always performing flawlessly in Padua.

Finally the morning came when we loaded the horses in the trailer and left for Padua, after a breakfast of bread and jam and fruit. I had to force myself to eat; my nerves took my appetite away. My whole family went, along with Bepi, who drove the horse van. Even Sandra dropped her bored-big-sister act and showed her excitement. She was proud of her little brother. Though we weren't certain of this as we headed to Padua, I was to be the only child in the competition. I tried not to think too much about it, because whenever I did I got huge butterflies in my stomach. The skies were clear and there was only a mild breeze; it would be a perfect day for jumping. The twenty-five mile ride took forever, but we finally arrived and unloaded the horses so they could stretch and move about. As I saw the other horses and their riders—all adults—I wondered what I was doing there. It had seemed such a grand idea only six days earlier. What had I been thinking?

"You'll do fine," Bepi said. "It's just you and Vespa, you and Pasquina. You know how to jump."

I nodded. I knew he was trying to give me confidence. I tried to look more confident, but I don't think it worked.

"Bepi knows horses," my father said, his hand on my shoulder. "He wouldn't have suggested you enter this competition if he didn't think you were ready for it. All you can do is do your best."

This settled me a bit; it was true that Bepi would not enter me in a contest where he felt I would do poorly. And I did know how to jump; I'd been jumping for five years now. I loved jumping. I'd just go out and have fun and see what happened. I smiled and nodded at my dad.

There were 15 jumps set up around the course. If you knocked over a barrier, you were penalized four points; if your horse initially refused to jump a barrier, you received a three-point penalty. The winner was the one with the fewest penalty points. In case of a tie, the win went to the faster rider.

Fifty-nine rides were entered; I was to ride Vespa in the 4th slot and Pasquina in the 56th. This didn't give me much time to get nervous or to contemplate how foolish I was to enter, as I went so early in the competition. I watched the first few riders and saw some horses knock over barriers, and this made me feel a little more comfortable. They weren't perfect, either. Maybe I would do all right.

Vespa had matured from a few years back, when she threw me a dozen times to the turf in Chirignago, but she was still frisky and skittish, graceful and strong but high-strung. With Vespa I had the chance to do very well or very poorly; her performance was harder to predict than Pasquina's. Pasquina was smooth and reliable and not so skittish.

I rode Vespa slowly to the starting line, aware of the 400 or so people in the stands watching me. A few officials raised their eyebrows when they saw how young I was. The head timer, a kind-looking man with wavy gray hair, asked me if I was ready. I nodded and tried to give the appearance of one who had been through this dozens of times. He surveyed the course, saw the white flags raised by officials on the course indicating their readiness, and then blew his horn to start my trial.

We were off, and Vespa cleared the first several jumps easily. I kept her under control, because I didn't want to pick up any penalties; I wasn't so concerned about the time. We were halfway through the course when Vespa spotted a horse warming up beyond the fence that encircled the course. She lost her rhythm and refused to take the next jump. "Come on, girl!" I prodded as we circled around to try it again. "Let's go!" She backed up, snorted, and finally took the jump, but we were penalized three points. From there on, we made each jump cleanly and smoothly. Even with the penalty points, this was good enough to lead the competition for quite a while. Had Vespa not lost her focus, we might have gotten through without being penalized. But I was thrilled to be leading.

My mother hugged and kissed me after I dismounted, and Sandra clenched and shook her fist in triumph and said I had ridden wonderfully. I looked at my dad and he smiled and said, "You handled her well, Paolo. You didn't panic out there. You pulled her through." I beamed, and Bepi's eyes were glowing with pride. "You rode like a champion," he said.

By the time I rode Pasquina, a couple of riders had surpassed my ride with Vespa. I was very calm on Pasquina. I had been through the course once, I had proven I could do well on it, and Pasquina was an easier ride. She wouldn't get distracted like Vespa; she wouldn't be looking around. She would obey me and focus on the jumps.

I rode Pasquina flawlessly. We made every jump without breaking stride, and we moved crisply from one jump to the next. It felt as easy as if we were back at the farm jumping the barriers we had jumped hundreds of times before. We completed the course without a single penalty point. The crowd cheered, in part for the flawless ride and in part because of my age. Two other riders had ridden flawlessly as well, but I had the better time. When the last rider knocked down a bar early on, I was ecstatic. I had won with Pasquina and placed fourth with Vespa. I received two plaques, one with a whip for the first-place ride, and I felt as if I had won the *Gran Premio di Milano*.

∞

The *Gran Premio di Milano* is to Italy what the Kentucky Derby is to America. Milan is about 150 miles from Venice, and I had accompanied my father to this event in 1938, when I was ten years old. "I am going to introduce you to a great man," my father said as we entered the track. As we walked in front of the stands, I saw several men milling about, talking about the upcoming race, reading newspapers, and eating sandwiches or pastries. The smell of cigarettes, coffee, and turf was in the air, mingled with the smell of the horses, some of whom were being walked nearby. Jockeys were standing by their steeds and talking with people I presumed to be owners or trainers, and the stands were quickly filling up.

We came to a man who had spotted us and was smiling broadly. He was a bit portly and was wearing a fedora and a suit and tie. This man and my father exchanged warm greetings and then my father turned to me. "Paolo, I want you to meet Frederico Tesio. Signor Tesio is the greatest horse breeder in the country." Looking very serious, I shook hands with the great man, who smiled. I wouldn't have felt more honored if I were meeting King Victor Emmanuel.

"Your father tells me you are an excellent rider," Signor Tesio said, causing me to blush.

"I like horses, sir. That is, I mean, I love them." I blushed again at my reply.

Signor Tesio smiled at me. "You'll see a horse today that you can love. This horse is my masterpiece. His name is Nearco, and he runs like the wind."

I of course had heard of Nearco. He was the fastest horse in Italy, indeed in all of Europe. I wanted to tell Signor Tesio that I knew that Nearco had never been defeated in his career and that he had crushed the field in his last race, the Gran Premio dell' Impero; he had won by a full six lengths. But I was too shy to say this. I just nodded, and, after saying our goodbyes, my father and I took our seats in the stands. My excitement mounted, because though I knew of Nearco, I had never seen him. I pictured a perfectly-formed horse, perhaps two hands taller than any other horse, muscles rippling, mane flowing, a magnificent creature that shook the ground he walked on. Nearco was a legend, and I was getting to watch him run, and I had met the man who had bred him.

True to form, Nearco quickly created two races at the Gran Premio di Milano: his own race and another race for all the other horses. Nearco glided home an easy winner, by three lengths, in the 3000 meter race, and I watched as Signor Tesio, seated not far from us, accepted the congratulations of many around him.

I was awed that day, but my appreciation for meeting Signor Tesio grew with the years as I understood more fully his greatness. Nearco remained undefeated in his career, his final race coming only six days after the *Gran Premio di Milano* when he won the Grand Prix de Paris after spending 36 hours on a train from Milan to Paris, arriving on the eve of the race. Nearco was then sold to British bookmaker Martin Benson for 60,000 pounds and sent to stud. His descendants, which include Northern Dancer and Secretariat, are legendary. Other descendants include almost all the great horses in the US and abroad over the last 50 years. When I asked Will Farrish, the owner of Lane's End, one of the leading stud farms in the country, of Nearco, he said, "He is the most important horse of the century. His bloodlines are the best."

And Frederico Tesio is widely acknowledged to be the best breeder of all time. For a kid who loved horses, it was a great privilege to meet Signor Tesio. It was Tesio who said, "A horse gallops with his lungs, perseveres with his heart, and wins with his character," and as I grew older I realized the application this had to people as well. You need your strength and health to succeed, to do well, but if you don't have the heart, you'll give up. And if you don't have the strength of character, you will be an also-ran in the field.

∞

My father had a passion for another type of racing as well: he loved car racing, or perhaps more specifically, he loved the *Mille Miglia,* the Thousand Mile race that in those days carved a figure 8 out of Italy. The race began and ended in Brescia, in northern Italy, and made its way south, going through Bologna, Florence, and then Rome before heading north through Grosseto, Siena, Venice, and other towns before ending again in Brescia. The course was marked with large red arrows pointing the drivers in the right direction. This race closed most of the main roads in Italy for a day, but people didn't mind because it was such an exciting event. In 1927, the first year of the race, drivers drove Alfa Romeos, Maseratis, Lancia Asturas, Fiats, and Mercedes-Benzes, and the average speeds were about 48 miles per hour. By 1957, speeds reached nearly 100 miles per hour, several fatal accidents had occurred on the roads, which of course were not built for racing, and the race was discontinued for 25 years before being resurrected in 1982 as a three-day touring event.

My father, who was president of the auto club in Venice, always took an interest in the race. As the 1934 version of the *Mille Miglia* approached, there were the usual pre-race reports in the Venice paper, the *Gazzettino,* about who would be entering, which drivers had decent shots at winning, and so on. Mixed among these reports was the entry of a mysterious "Mr. X" from Venice. Not much was said about "Mr. X," because not much, apparently, was known about him.

My father casually remarked one evening that the race was coming up, and added, as if the whole concept bored him, "What's the point of driving for a thousand miles if you end up in the same place?"

"The point," my mother immediately replied, "is that there *is* no point. It's men and their foolishness." My father smiled faintly but didn't reply. I felt he was testing her to see what she would say. The point, as he would have said, had he been more open about it, was to *win.* And I would have readily agreed. I would have gone so far as to say you didn't really need *any* point to race: racing was fun in itself. Wasn't that enough?

Imagine my mother's surprise, then, when, on the morning of May 6, 1934—the day of the race—she read this headline in the *Gazzettino:* "Mr. X is Max Oreffice."

I was with Mom in the kitchen when she found out. Her eyes grew big as she read, and her face blanched, and she put her hand to her mouth. Her look of shock and horror turned to worry mixed with anger. She would be nervous and anxious all day.

"What is it, Mamma?"

"Your father is in the *Mille Miglia.* He's going to drive for a thousand miles and end up in the same place." She didn't add *hopefully* to that statement, but I knew she was thinking it.

"Yea, Papá!" I cheered, raising my hands above my head. It was thrilling to me that he was in the race, and it was doubly thrilling that he was the mysterious "Mr. X."

There were several classes, and the race was run with a staggered start. My dad was one of the last to start, because he was in the top class. He was driving an Alfa Romeo, and he was in the midst of that "foolishness" my mother had described a few nights earlier. More to the point, he was, my mother was sure, headed toward his death. My mother tolerated cars, but didn't enjoy riding in them, and she had an innate fear of them. She refused to get her license and never learned to drive. Somebody else could drive her around. She would have put her foot down, hard, had she known that he was going to enter, and if she felt she had to, she would not have let my father out of her sight until after the race had started.

He, of course, knew that. So he had been training in secret, going out of his way on his business trips to Grosseto to take the roads that were used in the race. On these trips, he and his navigator—each driver had a navigator—plotted every curve of the road on a scroll that the navigator could pull out and read during the race. And he had entered the race as "Mr. X"—a man of daring and intrigue, a man who knew no fear, a man who was going to get an earful from his wife when he got home. *If* he got home.

Soon we huddled around the German-made Grundig radio in the living room, listening to the national broadcast for race updates, which were given every 100 kilometers. At 100 kilometers, my father was leading the race—something that didn't surprise me in the least. Even the great Tazio Nuvolari was behind him. I shouted and jumped up, giving my dad a big hurrah, and envisioned him flying along the roads near Bologna, the wind in his hair, people cheering him by the roadside.

The radio reports kept pouring in with good news: Max Oreffice was leading at 200 kilometers, at 300, at 400. At 400 kilometers, he was about one-quarter of the way through the race. This news came around lunchtime, and I thought how lucky I was to be at home, while poor Sandra was in school, unable to hear about the race. There was no doubt in my mind that my father would win the race.

Then something strange happened. When the announcer gave out the names of the leaders at 500 kilometers, my father wasn't first, or second, or third, or anywhere on the list that continued on for many more drivers. Finally the announcer said, "We don't know what has happened to Max Oreffice, who had been leading the race after 400 kilometers. As we find out we will pass along that information."

My mother stared at the radio, disbelieving, silently willing the announcer to say that Max Oreffice was fine, that his car had experienced mechanical problems. But the announcer refused to cooperate. My mother's worst fears, apparently, would be realized: her husband, she was sure, had been killed. He was lying dead on the roadside somewhere south of Ravenna.

She called her brother, Mario, and told him, in a querulous voice, that my father had disappeared from the race. Mario tried to soothe her and promised to find out what happened. She blinked tears from her eyes and bit her lower lip, which was trembling.

"It's okay, Mamma," I said. "He'll be all right."

Mom shrugged, unable to reply.

A few hours went by—a few of the longest hours in Mom's life—before a phone call from Uncle Mario cleared up the mystery. He had been able to get through, finally, to someone who told him what had happened. A spectator had come out onto the course somewhere near Florence, and Dad had swerved to miss the man, spinning out into a cornfield. He and his navigator weren't hurt, but the car's steering mechanism was broken.

Sadly, that was the only *Mille Miglia* for my family. My father had taken his shot, come up short, and received his earful, behind closed doors, when he got home. I had envisioned listening every year to the race, cheering him on, then entering the race myself when I was old enough. But my mother made my father promise to never race again, and I understood that that promise covered me as well. Cars were dangerous enough without racing them, and no Oreffice would be entering the *Mille Miglia*, whether under his own name or an assumed name.

❦

My father really had two passions in his life: horses and the land. I suspect that part of his love for horses had to do with their grace and speed; he certainly loved horse races as well as raising his own horses. And that appreciation for speed carried over to his desire to race in the *Mille Miglia.* While he passed down his passion for horses to me, I think he was always a little disappointed that I didn't share his passion for the land.

As a child, I had two dreams of my own. One, as I've mentioned, was to play on an organized soccer team, because Venice didn't have organized teams for kids. The other was to someday see the skyscrapers of New York City. As it turns out, I was destined to see those skyscrapers much earlier than I had imagined.

❧

CHAPTER 4

Rumblings of War

The appointment of Adolph Hitler as chancellor of Germany in 1933 was met in Italy with caution and reserve. No one was quite certain what this would mean for relations between the two countries, and while Benito Mussolini, in an August 1933 editorial in *Il Popolo d'Italia,* wrote, "Behold another great country creating a unitary, authoritarian, totalitarian, that is to say, Fascist State," he also spoke his thoughts on Nazi racial theories: "Nothing will ever make me believe that biologically pure races can be shown to exist today. . . . National pride has no need of the delirium of race." Indeed, Mussolini's first actions were not to forge a relationship with Germany, but to join in fortification against it. When Germany tried to incorporate Austria into the Third Reich in 1934, Mussolini mobilized 75,000 Italian troops to the Italo-Austrian frontier, ready to fight if Germany advanced on Austria. The following year, Mussolini aligned Italy with France and Britain to form the Stresa Front, protesting Germany's repeated violations of the Treaty of Versailles.

But when Italy invaded Ethiopia in October 1935, the pendulum began to swing the other way. In May 1936, Mussolini annexed Ethiopia, proclaimed King Victor Emmanuel III emperor, and Italian East Africa became a colony. Germany recognized this conquest, and in October 1936, Hitler and Mussolini came to an agreement in which each would support the other in pursuit of their common goals. I was not quite nine years old at this time, and I was much more concerned with riding horses and finding some fields to play soccer on than I was with national and international politics, but I noticed the scowl on my father's face as he read about these events in the *Gazzettino* or discussed them in quiet tones with my mother. I knew he thought Mussolini was terrible and that Hitler was worse. I held them both in contempt, as did my father.

Proof that the tide had turned and now favored a Rome-Berlin alliance came in March 1938, when Mussolini refused to aid Austria against Germany's takeover. Four years earlier, Italy was primed to defend Austria; now that Mussolini and Hitler had become cohorts, Austria was annexed, against its will, by Germany.

❧

The menace continued to grow across Europe. The fascism that Mussolini had set in motion in Italy in the 1920s had not been anti-Semitic until it became influenced by Nazism in the late 1930s. In fact, of the 47,000 or so Jews in Italy in 1938, more than 10,000 of them were members of the Fascist Party. But fascism took on a new meaning when Mussolini's doctrines became entangled with Hitler's. It was in 1938 that racial laws went into effect in Italy; these laws, among other things, excluded anyone of partial Jewish descent from civil and military appointments and administration. After about 75 years of equality in Italy, Jews and Catholics descending from a Jewish parent were once again relegated to second-class citizens. Their response throughout the centuries to this inequality was not to rebel, but to try harder to please, to become exemplary, productive citizens, to not rock the boat. Now their boat—my boat—was about to be rocked, and rocked hard.

It was in the spring of 1938 when the enormity of the Italian-German axis hit me full force. Those waves came, fittingly enough, from a boat floating down the Grand Canal in Venice. On the boat were Adolph Hitler and Benito Mussolini.

❧

I was in fifth grade, my second year in public school after being home-schooled, when my classmates and I were informed by our teacher, Signora Rossetti, to wear our *balilla* uniforms the next day. She didn't tell us why, but she made it sound very significant, as if the reason was so important it was not worth sharing with young students who could not fully appreciate it.

"I'll tell you why," my father told me that evening. "Hitler is coming to town. He and Mussolini are to motor down the Grand Canal. Doubtless Mussolini wants Hitler to see the bright-eyed, sharply-dressed Italian children paying homage to the two 'great men' as they pass by."

"I don't want to!"

My father shrugged. "I imagine the teachers aren't going to pose it as a question."

He was, as usual, correct. The next day I reluctantly showed up in my *balilla* uniform—dark gray shorts, black shirt, blue sash—as did all the other kids in the school. These uniforms were required of all elementary school children; we were showing our "national unity and pride" in wearing the uniform. In reality, we were being primed to become *giovani fascisti,* young fascists, smaller models of Mussolini's Black Shirts. Many children liked the uniform, which they were required to occasionally wear at parades and to practice military-like drills in the school yard, but only about half the kids bought into the idea behind the uniform. I wasn't among that half.

At about 2 P.M. Signora Rossetti told us to line up at the classroom door to prepare to go to the school courtyard. "But it's pouring out!" Giacomo said. Giacomo was pudgy and his shirt was sticking out; it was always sticking out.

Signora Rossetti gave Giacomo such a stern look that anyone who had thought of piping up in Giacomo's aid kept quiet. "Tuck your shirt in," Signora Rossetti said in a tone that implied to have his shirttail out was a heinous crime. Giacomo tucked his shirt in and we followed Signora Rossetti down the hall, through the double doors, and down the steps to the court-yard.

"This is ridiculous," I muttered to my friend Claudio, who was standing next to me. He nodded and rolled his eyes. To me, fascism meant stupid adults imposing stupid rules on people—such as standing outside in the pouring rain so we could listen to our school principal, Mr. Rosato, blather on about the tremendous honor we had in being allowed to view the two men my father hated the most, and how it was our grave responsibility to live up to that privilege.

The school administrators and teachers had umbrellas; the students got soaked as they listened to the dreary drivel of the administrators and of some muckety-muck local Fascist. This Fascist had a little pot belly that his black shirt couldn't hide, and he was so filled with his own importance that I thought (or wished) he would explode. He told us *where* to stand, *how* to stand, what to wear (our drenched *balilla* uniforms, which we'd have to dry that night), what expressions to wear on our faces, how to salute these two brutal dictators, how to cheer, *what* to cheer—"*Duce!*" and "*Fuhrer!*"—and, most importantly, what would happen to us if we did *not* show up and cheer. Our school had about 800 students, and it was made clear that there were *no* excused absences.

"He forgot to mention the blood sacrifice," Claudio said to me. "We're going to slaughter a goat and drop the horns on Hitler's head as he passes underneath us."

"Can't hurt his looks," I suggested.

"If you are not here at 8 A.M. sharp tomorrow morning," Mr. Muckety-Muck was saying, "We will come find you. We will dig you out of your home, yank you out of your bed if we must. You *will* be here tomorrow." He softened his stance for a moment, trying to win us over with his trust after battering us with threats. "I say this because sometimes students don't realize the honor and privilege that come their way, sometimes only once in a lifetime. It is hard to imagine that many of you will have a greater privilege. So I want you to take full advantage of this privilege." Talk about a back-handed compliment. If this was our greatest privilege, we were all in for woeful lives.

Incredibly, this presentation went on for nearly three hours. It was the most inane and senseless meeting I've ever been to—par for the course for the Fascists. They could have said, "Be there, 8 A.M., uniforms on, no messing around," and we could have saved three hours and gone home dry.

We could have at least gone home a little dryer if they had allowed us to wear the cape that went with the *balilla* uniform. But, befitting the intelligence of the Fascists, we were forced to keep our capes under wraps while we got soaked.

⚘

The next day we were all there, 8 A.M. sharp, driven out of our beds by the less-than-pleasant thought of Mr. Muckety-Muck barreling into our bedrooms to yank us out of our beds. It was not raining, but it was overcast and cool, and I had developed a sniffle from standing out in the rain the day before. We all knew our paces—who wouldn't, after three hours of hearing it over and over—and we marched fairly sharply in step from the school court-yard to the Accademia Bridge, which overlooks the Grand Canal. We lined up several deep across the bridge, facing a cool headwind, watching the empty canal below (all normal canal traffic had been curtailed until Mussolini's and Hitler's boat passed). Mr. Muckety-Muck was there, walking back and forth, inspecting the ranks, trying to make eye contact with each student to better spot any dissidents within the ranks. I refused to look at him but blew my nose as he passed by. He stopped for a second and I remained motionless; then he continued walking. Claudio, who was standing next to me, said, "That was a close one! I thought you had blown above acceptable Fascist noise standards." I cracked a smile, but I was feeling worse by the moment.

Il Duce and *Der Fuhrer* were, of course, late. Half an hour went by, then an hour. Kids shifted from one foot to the other, grumbling under their breath, making sure their grumbles did not reach the ears of any of our teachers or, worse yet, Mr. Muckety-Muck or the handful of Fascist friends he had brought with him.

An hour and a half went by. Still no boat. "Maybe they got the wrong day," Claudio cracked, and while I thought this was funny, I had no trouble picturing the Fascists, in their single-minded, idiotic zeal, screwing up. My throat was sore, my nose was running, my legs were tired, and I imagined us still standing on that bridge at 5 P.M., with Mr. Muckety-Muck telling us to stand at attention, look sharp, be ready, as kids, weakened from hunger, leaned on the railing, not a few contemplating jumping off to end their misery.

But around 10 A.M. the boat bearing *Il Duce* and *Der Fuhrer* mercifully floated into view. I thought Mr. Muckety-Muck was going to pee his pants in his excitement. "Attention! Attention!" he cried out. "They are coming! Be ready!"

There were a couple rows of kids ahead of me, so my view was somewhat obstructed, but I didn't care. The boat floated closer, and from the bridge dutiful cheers of "*Du-ce! Du-ce! Fueh-rer! Fueh-rer!*" began drifting down like rain-softened flower petals onto the boat. Many students seemed genuinely thrilled to see Mussolini and Hitler, but I was not so thrilled. I shared my father's disgust for them, and that was amplified by the sickness that seemed to be gaining strength by the minute, the sickness that had been prompted by standing in yesterday's rain in preparation for this moment. *Il Duce* and *Der Fuhrer* stood on the boat, Mussolini with his hand out and jaw stiff, looking like a tiny statue of himself, and Hitler with his head bobbing back and forth, turning slowly from side to side, as if it were on springs.

Both men looked ridiculous and small, and seeing them like this made me doubt that they could be so powerful.

As the boat slowly passed under the bridge, and the students around me were saluting and cheering, a teacher came and shoved me in the back, prodding me to cheer. I gave a half-hearted cheer, which quickly turned into a coughing fit. Mercifully, for as long as it took the boat to get there, it passed quickly under the bridge. Our cheering, for which we had practiced three hours in the rain and then waited two more hours to let loose, lasted about a minute and a half, and then the two dictators were gone.

I missed the next five weeks of school with a severe case of bronchitis. All things considered, I got off very lucky. The only way I could have been luckier is if I had gotten sick a few days earlier, and Mr. Muckety-Muck had come to our house and tried to drag me out of bed. I would have enjoyed seeing what my father would have done to him.

∞

As I say, the main impact the racial laws had on me and my family was when Sandra and I were assigned to Scuola Ebraica (Jewish School) in the fall of 1938, but this really wasn't a hardship, as the teachers were excellent and the classes were small, which was fine with me. I was one of eight sixth-graders; there were six boys—five named Paolo—and two girls. There were no sports, no extracurricular activities; there was no life in the school once the final period was over. As we lived about five minutes from the school, Sandra and I walked there and back home—often separately, as she had her own friends and I had mine.

∞

One evening in November 1938 I caught part of a conversation between my parents when they didn't realize I was in the hallway. They were in the living room, and while my mother was speaking in a low tone, I could tell she was upset.

"It's just going to get worse," she said.

"My work hasn't been hampered. We haven't been affected, except for school. And Scuola Ebraica is superior to the public school. They're actually doing us a favor," my father said.

"I'm not talking about the school, I'm talking about our lives. Mussolini is in with Hitler and Hitler is bloodthirsty. You saw what he did to

Czechoslovakia. And after last week, Jews are fleeing Germany—hundreds of thousands of them."

There was silence for a moment. Then my father said quietly, "I know it's bad over there. But that's Germany, not Italy."

Mussolini had supported Hitler in the recently-signed Munich Pact, which ceded territory in Czechoslovakia to Germany. Hitler truly had wanted to invade Czechoslovakia, and grudgingly accepted what he had demanded. He later called the acceptance of this pact his worst mistake; he really wanted to go to war against Czechoslovakia. (In March 1939 he seized the remainder of Czechoslovakia anyway.) As for the Jews fleeing Germany, I later learned that my mother was referring to what became known as *Kristallnacht,* the "Night of Broken Glass," where 76 synagogues in Germany were destroyed and another nearly 200 were set fire to, where nearly 100 Jews were killed and hundreds more beaten, where thousands of shops and businesses owned by Jews were looted and vandalized, and where 30,000 Jews were arrested and sent to concentration camps. This was merely a precursor of what was to come.

"He's not going to stop there," my mother said.

"Yes, but even Mussolini draws the line between Fascism and Nazism. The Fascists are fools, and anyway the majority of Italians don't truly believe in Fascism. It's like with Paolo last spring, being forced to salute Mussolini and Hitler. His heart wasn't in it. Neither were the hearts of probably most of those boys and girls. But to Hitler and Mussolini, they think everyone adores them and supports them. They're fools."

"They're fools with power," my mother corrected. "I think we should leave."

Leave! Leave Italy? The thought had never entered my mind. The hairs rose up on the back of my neck.

"This is our country," my father said. "We aren't going anywhere." There was another silence, followed by my father saying, "I fought for our country in the Great War. I didn't fight so that I could later flee. If Hitler and his army want to come over here, let them come. As for *Il Duce,* he and his Fascist followers will not be around forever. They will blow away in the first strong wind."

This conversation opened my eyes. When my mom had told Sandra and me that we would be switching to a Jewish school, I had put up a mild protest, though I didn't really care that much. Mom said we had to go there; we had no choice. That was the law. It was as if she were telling me all over again that I had to eat my spinach at dinner or I would eat it the next morning for breakfast. She presented it matter-of-factly, but now I realized that she had rising concerns and fears about the Fascist regime and about the safety of her family.

Of the four other Paolos at Scuola Ebraica, I know what happened to two of them. Paolo Ancona became a doctor, eventually settling in Israel. I believe his family survived. Paolo Sereni survived as well; he later ran a Murano glass manufacturing and trading company in Venice. But his parents, his brothers, and his sisters were all taken in 1943 by Germans to a concentration camp, where they were gassed. Paolo happened not to be home on the afternoon the rest of his family was taken.

∝

I heard no more dispute between my parents regarding whether we should leave Italy or not; indeed, they hadn't intended for me to hear what I had heard. The Rome-Berlin axis, formed in 1936, tightened its accord in May 1939 when Hitler and Mussolini signed a military assistance pact. A few months before this, Hitler had addressed the German parliament, the Reichstag: "In my life I have often been a prophet and . . . today I will once more be a prophet: if the international Jewish financiers in and outside Europe should succeed in plunging the nations once more into a world war, then the result will be not the Bolshevization of the world and thus the victory of Jewry, but the annihilation of the Jewish race in Europe."

Three months later, Hitler and Joseph Stalin, the Soviet dictator, signed the Nazi-Soviet Pact, in which the two countries agreed not to go to war against each other. The USSR had been courted by the other side as well, but were they to align with Britain and France, the reality of going to war loomed. What made the Nazi-Soviet Pact more lucrative was a part of it that was not published, giving the USSR freedom to operate as it wished in Finland, Estonia, Latvia, eastern Poland, and eastern Romania.

Hitler was sounding the bell for war and for the widespread destruction of Jews, and Mussolini—while clearly not so anti-Semitic in his stance—was nevertheless being sucked in. He was merely a pawn for Hitler, someone who could help him accomplish his goals, and despite *Il Duce's* desire to maintain Italy's identity apart from Hitler's influence, Nazi doctrine began creeping into Italy's policies. Italian Jews began to feel the effects of those policies— though the hardships on Italian Jews were nothing compared to German Jews. In Germany, Jewish families were ripped apart as the Night of Broken

Glass opened the floodgates of persecution against them; German Jews who did not flee or who were not deported were murdered, or placed in concentration camps; their rights had long been revoked. In fact, on September 15, 1935, the Reichstag had passed the Nurnberg Laws. The first law deprived German Jews of their citizenship; the second forbade intermarriage and sexual relations between Jews and Aryans. Three years later, German Jews were barred from medical and legal professions and were forced to sell their property to "true" Germans, those whose blood was not tainted with Jewish ancestry. In Italy, on the other hand, Jewish Italians were forced to go to separate schools, and were excluded, as I mentioned, from civil and military administrations. The difference was vast.

And yet, the message was clear: those of Jewish descent in certain European countries—specifically, Germany, and those influenced by or dominated by Germany—were in for increasing hardship and trouble. No one knew what that meant in Italy. My mother didn't want to find out. As it turned out, of course, my father's troubles stemmed from his antifascist stance, and not from his Jewish heritage, but it was impossible to predict where the backlash of Nazism and Fascism would be felt.

Here is another reason my father had no use for organized religion: in Germany, Catholic and other Christian church leaders stood by while Hitler imposed his anti-Semitic policies. As German Jews were deported, or beaten, or killed, the churches were silent. In Italy, Pope Pius XII neither criticized Hitler nor threatened to excommunicate him. The Vatican, fully aware of the extermination of Jews during World War II, never condemned the atrocities, claiming it had to maintain neutrality in international affairs. Hitler, a nominal Catholic, could order the slaughter of countless thousands of Jews during the week, then attend Mass and receive holy communion on Sunday. Everything about it was sickening, and the silence from the churches was deafening.

∽

By the time Hitler and Stalin had signed the Nazi-Soviet pact in August 1939, Sandra and I were in Switzerland. We had been sent, in June, to Champery, a beautiful village in the Alps. It's now a ski resort, though back then it wasn't a big resort. But it had a very good boarding school, *Ecole Superieure de Lausanne*, which had a large school in Lausanne proper and a smaller school in Champery, about an hour's drive northwest from

Lausanne. Our parents enrolled us in the Champery school for the summer term—so we could learn French, or so they said.

Neither Sandra nor I were thrilled about going to Switzerland for the summer. That meant leaving her friends, and to a fifteen-year-old girl that was a big sacrifice. For me, that meant giving up my horses and the beach at Lido. Why couldn't I learn French later? What was the big deal? Our parents didn't tell us anything other than that they had looked into schools for us and had decided on Champery. They didn't ask our opinion on the matter.

Before we left, we said our goodbyes to Grete, who planned to return to Czechoslovakia for awhile to look after her mother before coming back to Venice. Because I was disconsolate about going to Switzerland, my goodbye was distracted and less than heartfelt. "Paolo, your parents love you very much," Grete said as I sulked. "They're providing a great education for you. You should be thankful."

Grete spoke of my parents' love, but she left unspoken her own love for me, which I felt but didn't respond to. She expressed her love through actions, not words. At the moment I was too intent on the injustice of going to Switzerland to care about anyone's love—my parents' or Grete's.

It was true that Switzerland was known for its superior schools. It was also true that it was a neutral country. We were in Champery so we could learn French, but more importantly, so we could stay clear of the trouble that was looming in Italy.

My mother went with us on our trip to Champery; we hired a driver because my mother, as I've mentioned before, never drove. (When she was young, she attempted driving lessons, and seemed to have an affinity for every obstacle and ditch.) It was an all-day drive through some very scenic countryside, over the Alps in northern Italy and back down them in southern Switzerland. We stopped in Lausanne and stayed at the Hotel Beau Rivage, a beautiful hotel that overlooks Lake Geneva, with the Savoy Alps in the distance beyond the lake, to the south, and Lausanne proper rising up steeply to the north. I must admit it was a treat staying there, and it at least helped to soften the blow of leaving Italy for the summer. The hotel sat on ten acres of grounds, with terraced lawns, tennis courts, a half-indoor, half-outdoor pool, and had wonderful restaurants. It also had a ballroom with a marble floor that shimmered in the light let in through the glass dome above.

As we walked through the lobby, my mother smiled when she saw me looking around in wonderment. I had stayed in beautiful resorts, but this place was special. I think our parents wanted our first impression of Switzerland to be favorable, and mine was.

"You like it, Paolo?" she asked.

I shrugged noncommittally, like any eleven-year-old boy would. "It's all right," I allowed.

"It should be a wonderful summer for you and Sandra," she said. "You'll get to learn a new language, meet new people, and live in a beautiful setting. Your accommodations might not be quite like this at the school, but I know the setting itself is just as beautiful."

And she was right. Champery was lovely. I enjoyed the drive from Lausanne to Champery, northwest through the rolling hills, surrounded by the Alps, heading into pristine countryside with rushing streams flowing like veins from the mountains and rolling green meadows, sprayed with the bright colors of wildflowers, on one side, and dark green forests on the other. As our driver pulled up to the school, which was on a winding road near the center of the village, my stomach began churning and my throat tightened. We piled out of the car and got our bags, and my eyes moistened as we said our goodbyes to Mom. I was only eleven, and not used to being on my own, and here I was in a strange—beautiful, but strange—place, separated from my parents and from Sandra also, for the boys and girls had separate dorms. I fought a panicky feeling that seemed to crawl up my throat as I gave my mother a quick kiss goodbye.

"It won't be for long, Paolo, and I'll come visit you and Sandra."

I nodded and looked down.

"He'll be fine, Mamma," Sandra said. "Don't worry." If Sandra was nervous about being in a new school in a new country, she didn't show it. She looked slightly perturbed, but this time it wasn't at being separated from her friends, but at the attention Mom was paying me. Paolo, her baby, was disconsolate, and like a mother hen, Mom was tending to me. Sandra rolled her eyes, but she gave Mom a kiss when Mom approached her.

"I know he'll be fine, and you will be too," Mom said. "You take care of yourself. Study hard, and enjoy this land around you. I'll call you, and we'll plan on a visit or two. Maybe we can stay at the Beau Rivage again. Would you like that?"

We both nodded, though what I would really have liked was to get back in the car with our driver and return to Venice with Mom. But we went in to the main building to check in, and were received warmly, and were given a brief tour of the campus, including the cafeteria, the classrooms, the outdoor swimming pool, and the dorms, and soon Mom was gone, Sandra was in her dorm, and I was in the boys' dorm. I was in a room with four sets of bunkbeds, and I could see signs of other boys—books and bags were on or by several of the beds—but no one else was in the room. It was large, and comfortable, and as it was an end room, we had large windows looking out in two directions. Out one window I saw the main classroom building, but out the other was a green meadow, and a forest, and lots of beautiful mountains.

"Quel est ton nom?"

Startled, I turned from the window to see a boy, a little larger than me, with a mop of dark, wavy hair that looked like it would be impossible to brush through, and a broad face with a ruddy complexion.

"Pardon?"

The boy nodded with an I-knew-it look. "You don't speak French, do you?" he said.

I shook my head and told him I spoke only Italian and German.

"I said, *What's your name?*" He said this in perfect Italian, loudly, as if I were deaf.

"Paolo," I said. I wanted to ask him his name, but I was too shy. I hoped he would proffer it.

"Where are you from?" he continued in Italian. He demanded this information, but in a cheerful enough way.

"Venice. Italy."

He laughed. "Where else would Venice be, but Italy? It's always been there, hasn't it?"

I didn't know what to say to this, so I said nothing.

"Do you play football?" he asked.

I nodded. I half expected him to question my experience and to require references, but he didn't. Instead, he crossed the room, reached under a bed, pulled out a soccer ball is if he were pulling a rabbit out of a hat, and said over his shoulder as he retreated out of the room, "Well, come on then. No use hanging in here all afternoon."

So I followed him outside, and as we walked toward a field, where I could see some other boys waiting for us, he told me that this was his second summer at the school. He carried himself as if he *owned* the school, as if he were the headmaster with the power to expel anyone on a whim.

I marveled at his bluster and confidence. He seemed to be my polar opposite in personality. I wondered how he got along with his teachers, whether he allowed them any time to talk, or if he kept correcting them as they stumbled along in their instruction.

As we neared the field, he stopped talking to breathe for a moment and I got the courage to ask him where he was from. This was easier than asking his name, which was more personal. He stopped and looked at me as if I had tugged on his sleeve and asked him what time it was as he was reporting, to worldwide media, the most amazing scientific discovery.

"Dijon, of course," he said, and then he continued to the field, punting the ball to a boy who yelled for it.

"Come on, Andre!" someone yelled at him. Andre jogged onto the field, scanning the boys gathered there as if he were a general inspecting his troops shortly before battle.

"We have a newcomer," he said. "Paolo." And he held his arm out toward me, as if I were Exhibit A. I looked shyly at the other boys, who all appeared normal enough. Some grinned, some nodded at me, others squinted in the sun. One said, "Let's go!" and soon enough we were playing. As I ran up and down the field, I blended in with the others, and enjoyed the afternoon, and some of my homesickness faded. Andre was not a very good player but he bellowed good-naturedly for the ball the entire game and fouled any opponent who ventured near enough for him to reach.

I quickly learned Andre and I were not the only foreigners at *Ecole Superieure de Lausanne*. In fact, there were many more kids from other countries than from Switzerland. From France, besides Andre, there were Etienne, Bernard, Dominique, Luc, Antoine, and Henri; from England, I recall Peter, Adrian, and Jack; from Germany came Dieter, Claus, Franz, and Carl; and Arend hailed from Holland. There were many other non-Swiss residents besides. It was not hard to make the best of it in such surroundings, and playing soccer helped bring me out, make me feel part of the group. We took lots of hikes in the nearby forest, and while French was the only language spoken in class, German, French, and Italian were all spoken outside of class, and so I had an easier time of it, language-wise, than the boys from England. The school was for grades 6 through 10, and I was just entering sixth grade, and as usual was the youngest and smallest of my class, but the relaxed atmosphere of the school, the beautiful surroundings and weather, and the abundance of recreational time we had made it an easier transition than I expected. I saw Sandra often, in the cafeteria and in the hallways, and she was enjoying it, too. We talked on the phone weekly with our parents, and Mom came over two or three times to visit us—treating us to weekends at the Hotel Beau Rivage in Lausanne each time.

She came over on her birthday, August 15, which is a holiday known as *Ferragosto* in many European countries. *Ferragosto* means "middle of August," or middle of the holidays. The school was celebrating the holiday by holding swimming races in its outdoor pool in the morning and afternoon, with lunch in between. I was a lousy swimmer, but I was entered in the novice division, which apparently was filled with even lousier swimmers, as I greatly surprised myself—and delighted my mother—by winning the race. After downing a big lunch, we returned to the pool to watch the afternoon races. If I was surprised at winning my race in the morning, I was even more surprised at hearing my name called to compete in an afternoon race. The winner of each morning race competed against each other in a final race. I had changed out of my bathing suit, and someone quickly lent me a suit that was too big. I had to hold it up as I swam to keep it from slipping to my knees. Needless to say, I didn't win this race. Still, I was in an idyllic world, and though I missed my horses and the beach, I had come to enjoy my time in Switzerland.

❧

"Paolo! Come here!" It was Luc, one of my roommates; he was standing at our window in early morning, the one that looked out on the school grounds. Beyond the grounds was a road that led to the French border. And on that road, men were marching—men in uniforms, with rifles slung over their backs.

"Who are they?" I said, looking at the men and rubbing the sleep out of my eyes.

"It's the army, the Swiss army!" Luc said, his voice husky with excitement. "There's a war on!"

Dieter, a boy from Germany, came to the window and looked out. He said nothing, but his face looked pinched and his brow was furrowed. I thought about my father's hatred of Hitler, and his distaste for Germans in general, and as I looked into Dieter's kind but troubled eyes, I felt sorry for him.

It was the morning of September 2, 1939. The term would end the next day and parents would be arriving to take their children home. But more importantly, one day before, Germany had invaded Poland. Now the Swiss army was on the move, and our classes were suspended so that we could go, with our teachers, to the road a hundred yards or so from the school and watch the troops go by.

It was a sight I will never forget. It's closing in on 70 years ago and it's as clear to me as if it happened yesterday. My neck hairs still prickle as I remember watching this strange army march past. I remain incredibly impressed with the Swiss army and with their organizational skills. It amazed me then and amazes me still that the army was formed largely of citizens who, by government decree, were allowed to keep their weapons at home. As a result, when they were needed, they simply dropped what they were doing, picked up their weapons, and fell into line with their fellow citizens. (We learned that the army was made up of every male between the ages of 20 and 42; the country had, in effect, a huge army reserve, each reservist equipped with a uniform and a rifle or other weapon that they kept at home. What were bread trucks and other delivery trucks the day before were now army trucks, carrying men and weapons.)

It was amazing to see how swiftly the country responded, how ready the Swiss were to defend their country. They didn't have high crime rates as a result of being able to keep weapons at home. They were just prepared to defend their country. This ability to organize and to move swiftly greatly influenced my philosophy later in life as an executive. I figured if I could position our organization half as well as the Swiss did in preparing to defend their country, and trust my employees to the level that the Swiss government trusted their citizens, I would be doing a good job.

As we watched the troops head north, toward France, the rich smells of a nearby bakery wafted over us. Our teachers told us that there was no fighting in Switzerland but the army had been mobilized to protect all its borders against possible German attack. More and more troops marched northward throughout the day, past our school and toward the border, less than 10 miles away.

Hitler had about 1.5 million troops at his command, and the most sophisticated weaponry in the world, including six armored and four motor-ized divisions and 1600 aircraft. It was in the weaponry, and not the numbers (the Poles had about 1.8 million troops), that Germany found its advantage. That, and their alliance with the Soviet Union; as Germany executed its *blitzkrieg* (which means "lightning war"), infiltrating Poland's western border and targeting railroads to cripple the Polish military mobilization before moving toward Warsaw, the Soviet Union invaded Poland from the east on September 17. The Poles were defeated by the end of the month. By then, however, the Oreffice family had more immediate concerns. My father disappeared on September 29.

∞

When my father disappeared, as I related in chapter 1, my mother told Sandra and me he was away on a business trip. We never quite believed that, but I was not ready to believe the truth, either. The truth seemed too shocking, too preposterous. Italy, I believed up until that point, was still civilized, still a good and safe place to live, despite being under Mussolini's hand, despite its shameful part in forming the Rome-Berlin axis, in being on the same side as Germany. When Germany invaded Poland, this shone a spotlight on the axial relationship formed by Hitler and Mussolini. *Il Duce* had been strong in his support for the Munich Pact in 1938; would he be swift in coming to Hitler's aid as World War II began?

The immediate answer was no. Mussolini said he had made it clear to Hitler that Italy was not prepared for military action until 1942, and Italy held back as the German troops surged forward. There was plenty of unrest, of course; perhaps in response to the military action in Poland, the Fascist movement in Italy reached a fever pitch in the fall of 1939; my father's arrest resulted from the stepped-up Fascist furor that swept across Italy that fall. While it might be true that the majority of Italians belonged to the Fascist party, they were not real Fascist or Fascist sympathizers. Rather, the Fascists who were in place were agitated by the war on the eastern part of the continent and by Mussolini's escalating rhetoric. The churlish dictator was drawing a line in the sand, separating Fascists from antifascists, and giving greater power to the Fascists to shut down those who spoke out against the regime. Italy might not have entered the war yet, but Fascism's dark shadow was spreading across the land and, with each passing day—I realize now, in retrospect—the dangers of living in Italy, as an outspoken antifascist or a relative of one, increased.

As it was, I was not aware of so much danger, at least for myself, even after learning of my father's arrest, and then welcoming him back home as he remained under house arrest in the fall of 1939. Sandra and I, freshly returned from Switzerland, enrolled again in the Jewish school in Venice, where we spent the fall term in rather quiet fashion, despite the winds of change that were undeniably swirling around us—at least I see them as undeniable now. When my father was missing, my mother did a superb job of not transferring that worry to her children; when he was home, under house arrest, they both did all they could to live as they had always lived, to show no alarm or concern; indeed, my mother took to preparing sandwiches and serving wine to the Black Guards who would come check on my father in the night. As I think back, this was not an act of submission on her part; rather, it was a show of power: *You are in my house now. I will take care of you.* Like any good Italian woman, my mother was feeding those who entered her house, regardless of their guise or mission. Though we didn't see these feedings, Sandra and I knew of them, and the message Mom was sending to us was clear: *We are in control here; they aren't. They are misled guests in our house, and we will take care of them and send them on their way.* It was as if they were scouts lost in the wilderness, stumbling upon a house, and being welcomed in to regain their strength and their bearings. In their case, they didn't really regain their bearings, but they always left with full bellies and empty hands, which was what we wanted.

And so we lived in this uneasy equilibrium for the fall, this strange new world in which my father was freed yet under house arrest, in which Italy was in cahoots with Germany, yet not at war, when Sandra and I were back in school in Venice, yet not at the old public school, but at the new Jewish school, apparently so our thoughts wouldn't infect the minds of non-Jewish kids. The USSR declared war on Finland on November 30, beginning a poorly-fought war on their part that ended three months later with Stalin gaining some Finnish territory but Finland retaining its independence.

No one knew who was going to strike next, or where. On the surface, things were not horribly disfigured yet, but underneath, a cancer was growing, and my father—the son of a doctor—knew it. A year earlier, he had not been ready to admit to my mother that it was time to leave Italy; now, in the fall of 1939, he recognized the inevitable: to live in Italy as a known antifascist was putting not only himself, but his family, in greater peril with each passing day. Just as no one knew how far the war looming in the east would spread, no one knew how quickly the Fascist cancer would spread in Italy, and how deadly its effects would be. And no one could trust Mussolini when he said that Italy would not enter any war until 1942.

Sensing the danger, my parents sent Sandra and me back to *Ecole Superieure de Lausanne* in Champery after the winter holidays in 1939. This time we understood why we were being sent abroad. We attended the Champery school for the spring term, and we sharpened our recently-acquired French lingual abilities as German warships sailed in early April to Norway and Denmark; the Danes surrendered immediately but Norway was determined to fight, and were aided by British and French troops. On May 10, Germany attacked Belgium and the Netherlands, and four days later, after bombers destroyed the business section of Rotterdam, the Netherlands surrendered. On the same day of their surrender, more German troops emerged from the Ardennes Forest in northern France, pushing west toward the North Sea. On May 20 the Germans occupied Abbeville, close to the coast, and then began to push north along the coast, driving back British and French troops and causing Belgian troops to surrender. The Germans were blitzing northern Europe, and while they were meeting opposition, they were not being stopped. Indeed, France was to sign an armistice with Germany on June 25, giving Germany control of northern France and the Atlantic coast.

By then, we were long gone—not just from Switzerland, but from Italy.

PART II
TO ECUADOR AND BEYOND

※

CHAPTER FIVE

Bound for America

"Paolo."

It was my mother's voice, crackling through the phone line from Italy. I was on the phone in the foyer of my dormitory at *Ecole Superieure de Lausanne* in Champery. It was early May 1940.

"Mamma, hi. How are you?"

"I'm good, Paolo. And I have some big news."

"Yes?" By now, I was conditioned to be wary of big news. I held my breath.

"I'm coming to get you and Sandra in a few days. I'm going to bring you back home."

"But the term's not over until June." Then a panic gripped me. "Is it Papá? Is he okay?" A few months earlier he had been acquitted of the ludicrous charges against him, but the Fascists still had him under house arrest. Maybe they had done something to him, beaten him again, thrown him in jail, or worse. My heart was pounding hard.

"No, no, no, Paolo, he's okay, he's fine. Don't worry. It's good news, but it's something I want to tell you and Sandra in person. But above all, don't worry. There's nothing to worry about."

I exhaled deeply. "Okay, Mamma. But can't you tell me over the phone why we're leaving school early?"

"You'll find out in two days, sweetheart. That's all I can say for now."

I was, of course, only too happy to oblige my mother by leaving school early, though I had grown to like it at *Ecole Superieure de Lausanne*. But I was tremendously curious as to why my parents would pull me out of school early, and waited impatiently those last two days before my mother arrived with our driver. I was called down to the foyer of my dormitory, where they waited for me, along with Sandra. My sister looked expectant and excited, and I couldn't tell if she already knew the news or not. I ran over and hugged my mom, and she gave me a big smile as she put her hands on my shoulders. But before she could speak, I looked over at Sandra.

"Do you know?" I asked.

She shook her head. "She wanted to tell us together."

"Paolo," my mother said, "we have tickets to leave Italy, to go live someplace else for awhile. We're going to Ecuador."

I was stunned. I imagine my face registered nothing, because I didn't know what to think. Ecuador? Other than in South America, I wasn't even sure where it was.

I glanced over at Sandra, whose excitement had turned to near tears. "Ecuador!" she said. "What do you mean? Why would we go there? I don't want to go to Ecuador!"

I was still too shocked to say anything. Mom turned to Sandra and said, "It'll be a great adventure. Don't worry about it. You were worried about coming to Switzerland, and that turned out well, right?"

"Yeah, but that's because we knew we were going back to Italy," Sandra said.

My mother smiled patiently at Sandra, whose sadness was mixed with anger at the thought of leaving her home, her friends, her country. "I'm not saying we'll never return," Mom said. "I'm saying it's time for us to go."

"Where exactly is Ecuador?" I finally managed to say.

"It's on the western coast of South America," mother said. "It's a lovely country, with the Andes for mountains, instead of the Alps, and the Pacific for an ocean, instead of the Adriatic. We'll all love it, I'm sure."

"When are we leaving?" I asked.

"May 24th. Our visas came through a few days ago."

"But why Ecuador?" I was neither angry nor sad; rather, I was in a daze.

"Because it's the one country that would welcome us," my mother said. She managed a smile; she was trying to win us over. "You like adventure, don't you?"

I shrugged; I wasn't sure. Sandra quickly replied, "Yes, I like adventure—in Italy!"

I returned to my room to grab my bags. Andre and Dieter were there; the others were down in the cafeteria. "Well, I'm off," I said.

"Lucky stiff," Andre replied. He was pulling on a shirt; Dieter was tying his shoes. Andre was always the last one out of the room for meals, for classes, for anything. "Getting to go home early."

"I'm not just going home," I said with some importance.

"You off on holiday, then?" Andre said, trying to pretend he didn't really care. He was going through the motions of trying to brush his unruly hair. He stopped brushing and peered more closely in the mirror. "Look at that, will you? Another pimple!" he said in disgust.

"We're going to Ecuador. To live."

Both Andre and Dieter stopped what they were doing and turned to me.

"Ecuador? Where in blazes is Ecuador?" Andre demanded.

"On the west coast of South America," I said, pleased that I knew something that Andre didn't.

"South America! That's half a world away!" Andre said.

I shrugged and nodded, as if moving halfway across the world was rather routine for me.

"Good luck, then," Dieter said. I thanked him and wished them both luck as well. As I left the room, Andre called out, "Hey Oreffice, show them how to play football, European style, down there!" I grinned, thinking of Andre's own brand of play, which was short on finesse and technique and long on physical pounding.

As we drove through Switzerland and then Italy, my stomach was churning. I was excited—I had bought into Mom's talk of adventure more than had Sandra, who spent much of the ride home sulking—and I was also a bit nervous. I peppered Mom with questions about what Ecuador was like, and she gave me some answers, but they didn't satisfy my curiosity. I learned the country exported cacao and coffee and bananas and pineapples, a fruit I had never tasted; that it had a big fishing industry; that the Andes ran through the entire country from north to south; and that the people spoke Spanish.

Another language to learn.

"Well then why did we waste our time learning French?" Sandra said.

"Learning a language is not a waste of time, Sandra," Mom replied.

"What about Nonno Vittorio and Nonna Emma?" I asked.

Mom shook her head. "They're staying."

"And Nonna Alice?"

"She's staying as well."

"Then I want to stay with Nonna Alice or Nonna Emma!" Sandra said.

"You're going with us," Mom said in a tone that let Sandra know the discussion was closed.

I was sad to think that I would be separated from my grandparents and my extended family. I sat quietly for a while, thinking of them all, of our times in Venice and of Nonno Vittorio's birthday celebrations in Chirignago. Gradually my mental image shifted from the pleasant ones of my relatives, now tinged with sadness, to one of Hitler and Mussolini, floating down the Grand Canal, with the Fascist official prodding my classmates and me to cheer these two evil men. It was because of them that we were leaving. I despised them for what they were doing—Hitler across Europe and Mussolini with his Fascism in Italy. Though Hitler would be judged the more cruel and brutal of the two, and rightly so, it was Mussolini in particular that I scorned. Were it not for Mussolini and his own brand of national terrorism, we would not have been forced to leave our homeland.

It was this injustice that angered Sandra; we were forced to leave what we knew and loved. She wasn't really angry with Mom and Dad for making the decision; she was angry that her country had become a place where you could not safely speak your viewpoint, state your opposition to degrading and unjust policies. If you opposed the government, you could be beaten, tortured, perhaps even killed. Thank goodness my father was able to receive a fair trial in the midst of this madness; but even then he remained under house arrest. The immediate future for known antifascists in Italy, as World War II escalated and the Rome-Berlin axis tightened, was at best unknown. To remain in Italy was dangerous, perhaps even foolish. My father loved Italy, and he detested leaving, but he was not foolish. And he didn't take chances when it came to his wife and children.

Sandra had every reason to be angry, as did I. But our anger was misplaced if we spent it on our parents. It was better spent on the men behind the Axis Powers.

☙

As the war had rumbled across the northern portion of the continent in the spring of 1940, and as Sandra and I had continued our schooling in Champery, my mother had not sat idly by. She had gone into high gear, with a singular goal on her mind: to acquire visas for us to leave the country. Because of my father's house arrest and political status as a known antifascist, it was up to my mother to do most the work in obtaining the visas. She went at this task just as tirelessly as she had gone about getting my father out of jail, not stopping in the latter case until she had talked to Mussolini's son-in-law. While obtaining visas for us to leave Italy didn't have the same urgency attached to it as did the mission of freeing my father from jail, it did have an importance to it, one that grew as the war, and Fascism, spread. Mom tried to get visas to a number of countries: Brazil, Argentina, Chile, and Venezuela, in addition to Ecuador. We had some close cousins on my father's side in Brazil; they had smelled trouble brewing in Italy in 1937 and had left. Because of them, Brazil was my parents' first choice. Our cousins tried to get us visas, but things moved too slowly with the Brazilian bureaucracy.

Because it could take a minimum of six months to get an immigration visa to the United States, the US was not a consideration. My parents wanted out, and they wanted out quickly. My father knew someone who had family and friends in Ecuador, and this man helped expedite getting our visas. Even while the visa process for the other countries was still going on, they received word in late April that we had been granted visas to Ecuador, and they didn't wait to hear from the other countries. Ecuador would be it.

We came home on May 4, 1940. My dad took the following day, his birthday, off—very unusual for him. Birthdays were big for kids but not so big for adults. But he took May 5 off, spending the day with us, treating us to *gelato,* going for a walk with me in the afternoon. We kept our walk confined to the area of Venice prescribed by the Fascists as allowable territory for my father to be in, passing by businesses and houses that I had seen my whole life and soon would leave behind. During our walk he asked all about Switzerland, had me show off my improved fluency in French, and praised me for doing well in school and for making the adjustment. "You and Sandra have made a lot of adjustments in the past year, haven't you?" he noted.

I thought of his being beaten, being thrown in jail for no cause, being put on house arrest. In comparison, going to Jewish School in Venice and then to school in Champery didn't seem such a hard adjustment.

"It hasn't been so bad," I said.

He smiled at me. "And now we have more adjustments to make." His smile tightened as he gazed off into the distance, not seeing the landscape around us, but trying to peer into the future ahead of us. "Three more weeks," he said, as much to himself as to me.

"Papá?"

"Yes?"

"What will it be like in Ecuador?"

He stopped and turned to me. "What do you want it to be like in Ecuador?"

I shrugged. Other than *good* or *nice*, I didn't know what I wanted it to be like.

"It will be, Paolo, what you want it to be, what you make it to be," he said. "It will be very good, Paolo. You'll see. We'll all love it there."

We walked on a bit more. "Papá?" I said again. "What will you do there?"

Without hesitation he replied, "Why, I'll do whatever I want there."

I was bolstered by his confidence and optimism, but I couldn't shake the feeling that something was bothering him, something beyond the obvious dissatisfaction with being forced to leave his own country to protect his family. He seemed worried, and no matter how he tried to cover it, worry was so unnatural for him that he could not fully conceal it.

We celebrated his birthday that evening, but the celebration was subdued, and the merriment, while not forced, was colored by the preoccupation of what lay ahead of us in our final few weeks in Italy, and of our lives beyond that, in Ecuador. My parents, in fact, seemed uneasy and tense, and after a short while we gave up trying to have fun and just went to bed.

∽

We had 19 days from my dad's birthday until the day we were to sail for Ecuador on the SS Rex, the largest steamship owned and operated by the Italian Line of Genoa. The ship—which my mother booked us on, and had a brochure of—had been launched in 1931 in the presence of King Victor Emmanuel III and Queen Elena. It had white funnels, red tops, and a green stripe, cruised at about 24 knots (about 28 miles per hour), and was 880 feet by 106 feet, rising up 37 feet above the water. It was one of the few Italian ships that had continued to run after the war started; in doing so, it was supposedly, I learned later, a symbol of Italy's neutrality to that point.

All I knew at the time was the Rex looked regal. Pictures in the brochure showed outdoor swimming pools and lido areas, with sand scattered around the pools to make it seem like a beach. The ship brochure captured my imagination and helped me become more excited about the trip. It made the trip somehow more real: it was happening, and it was happening soon. Thus inspired, I even cracked a geography book that I had in the house and read up on Ecuador. I learned some more about their major industries and exports, their climate, their landscape and environment, their history. I learned, among other things, that they had plenty of yellow fever, malaria, and tuberculosis to go around, and that malnutrition was a common problem. The land might be beautiful, and the Andes majestic, and the seaport towns must surely be nice, but we weren't heading toward any quixotic paradise. We were simply leaving Italy, heading toward any country that would take us in.

Much had to be accomplished in the 19 days we had left. My parents had been busy before we got home from Switzerland. Dad had just sold his interest in the farm to his business partner, Cugnasca, unfortunately for a fraction of what it was worth. Cugnasca had him over a barrel and they both knew it. Dad met with Bepi Rosini, the head of our stables, and told him what was happening. He helped Bepi financially and asked him to take care of the family silver. Dad trusted Bepi not only in horse matters, but in all matters. Bepi took the silver and distributed it among several different farm families. Years later, after the war, my parents returned and all the silver was intact.

It was no different with the horses. Bepi oversaw the sales of Vespa and Pasquina to two separate people whom he knew would take good care of them. Before they were sold, I rode each of them again, and my heart was heavy as I thought of all the riding and training I had gone through with them, and of the *Gran Concorso Ippico di Padova*, where I had placed fourth on Vespa and first on Pasquina in the jumping competition. Now I would never ride them again.

"Don't worry, Paolo," Bepi told me one afternoon after I had ridden them for one of the last times. "I'll make sure they are placed in good hands."

I nodded and turned away, feigning interest in a car that was driving past on the road by the farm. As tears welled in my eyes, I realized I was sad to be leaving Vespa and Pasquina, but far sadder to be leaving Bepi. He had taught me a lot about horses, and I had come to look on him as a second father, a wise and kind man who was soft-spoken and loyal to my father. This loyalty was magnified by the number of people who had betrayed my father in recent months.

As Bepi led the horses to their barn, I peeked over my shoulder at him. He nodded, smiled a sad smile, and looked down as he kept walking. I wasn't sure if I would see him again before we left, so I said, "Goodbye, Bepi," and he turned and nodded again, his smile brighter this time.

"You'll do well," he said, and then he turned again and walked on. Not, *You'll be fine* or *You'll be okay,* but *You'll do well.* For some reason, this calmed me, just as his encouragement right before the *Gran Concorso Ippico di Padova* had calmed me. Sometimes all we need is someone to believe in us to get us going in the right direction.

As our departure date of May 24 neared, Dad took care of financial matters, closing bank accounts, giving some of the money to Uncle Mario for safekeeping, and exchanging some of the lire for dollars. Officially, we were allowed to take only $100 per person, so Dad was forced to try to raise additional money in other ways, because we wouldn't have gotten very far on $400.

Because anything above the $100 per person limit was illegal, my father was between a rock and a hard place. No papers could be exchanged showing any financial transactions taking place; such records would put my father's ability to depart in great peril, were he to be searched. So he didn't deal with banks, but with individuals who were temporarily in Italy and looking to exchange dollars for lire—to pay for their hotels, meals, and so on. A few of the people he dealt with happened to be associated with banks, but he dealt with them on an individual basis and not with them as representatives of their banks.

The rate of exchange at that time was 20 lire to the dollar, but Dad was willing to pay double or even triple that rate if he could find people who could provide him the money quickly. He found one such person in the Swede Raoul Wallenberg, who in a few short years was to become famous for saving 100,000 or more Jews from death in Nazi concentration camps. My father knew Wallenberg, who was in Venice on business at the time; they met and Wallenberg agreed to exchange what currency he needed for his stay in Venice with my father rather than a bank, but he refused to do it at a rate that was higher than the official exchange rate. The amount wasn't great, but Wallenberg came through on his end of the deal: our money was waiting for us in New York where he had deposited it in cashier's checks at our hotel.

Unfortunately, the same can't be said for a vice president of what was then known as the Chase Bank. My dad met with this Chase banker, who demanded three times the exchange rate. My dad paid the rate, trusting that the money would be there on the other end.

My parents scrambled for money in other ways, too. My father had what he believed was a Monet original; he took it folded in a suitcase, but an appraiser in New York told him it might or might not be a Monet. Had it been an original for sure, he would have sold it for a princely sum. My father later admitted he would have been better off buying diamonds in Italy and reselling them in America or Ecuador. But he didn't know if he would be frisked and the diamonds taken as contraband, with him thrown in jail. It was just too risky.

A few days before we were to sail on the Rex we had dinner with Nonno Vittorio and Nonna Emma. "You're all set, then?" Nonno Vittorio asked.

"We're ready," my father said. I noticed he looked tired, and had that same worried look that I had first seen when Sandra and I had returned from Champery.

"It's hard to believe that in a few days we'll be gone," Mom said. She, too, looked pensive; maybe it was just the stress of leaving. She mentioned the friends she had placed Maria, our cook, and Angela, our maid, with, though they wouldn't leave until after we had departed. They would stay on to supervise the storage of our furniture and other belongings before moving on to their new situations. My parents compensated them handsomely in their final settlement.

Nonno Vittorio and Nonna Emma seemed unusually subdued that evening. The talk was kept intentionally light, and drifted back to remembrances of birthdays past at Chirignago, to holidays at the beach at Lido, to summers at *Prati Nuovi,* and to our horses. The war was mentioned only briefly, though the Germans had been relentless in the preceding six weeks. Germany had invaded Denmark and Norway in April, and in May had invaded France, Belgium, Luxembourg, and the Netherlands. Nonno Vittorio and Dad mentioned the Nazi advances in low tones and almost in passing. It grated on my dad that Italy was allied with Germany; he had such a hatred for Germans that he couldn't talk about them, knowing that he was leaving. He would have much rather stayed and fought them. Brief mention was also made of Winston Churchill, who a few weeks prior had become British prime minister. The new prime minister had just met with Mussolini to try to convince him to keep Italy out of the war.

"Churchill will be a good prime minister," Nonno Vittorio said. "Let's hope Mussolini listened to what he had to say."

"Don't count on it," my father said. "Mussolini is aligned with Hitler, and he has stated that Italy will not enter the war for at least two years. Therefore, my guess is that Italy will enter the war, and soon. You can't trust Mussolini, and you know he won't listen to reason."

Mom, seeing Dad's agitation, changed the subject, asking her own mother to look in on Nonna Alice, my dad's mother, from time to time. "She seems especially worried, and is all alone," Mom said. "And she's sad, too, that we are leaving." For the first time I thought about our departure from my grandparents' angle; they were losing, for an unforeseeable time, a son, a daughter, two grandchildren. Nonna Alice was 70 years old; Nonno Vittorio would be 80 in a few months; and Nonna Emma would turn 70 in six weeks. They were in reasonably good health, as far as I knew, but they seemed very old to me, and I realized that I might never see them again. I was quiet that evening, even quieter than usual, holding this heaviness in my heart and not knowing what to do with it.

Sandra was quiet as well; she had become reconciled to leaving, and had said goodbye to most of her friends, and she had gone around teary-eyed for the last few days. She no longer was lashing out about leaving, and simply appeared sad and a little frightened, and I felt sorry for her, because she was leaving behind so many friends. Being sixteen, she was a little more settled in her world, and her friends meant a lot to her. I had friends as well, but the bonds weren't as tight as they were for Sandra, and saying goodbye wasn't as hard for me.

Sandra's best friend, by the way, was Giuliana Camerino, whose *nom de plume* is Roberta di Camerino, internationally famous in the fashion world. Born Giuliana Coen, she escaped with her family to Switzerland during the war, staying in the same refugee camp that some of my relatives stayed in to escape the Nazi regime. While in the camp, Giuliana began making purses to earn herself some spending money. She was awarded an "International Fashion Oscar" by Nieman Marcus in 1956, and now designs handbags, suitcases, jewelry, clothing, and other products, with offices in Switzerland, Tokyo, Shanghai, and New York.

To Sandra, she was just Giuliana, a great friend left behind. To me, they were just teenage girls being a pain!

When we got home that evening, we quietly went to bed after bidding Maria and Angela good night. I would miss Maria and Angela, but not nearly as much as I would miss Grete, who, as I mentioned, had returned to Czechoslovakia. I hadn't seen her for nearly a year, since right before Sandra and I went to Switzerland for the first time, in the summer of 1939. Now I recalled how I had sulked about having to go to Champery over the summer, and how Grete had said it was because my parents loved me, and I recalled how my goodbye with Grete was dominated by my self-pity, and how I had hardly said goodbye to her at all. I assumed I would see her again, but leaving the country—the continent—made me wish I had said a better goodbye. In my bedroom, I looked out my window to the north, toward Czechoslovakia, and said *Goodbye, Grete Grossman, until we meet again.*

❧

On May 22, one day before we were to drive to Genoa to embark the following day on the Rex, I walked into the dining room where Angela was preparing breakfast. Both Mom and Sandra had steaming cups of coffee. Dad was nowhere to be seen.

"Well then, what are we going to do?" Sandra was saying. "Are we going to stay?"

"We are not staying," my mother said firmly. "We will find a way. There must be other ships sailing."

"Other ships?" I said. "What happened?"

"Sit and eat, Paolo," Mom said, and Angela placed a slice of toast with strawberry jam on it in front of me.

"What's going on?" I repeated.

"The Rex was canceled!" Sandra said. "All Italian ships were canceled!"

"Canceled! By who? What do you mean?"

"By the government. By Mussolini," Sandra said. "He announced that it was too dangerous for people to be on these ships anymore. So he just canceled them all!"

"You're kidding!"

"Do I look like I'm kidding?"

She didn't. I was dumfounded. I looked at my mom, who said, "So help me, Paolo, we're going to find a ship somewhere that's leaving Italy. Or if we have to depart from another country, we'll do that. We will find a way out. He can't keep us here if we don't want to be here!"

It had become a personal confrontation between Mussolini and our family. My father was arrested and beaten and jailed under Mussolini's juris-diction, he was released in part on Mussolini's son-in-law's command, and now the dictator's latest decision directly impacted our ability to leave the country we loved to head toward a country I had barely heard of.

"Where's Papá?" I asked.

"Talking to Signor Vaccari, the *prefetto*," Mom replied. "Finding out about other ships."

"But they're saying there *are* no other ships!" Sandra said. "You heard them!"

"I've heard Mussolini say a lot of things," my mother said. "Believe me, I don't place much stock in what he says."

"All I want to know is, are we supposed to unpack or not?" Sandra said.

"Absolutely not," my mother replied.

"Fine," Sandra retorted. "Why don't we just float over on a raft, then."

Mom, ever understanding and patient, chose to ignore that comment. "Your father will be home soon," she said. "When he is, we'll find out what ship we can get on."

Dad didn't get home until early afternoon. By then we were all dying to know our fate. Were any other ships sailing? Could we get on one of them? Would we have to go to another country to leave Europe? Would we leave at all, or would we stay? What would happen to Dad, to all of us, if we stayed and Italy—despite Mussolini's declarations otherwise—entered the war? We had so many questions that we nearly leapt on Dad when he got home.

"What did you find out?" Mom asked.

"It's as they said, all Italian ships are canceled," my father replied. "The official word is it is for the safety of the passengers. The unofficial word is it is in preparation for Italy to enter the war."

"Italy's going to enter the war?" Sandra asked. She suddenly appeared not so eager to stay in Italy after all.

"That's the rumor," Dad said. "No one seems to know for sure, or at least no one is saying."

"Well, what do you think?" Sandra said, panic rising in her throat.

My dad looked at Sandra for several seconds, measuring his reply, not wanting to frighten her. He shrugged. "It will probably happen, but it's hard to say when. And by that time. . . ."

I looked at Mom; her face had gone pale. Dad noticed this too, and smiled at her. "By that time, we will be long gone, I assure you."

"Did you find a ship?" Mom asked, nearly breathless.

"The SS Manhattan is bound for New York on June 2. Marcello Vaccari believes we can get on that ship, if we can get 30-day visas for the US in time."

Mom and Sandra did an impromptu victory dance; Sandra had gone over completely to the side of leaving. I was quite happy—and relieved—too. "Let's go get the visas then!" I shouted, as if we could all walk down to the corner store, get our visas, and end the excursion with a *gelato.*

"It's not quite that simple," Dad said. "Venice doesn't issue those visas. We have to go to Trieste, or maybe Rome."

The smile vanished from Mom's face. "But you can't travel outside of Venice," she said.

"Marcello is talking with Foscari," he said. "He thinks Foscari will not be sad to see me go, as he lost his battle in trying to get me imprisoned or killed." Ludovico Foscari, the head of the Fascists in Venice, considered dad a traitor to his country; if he couldn't kill him, the next best thing would be to have him leave the country. Ironically, dad's antifascist stance and high profile could be in his favor as he attempted to get his family out of Italy.

Foscari did not ease up on the house arrest restrictions for my father, but he did not stand in the way of my mother going to the US consulate in Trieste to try to obtain 30-day visas for the US. She met up with plenty of uncooperative people and lots of red tape, but by this time she was used to that treatment, and she eventually found a consul who understood the gravity of the situation, with my father being a political prisoner, and she was able to obtain the visas.

Several days before the SS Manhattan's departure date of June 2, we purchased tickets to travel on it to New York City. We were—once again—set to leave Italy, though the time from May 24, our original departure date, to June 2 seemed to stretch on forever. I awakened each morning wondering if the Manhattan would be canceled as well, or if our visas would be revoked, or our tickets would fall through. I had gone in a short span from not wanting to leave Italy to being very ready to leave.

A few days before we were to leave for Genoa, from where the Manhattan would sail, we paid a visit to Marcello Vaccari. As the *prefetto* of Venice, he was of higher rank than Foscari, and he and my father had been friends for years, and had played bridge together as members of *Casino di Commercio,* Venice's chamber of commerce.

Vaccari was in his office in downtown Venice, working, but he immediately received us in his outer office. The *prefetto* was a tall, distinguished-looking man with gray hair and a kind smile. His eyes were dark brown and when he smiled, his whole face—indeed, the whole room—lit up. He somehow gave the impression of both being very busy and yet having all the time in the world for us.

"Elena," he said. "You're looking lovely as ever." He made a small bow and took her hand warmly in his. Mom smiled graciously and a little shyly, but she couldn't help but glow—not only at the compliment, but at the thought that we had tickets on a ship that was still scheduled to sail, and we would be gone in a few days. Her relief since we'd gotten the 30-day visas and the tickets for the Manhattan was noticeable.

"Thank you, Marcello," she said. "And we all want to thank you for what you've done for us."

"Me?" he said, putting his hand on his chest and raising his eyebrows in pleasant surprise. "I've done nothing that I know of, nothing at all. But I take it from your comment that you did indeed get the visas?"

"We did," my dad said. "We're bound for America."

A worried look drifted over Vaccari's face. This struck me as odd, seeing as we had our tickets and our visas. "When do you leave?" he asked.

"June 2, from Genoa," my dad replied.

A look of relief flooded Vaccari's face. "That's good. That's great, Max. You're just in time. Just in time," Marcello said. "Come with me for a minute, Max. Excuse us, will you?" He opened his inner office door for my dad and then followed him inside, shutting the door behind him.

"So is this ship going to be as nice as the Rex?" I asked Mom. I hadn't seen a picture of it, but I hoped it would have a swimming pool and be as impressive as the Rex.

"If it floats and it gets us to New York, it will be the nicest ship in the world," Mom said.

A few minutes later Dad came out of Vaccari's office, and after saying our goodbyes, we left. On the street, my mom asked him what Vaccari had said inside his inner office.

"Oh, nothing much," Dad shrugged. "Just wished us luck, asked about our travel plans, that sort of thing."

Mom looked at him for a moment and then decided not to press the issue. Later, Dad told us that Vaccari had told him that he still had the papers of *confino* that were meant for my father, and that Foscari and no other Fascist in Venice knew of the papers that had come from Rome. "They're as disorganized as they are contemptible—luckily for you," Vaccari had told my father. Vaccari also told my father why we were getting out just in time: because Italy was going to enter the war any day now, and once Italy was in the war, no ships other than warships would be sailing. Finally, Vaccari allowed that it was possible that in the ensuing confusion after Italy entered the war, the papers of *confino* might be lost. Such are the vagaries of war, he said. At any rate, once my father was out of the country, he would be safe.

✣

The last few days before leaving for Genoa went very slowly. I couldn't shake the fear that Black Shirts were going to come into our house, yank my father out of bed, and drag him away from us forever. (This vision was doubtless aided by the threat of two years ago, when Mr. Muckety-Muck promised to yank any schoolchildren out of bed, dare they not show up to pay homage to Hitler and Mussolini floating by on the Grand Canal.) Sounds of people passing by on the calle outside gave me a start; I dreaded the nights, when the Black Shirts were most accustomed to calling. Strangely, they had paid us only irregular visits in the last few weeks; either they had gotten tired of policing my father, or their attention was diverted by other things. Either way, these irregular visits served to heighten my fears, not allay them, because now I didn't know what to expect—and I couldn't help but expect the worst. True, we had been allowed to obtain the 30-day visas to America and to get passage on the Manhattan, but I kept seeing stubble-faced Black Shirts at the port in Genoa, greasy grins on their faces, devilish eyes shining, waiting to drag my father off as he tried to board, hooting at the great jest they had played on my family. I hated them and feared them and hated that I feared them. I remembered what my father had told me the previous fall, when he was released from the Black Shirts' jail: *We cannot live in fear. That's what they want.*

I understood that; it was just hard to follow.

We had been prepared to leave more than a week earlier, so the last few days I had some time to myself. I spent some of it saying goodbye to friends in the neighborhood, and some just walking, taking in the sights. I crossed the Accademia Bridge, under which I had watched Hitler and Mussolini float, and I went to Piazza San Marco, looking at the centuries-old structures as if I were a tourist, taking in their beauty and elegance as if I had never seen them before. There were Saint Mark's Cathedral, first built almost 1,200 years ago, then reconstructed after being nearly destroyed by fire and rebuilt again after that, and the Doge's Palace (Palazzo Ducale), slightly older than the cathedral, destroyed four times by fire, and each time rebuilt on a more magnificent scale. I took solace in the lasting power exhibited by these edifices; they had endured through 5,000 generations, and though they were all but destroyed by fire, they had come through the fire, were rebuilt to be stronger and more beautiful, and were lasting monuments to what I saw as the triumph of good over evil. Piazza san Marco had outlasted kingdoms good and bad, and surely it would outlast Mussolini, and Venice and Italy would one day be restored, just as Saint Mark's Cathedral and the Palazzo Ducale were.

Near the Palazzo Ducale, I looked at the Bridge of Sighs, which connects the palace with the old public prisons. As prisoners were escorted from the Palazzo Ducale, where they had their cases heard and sentences handed down, I imagine their collective sighs and wailings gave rise to the name of the bridge. I heaved a small sigh of my own off that bridge, and perhaps it drifted upward, toward the bell tower of the cathedral, because in a few moments the bells rang. Though I was not particularly religious, and knew the bells ringing were a coincidence, still they offered me some small comfort, as if my sigh had been heard, my concerns and desires acknowledged.

∽

June 1 dawned clear and beautiful. We had said our final goodbyes to our grandparents, so after a rushed breakfast we loaded our suitcases in Grandfather Vittorio's motorboat. His chauffeur took us to the Piazzale Roma, which contained the world's largest parking garage at the time (it might still be the largest). Oreste, grandfather's driver, was waiting for us there. He drove us—in his inimitable, slow style—toward Genoa, the huge Lancia all but crawling over the highway.

I was still unsettled, and vaguely fearful, and I think it's safe to say we each carried a mixed bag of emotions with us as we left Venice and headed west, from one coast to the other. We drove through Padua and Verona in the morning, stopped near midday in a small roadside restaurant for lunch, then made the final leg of the journey, southwest to Genoa, arriving in late afternoon. We made small talk along the way, but our hearts were heavy, our minds troubled, and we spent most of our time silently saying goodbye to the land that we knew, uncertain of the future, unsure even of what—or who—we might encounter in Genoa. I continually saw Black Shirts in my mind's eye, and tried hard to just take in the countryside, with its vineyards and its meadows with cattle dotting the rolling hills, hoping that we were leaving the Black Shirts behind forever.

Genoa is a port city on the Gulf of Genoa, on the Mediterranean; it lies beside a harbor at the foot of the western Apennines. We stayed in a hotel in the old quarter of the city. A doorman in crisp maroon livery and a black top hat opened the large glass doors for us and we walked into a high-ceilinged reception area with a marble floor and Renaissance paintings on the wall. After we checked in we drove to the harbor, over which towered the Palazzo

San Giorgio, built in the 14th century, not far from the Church of Annunziata, which has numerous fine works of art lining its interior. The ocean liners docked near the church, and I must admit, as beautiful as the frescoes and paintings were in the church, I was more enamored with the elegant beauty of the ship in the harbor, the SS Manhattan. For it was that ship, and not the church, that promised us deliverance from the Black Shirts.

As I laid eyes on the Manhattan and on the waters beyond, my spirits lifted. The ship was there, it was real, and it was still scheduled to depart the next afternoon. I thought fleetingly of Christopher Columbus, a Genoa native, and felt a surge of excitement, perhaps not unlike Columbus did in 1492 when he set sail westward from Spain to find a shorter route to India and China. Columbus didn't know exactly where he was going, but then neither did we, other than the name of the country, Ecuador, and a few raw facts about it.

And so we returned to our hotel, ate dinner, and went to our rooms to sleep. It took me a while to get to sleep, which was unusual; it was partly in excitement about the next day, and tinged with the remnants of the fear of hearing pounding at our door, and opening it to see two Black Shirts ready to haul Dad away.

But I finally fell asleep, and awoke to another gorgeous morning. We had breakfast in the hotel, and the food tasted wonderful, the servers were professional and kind, the doorman was smiling and pleasant. We were ushered out into a new day under a bright blue sky, and as we returned to the harbor, I saw my parents smile at each other without a hint of the stress that had been hanging over them, over all of us, for the last month, and I was happy. There were no last-minute ship cancellations when we got to the harbor, no Black Shirts, nothing to stand in our way. Someone checked our papers and tickets and we were allowed to board the Manhattan. We brought with us a few suitcases, and Mom and Sandra were ushered off to their accommodations while Dad and I were shown ours. The Manhattan normally carried about 800 passengers, but on this day that number had swollen to about 2,400, many of whom were Americans returning to the US. Because of the overflow of passengers, cabins for two became cabins for six or eight, salons were turned into dormitories; women boarded with women and men with men. Mom and Sandra were in a cabin with six other women, while Dad and I were in the ballroom with about 200 other men. We had cots to sleep on and kept our suitcases under our cots.

No one complained, though. The ship was clean, the food was good, and everyone was just happy to be sailing, to be leaving Europe and Italy. We all considered ourselves lucky to be on board.

The Manhattan turned out to be the last ship to sail from Italy before Mussolini reneged on his word and entered our country in the war, and normal limitations and procedures were scrapped. The Manhattan became, in effect, a luxurious liner transporting a few thousand refugees. It, too, would be affected by the war, as would the harbor and Genoa itself. The Manhattan became, in June 1941, a Navy transport called the Wakefield; Genoa and its harbor suffered heavy damage in bombings. But both Genoa and the Manhattan were unscathed by the war as of June 2, 1940, and the Manhattan sailed with its neutrality clearly marked on the sides, by the name of its ship, its ship line, and by the American flag posted. All of these were very large, easily seen from a distance, with the intent being to protect the passengers on board.

The passage was uneventful until after we crossed the Strait of Gibraltar, where the ship received warnings that German submarines were in the area. I peered out anxiously over the waters, hoping and expecting to see nothing, but knowing that submarines could well be prowling underneath, and that we could be the target of an attack at any moment. Maybe a submarine would mistake us for a warship, or maybe the Germans had knowledge that many Jews were on the Manhattan, and they were going to sink it even though it was a nonmilitary ship. I turned to my dad, who was peering out over the waters as well.

"Do you think there are subs nearby?" I asked.

He paused, then said, "No, I don't think so. Why would they be over here?"

I nodded, but he kept looking out over the waters, and I wasn't certain that he believed his own words.

So we spent a few uneasy hours shortly after passing through the strait, but we relaxed as we got farther from the strait and nothing happened. We were in the Atlantic Ocean now, with nothing between us and America but water.

We were on the Manhattan for eight full days, and it was my first experience with the big heart of Americans. No other country's ship would have gone to the extent that the Manhattan did to save as many people as possible from the war. The crew could not have been nicer; they did everything to make the trip as pleasant as they could under the circumstances.

✃

I met a French boy who was a year older than me, Bernard, and he and I struck up a casual friendship. He had been to America once, to visit relatives, and now he and his parents were moving there for good. When he found out I had never been to America he felt it his duty to enlighten me about the country.

"Are you Jewish?" he asked.

I shrugged. "I guess."

"What do you mean, 'you guess'? Either you are or you aren't."

"Well, I am, but religion has never been part of our lives."

"So that's why you're going to America—to escape the Germans."

"Actually we're escaping Mussolini's fascists."

"The World's Fair is going on in New York right now. We're going to go. Are you?"

"Of course," I said, though I had no idea if we would go. We hadn't talked much about what we would do once we got to New York; we were just intent on getting there.

"In Central Park, people sunbathe in the nude and no one says anything," Bernard said.

"Really?" I doubted this statement, and much of what Bernard said on the trip, but he was fun to be around, very energetic, and seemed intent on entertaining and impressing me. He told me he was a ping pong champion in his hometown of Aix-les-Bains in the Rhone Alps. I had never heard of Aix-les-Bains, but either the town wasn't very big, or it didn't have very many good ping pong players, because I beat him handily every time we played.

"I'm taking it easy on you," Bernard explained after I had beaten him three games in a row the first time we played. "Besides, I sprained my wrist and I can hardly bend it." He wagged it to show me how hurt it was; it seemed to bend fine then, but he winced as if in great pain.

Bernard and I occasionally passed our time at the few slot machines on board. My dad would give me a few quarters to play, and I won a few coins here and there. Bernard didn't win much, either, but he said he had once won 5,000 francs playing roulette in a casino in Nice.

"They let thirteen-year-olds in casinos in France?" I said.

"I passed for twenty-one," he said. I looked young for my age, and he looked even younger, with his pimply face and youthful features.

Bernard made the trip fun for me. He kept things interesting, and my parents were happy that I'd made a friend on board. I spent a lot of time with my family, too, of course; sometimes we played board games and at other times our talk drifted to what our lives would be like in Ecuador. But we never got very far, in part because we were excited to be stopping in America, even for a short time, and in part because we simply didn't know enough about Ecuador to venture to guess what life would be like there. And that was all right with me; I knew that, whatever it was like, we would be all right.

∞

One of the many things the crew did to make things enjoyable for the passengers was to organize a ping pong tournament. I was far from a confident kid, but I loved ping pong and was pretty good at it. So, encouraged by my parents and with a lot of time on my hands, I took a deep breath and decided to enter the tournament. (Bernard was unable to enter the tournament, he claimed, because his sore wrist was killing him.) Sixty-four people were in the tournament, and I was easily the runt of the litter. I was not only young, but small for my age, but my cousin Paolo had given me the nickname *Il Muro*—"The Wall"—because I could return virtually every shot. Or at least so it seemed. I wasn't much at attacking, because of my size, but it was hard to get a shot to fall on my side.

I won my first match, and my second, and I began to gain a little confidence. I could play with these guys. In fact, the first two matches were pretty easy. I had survived the first day, and only sixteen players were left. The next day, my third match of the tournament proved more difficult; the competition was getting decidedly stiffer. But I won that match, and made it to the round of eight. I won my next two matches as well, and that put me in the championship match against a very good 25-year-old player from Chile. He had breezed through his matches, and he showed up with his own paddles (I of course was using the ship's) and with his own cheering section, headed by four adoring girls who followed his every move. He was trim and lithe, very well dressed, with slicked-back dark hair and an air of complete confidence about him.

I didn't have four adoring girls watching my every move, but I did have the majority of the crowd—and a large crowd had congregated—pulling for me, because I was a little kid playing against a polished veteran. To the delight of the crowd, the little kid won the best two-of-three match. I was elated. The win was an enormous confidence boost, not just in ping pong, but in other activities and situations later in life where I was clearly an underdog. I began to believe in myself and my abilities, and a turning point in doing so happened on that ship.

∞

On the morning of June 10, on our eighth day at sea, we saw New York Harbor and the American shoreline in the distance. After awhile we spotted the Statue of Liberty, and an electrical surge of excitement passed through me. Sandra and my mother and I posed for a picture with the statue in the background as we neared the harbor. Shortly after the picture was taken, the captain came over a loudspeaker and asked us to listen to an important announcement. The next voice we heard was that of the proud and haughty Benito Mussolini, broadcasting from the Palazzo Venezia in Rome:

> *Combatants on land, sea, and in the air, Black Shirts of the Revolution and of the Legion, men and women of Italy, of the Empire, and of the kingdom of Albania, listen: An hour signed by destiny, is ticking on the skies of our country; an hour of irrevocable decisions. A declaration of war has been given to the ambassadors of France and England.*
>
> *Our conscience is absolutely tranquil. The entire world is witness to the fact that Fascist Italy has done everything possible to avoid the storm that is now unleashed upon the world.*

Mussolini paused several times in his speech to give his great crowd of supporters a chance to roar their throaty approval. His words had a much different effect on those on board the Manhattan: first a silence, as people digested the declaration, then a murmur went through the ship, and groups of people discussed the speech, shaking their heads in disapproval.

I later learned that Mussolini was entering the war because he felt Germany was on the verge of victory and feared that Italy would lose out on the spoils, through which he hoped to build Fascist Italy into a new Roman Empire. Speaking to the Italian Army's Chief of Staff, Marshal Badoglio, *Il Duce* said, "I only need a few thousand dead so that I can sit at the peace conference as a man who has fought."

The speech took the wind out of my sails. I was more grateful than ever to be on the Manhattan, but the thought that Italy had joined forces with Germany and was fighting against Britain and France sickened me.

It sickened Bernard, too. My French friend whom I had spent so much time with on the ship turned on me. He found me on deck with my family, and he told me what he thought of Italy and all Italians, and it wasn't much.

"And that goes for you, too!" he said, and spat at my feet. I wanted to tell him that I hadn't entered Italy into the war, and I didn't agree with Mussolini's stance, but it would have done no good. So I just listened to him and said nothing. Finally he stomped off, hurling curses over his shoulder at me as he did.

My father put his hand on my shoulder. He was struggling with his own thoughts about Italy entering the war; the last time Italy had entered a war, he had given up his education and risked much to get back to Italy to join the military and fight. Now, some twenty-five years later, he was running away from his country, and as Italian officers were leading their troops toward France, he was an expatriate leading his family to distant shores, far from the battles that would rage across the European continent in the next several years.

"Don't feel bad," he said to me. "He was just venting. He has a right to be angry."

"But not at me," I said.

"No. Not at you."

Tears welled in my eyes; they sprang up quickly and surprised me. I felt bad, because I thought Bernard was my friend, but he had turned on me without hesitation and with no provocation—at least from me. He was judging me unfairly, and the injustice left a bitter taste in my mouth. I wondered if Andre, Etienne, Luc, and the other French boys I had met in Champery would react in the same way Bernard had. I had the faintest taste of what it was like for my father to be falsely accused of being a traitor to his country, and it deepened my respect for him.

"So what do you think?" my father said, smiling and pointing toward the Statue of Liberty and the harbor. I could make out the skyscrapers of the city, and another thrill went through me. That had been one of my goals in life, to see the skyscrapers of New York, and on this tumultuous day, I was realizing it.

I wiped my eyes and sniffed. "I think it's incredible," I said, smiling. A thought struck like a jolt of lightning: with Italy in the war, the Black Shirts would have even more power and would go berserk. It was like stirring up a hornet's nest. They would not have been content with checking in on my father, keeping him under house arrest. On this very day, had we remained in Italy, my father would have been rounded up with all the other so-called traitors and placed in *confino*—or worse. I shuddered and hugged my father tightly. He hugged me back.

"We made it, Paolo," he whispered. "We're safe. We're going to be all right."

CHAPTER 6

The Ship from Hell

We had made it all right. We were in America! Though we had always had plenty of money in Italy, and our lives had not been difficult until the last couple of years, I had a sense of what poor immigrants from Europe must have felt upon arriving at New York Harbor and being sheltered under the shadow of the Statue of Liberty. It was a sense of relief, of gratitude, of excitement, and most of all, of hope. We had escaped Mussolini and his Black Shirts, we were free, and we had our lives in front of us.

As we walked down the gangway connecting the ship to the shore, I saw many people hugging on the ground below us. One older man with a long beard even bent his stiff frame to the ground and tenderly kissed it. Others were greeted by friends and family, backs were clapped, greetings shouted, and more than one man completely lifted the woman who greeted him off her feet, swinging her as if they were dancing. The atmosphere was festive, and my first impressions of America were that it was a boisterous and happy place, a land where old acquaintances are renewed and new beginnings are launched. Most of all, it was a land of freedom. That's what we yearned for, and though we weren't staying long before heading to Ecuador, that's what we knew we had found.

I was amazed at how quickly we passed through the immigration station and customs. I was also disarmed by how nice and kind the customs officials were. Our arrival was handled in a way that said, "You're welcome here." As we went through customs at the dock off West Side Highway, I caught a glimpse of Bernard, who was standing about twenty yards ahead, with his parents. He was looking directly at me, glowering, as if I had personally betrayed him. I shifted my glance from him to the right, where I saw the skyscrapers of New York City—magnificent edifices rising so much higher than any buildings I had ever seen. Then I looked to my left, and I saw the Statue of Liberty again, towering more than 300 feet above the immigrants that entered her land, fleeing their own barbarous governments or looking for greater opportunities. Millions of immigrants have come to America through New York Harbor, and those millions must have gazed in awe at the statue—which, ironically, commemorates the alliance between France and the US during the American Revolution, was created by a French sculptor, and was a gift from France to the US. Bernard probably didn't know this, and he certainly wouldn't have cared to hear it, at least from me.

A few days later we got to tour the statue. I was aware of the burning torch held high in the woman's right hand, and knew this represented liberty, but I hadn't seen what lay at her feet: the chains of tyranny from which she had escaped. I also hadn't read the poem by the American poet, Emma Lazarus, which was written in 1903 and inscribed in bronze at the base of the statue. I couldn't read it when we first arrived in America, because I knew essentially no English, but I later was able to read, and fully appreciate, the poem:

> Not like the brazen giant of Greek fame,
> With conquering limbs astride from land to land:
> Here at our sea-washed, sunset gates shall stand
> A mighty woman with a torch, whose flame
> Is the imprisoned lightning, and her name
> Mother of Exiles. From her beacon-hand
> Glows world-wide welcome; her mild eyes command
> The air-bridged harbor that twin cities frame.
> "Keep, ancient lands, your storied pomp!" cries she
> With silent lips. "Give me your tired, your poor,
> Your huddled masses yearning to breathe free,
> The wretched refuse of your teeming shore.
> Send these, the homeless, tempest-tost, to me
> I lift my lamp beside the golden door!"

We were certainly tired, and we were poor, as we were allowed to take very little money with us on our passage; and most of all, we were yearning to breathe free. The Mother of Exiles was welcoming us to America, as she had welcomed millions before us, and the scowl and epithets of a small-minded French boy could not dim the glow that issued from the woman and her torch.

So June 10, 1940, was a significant day in my life. It was also significant in the escalation of World War II. Not only did Mussolini enter Italy into the war on this day, but Germany's 7th Tank Division, under the direction of General Erwin Rommel, reached the English Channel; Norway surrendered to German forces who had invaded its country; and Canada declared war on Italy, sending its navy to join in the defense of Atlantic convoys against submarine attack.

I knew none of that at the time, of course—except for Italy entering the war. We were intent on getting through customs, claiming our bags, and finding our way to our new, temporary home: the Park Plaza Hotel, on West 77th Street. In 1940, it was a neat, clean, no-frills hotel that cost $20 a week for a two-bedroom suite. It was exactly what we were looking for. A cousin of my father's, Giulio Oreffice, had made the arrangements for us and drove us there from the dock.

On the ride to the Park Plaza, I gazed out the window in gape-mouthed awe. The city was sprawling and magnificent, teeming with life and color and sound, inhabited by people from all over the world. We passed Central Park on our right as we made our way to the Park Plaza, but my focus was on the incredible skyscrapers of Manhattan. I had never seen anything so grand, and the war and our troubles seemed a million miles away as we made our way through Manhattan.

"What do you think now, Paolo?" my father said, patting me on the knee. I had no words then to describe what I was thinking, so I just kept staring at the skyscrapers. When I glanced over at Sandra, she looked awestruck, too. Mom looked happy; she had gone through tremendous pains to free my father and then to get us visas and passage on first the Rex and then the Manhattan. She had never complained about it, but she had been under stress for the greater part of two years. This ride through the streets of Manhattan must have felt like a victory parade for her.

The Park Plaza was a microcosm of New York. The doorman was black, one of the bellhops was Chinese, some of the waiters in the restaurant were Hispanic. The man who registered us was Italian, and he welcomed us warmly, making us feel as though the whole hotel had been expectantly awaiting our arrival, and asking us news of Italy, especially in light of the speech by Mussolini earlier in the day.

"We're just happy to be here," my mother said in a huge understatement.

"And we're delighted that you chose the Park Plaza to begin your stay here," the man replied.

We were shown to our suite, which was on the fifth floor. The sitting room looked out on a street far below; I dashed over to the window, pulled back the thick curtain, and watched the cars crawl on the street.

We did everything together as a family in New York, though Dad would sometimes go off on his own to tend to business: trying to collect from the Chase Bank vice president and some others on the money that was owed him through the exchange he had made in Italy, and getting our tickets for the next, and final, leg of our trip to Ecuador.

"Mamma," I said one morning at breakfast in the hotel, "can we go to the World's Fair?" I remembered what Bernard had said on the ship about the fair, and the thought of going excited me.

"We'll see, Paolo," she said. Unlike many parental *We'll see's*, this one turned into a *Yes*, and the next morning we paid a nickel each to ride the subway to the fair, which was spread out over more than 1,200 acres in Flushing Meadows. Admission to the fair was 50 cents for adults and 25 cents for children under the age of 15. The fair, which had opened in April 1939, reopened in May 1940, and would run through that summer, was entitled "Building the World of Tomorrow." Ironically, the fair's proclaimed theme was one of international cooperation; many European countries were represented at the fair even as these countries waged war against each other overseas. The Soviet pavilion, which was up for the 1939 fair, was gone, and the British, Polish, Czechoslovakian, and Finnish pavilions had exhibits that acknowledged the reality of the war going on. Norway and Denmark had exhibits that were greatly trimmed from the previous year. In 1939, the war in Europe was labeled the "Phony War" by US newspapers; a year later, it was acknowledged as real, and though it would be a year-and-a-half before the US would enter the war, its reality had worked its way into the consciousness of Americans. Still, Americans are nothing if not hopeful, and that hope for a brighter tomorrow came shining through in resplendent fashion at the World's Fair.

The fair's real theme was on science and technology, on the newness of ideas, forms, and consumer products, and as we visited many of the exhibits, my mind opened to a whole new world of endless possibilities. The Consolidated Edison Building was fronted by 9,000 square feet of water shooting from fountains that sent the water more than 40 feet into the air. The circular Glass Center Building contained more than 25,000 square feet of exhibits and a blue plate-glass tower reaching more than 100 feet above the top of the building. The DuPont Building showed off its research and laboratory processes and how its products made life better. In the Hall of Inventions, the varied uses of plastics was touted as part of our great future; ironically, it was to be a central part of my own future. The General Electric Hall of Innovations was mind-boggling with its repertoire of futuristic refrigerators, stoves, and other appliances, as well as lighting systems. The Trylon and Perisphere were the grand icons of the fair, the Trylon rising 700 feet above the ground, connected by a giant ramp to the Perisphere, which was as wide as a city block and housed a model of the urban and exurban future. The RCA Exhibit Building was shaped like a radio tube; inside, it showcased the marvels of communication, including television.

While I was impressed with the idea of television, I was convinced it was one of those wildly optimistic ideas about the future that wouldn't fly. I recall seeing a Yankees game, telecast from the nearby Bronx; the picture was small, fuzzy, and black and white, and transmitted only over a short distance. I figured that once the fair closed, television would quietly slip away, because it just couldn't work.

My father's meeting with the vice president from Chase was not successful. The banker—the same one who had made a deal with my father just a few weeks earlier in Italy—purported not to know my father. Unfortunately, this was the largest single exchange my father had made. This banker was no better than Cugnasca or Ghirardelli or Foscari or any of the others who betrayed my father in Italy. My father was angry and persisted in his attempts to get his money, but was turned down. (After much pressure, my dad did receive his money, about five years later, after the war, and not when we needed it so badly.)

For the most part, though, our time in New York was splendid and almost dreamlike. Having all day long to explore, we went to Macy's and Gimbel's and roamed these immense department stores. We had seen nothing at all like them in Italy, where there were shoe stores, clothing haberdasheries, perfume shops, kitchen supply stores, hat shops, but they weren't all rolled into one sprawling store. Macy's alone had over one million square feet of retail space, with seemingly everything imaginable under the sun on its floors. Navigating the store's aisles seemed no less complicated than finding our way through the streets of New York. But we couldn't really get lost in the store, because we had no final destination in mind; we were content to wander the aisles and gawk at all the items for sale.

Two other concepts new to me were those of the cafeteria and the automat. We had nothing like those in Italy, and the idea of reaching into a machine after serving it a coin, or sliding a tray down a line and picking from an assortment of foods was, in its own way, as futuristic as many of the things I saw at the World's Fair. It was in New York that I discovered, and fell in love with, chicken salad sandwiches. I also fell in love with the American way of life. Though I could understand little of the language, Americans were almost uniformly friendly. We were treated with respect and dignity, and as we played the tourists, taking in the Rockefeller Center, the Empire State building, Radio City Music Hall (where we saw *Gone With the Wind*), and other attractions, many Americans went out of their way to be helpful. This treatment helped ease our pain of leaving our old world behind. Indeed, we were saddened to leave New York after only a few days, but as our date approached for boarding the Santa Lucia, bound for South America, I began to prepare myself for the final leg of our journey to our new home.

⚓

Dad had managed to book us on the ship, but because of the scant money we had, he booked Mom and Sandra in second class, while he and I took third class. The Santa Lucia was supposedly a large luxury liner, with outside staterooms and the largest tiled swimming pool of any ship afloat at that time. The dining room had high ceilings, and off the promenade deck was a roll-back dome that allowed the first-class passengers to dine under the stars, but the experience in first class was as far removed from third class as Italy was from Ecuador. (Second class didn't have it so bad, either, with its inside state rooms and good food. It was nice, if not as ritzy as first class.)

It was the middle of summer, and it was hot, with no air conditioning of course, and as we made our way south it got hotter and hotter. My father and I were on double-decker bunks with about sixty other men in steerage, separated from all the other passengers by a four-foot fence. It was as if we were animals to be kept from the passengers, or prisoners being deported.

Our first night in steerage, Dad hung his watch on a broken spring on the end of his cot; in the morning, it was gone. Our bags—stowed under our cots—were still there, mainly because it would have been harder to steal them and dispose of the evidence. My father slept with his wallet under the center of his pillow, and we all slept with cockroaches scrambling over the floors and walls, and sometimes over us. As I was getting up one morning, a nearby sleep-eyed boy—the only other youngster in steerage—was pulling on his shoe. He came to life suddenly and yanked out his foot. One cockroach scrambled out of the shoe and another skittered up the boy's leg before the boy screamed and knocked it off. As it ran under his father's cot, he tried to hit it with his shoe, but instead he hit his father, who was lying on the cot, in the back. After that I carefully checked my clothes and shoes before putting them on.

With those sixty men we shared a bathroom with four toilets and sinks and three showers, the latter of which were out in the open. The smells drifted back through our common room, and no matter how many showers we took, we were always hot and sweaty. (It didn't help that there was no soap in the showers; if you didn't have your own soap, you were out of luck. My dad had a bar of soap, which he guarded tighter than he had his watch, as it had to last another twelve days.) Most of the other men ignored the showers, and the smell in steerage quickly became powerful and nauseating.

Some of the breakfasts– breads and coffee—were okay, but lunches and dinners were inedible. On the better days, when the meat wasn't filled with vermin, it tasted, as my father put it, like the leathery sole of a shoe. We were able to converse with Mom and Sandra during the day, and Mom of course was worried about her little Paolo and how he would survive in the hole with such horrible food. So she and Sandra took to saving portions of their meals, which were quite good, and handing them over the fence to us. In a sense it was like bringing food to caged dogs, but my stomach took precedence over my pride, and I gratefully took the offerings and gobbled them up before any of our steerage brethren could snatch it out of my hands. After all, no one else in steerage was eating the steaks and chicken and seafood, not to mention the desserts, that were reserved for the first and second class passengers. This food transferral quickly became the highlight of my day, something I eagerly looked forward to.

Besides the physical barrier between second and third class, my father and I had a language barrier between us and most of the others in steerage. Most of them spoke Spanish, and our mastery of the language was minimal at best, so we kept pretty much to ourselves. Some of the men looked pretty scary, with their stubbled faces and greasy hair. Our common room was pretty crowded, with not much space besides the cots, so my dad and I spent as much time on deck as possible. At first we weren't allowed on the same deck as the first and second class passengers, so our time with Mom and Sandra was limited to when they passed portions of their meals to us. After three days, my mother, ever the lady of action, talked the captain into letting my father and me spend some daytime hours with our women. That was a great improvement.

Otherwise, Dad would devise math problems and crossword puzzles for me, and he and I studied Spanish together, trying to pick up the language that we would need to speak in our new home. Knowing two other romance languages, Italian and French, made the rudiments of Spanish easy to pick up.

We also had lots of time for talking. I liked the evenings the best, right after dinner, when the sun was going down and the air was cooling and Dad and I could sit on the deck and watch the ocean roll below us as the clouds turned pink on the western horizon.

On one such evening my father shook his head as he looked out on the ocean. We were sitting side by side. "I don't like putting you and Sandra and Mamma through this," he said.

"It's not your fault."

He looked at me and raised an eyebrow. He had a slight smile on his face; I think he appreciated me saying that, because, in a way, he did blame himself. If he'd not spoken up against the fascists, we wouldn't be on this ship. But then, given the turn of events in Italy, I wasn't so unhappy to be on board, even if the accommodations were less than luxurious. I didn't like it, but I knew the trip would soon be over.

"Our country is in the hands of a madman right now," he said. "He's destroying all that's good in Italy. Or at least he's trying to."

"Papá? What was it like? When you were in jail, I mean."

Dad looked out over the ocean for a long while, as if he were searching for the answer on the waves, and then he bent his head and looked down at the deck. "I don't want to talk about that, Paolo." He looked up at me. "I'm here. We're on a ship sailing far away. We're safe, we're free, we're headed toward a new life." He smiled at that thought.

"Quito is beautiful," he continued. "It's in the mountains, and the ocean is less than 200 kilometers away. Quito is the capital of Ecuador. Because it's in a mountain valley, the weather is pleasant, not hot and burning like this." It was true that even at night, unless the air was moving over you, the heat was stifling.

"Where will we stay, and what will we do?"

"We'll find a place to stay. I don't know yet until we get there. As for what we'll do, we'll learn the language, you and Sandra will go to school in the fall, and I'll find work." He told me of a new pharmaceutical company, L.I.F.E., that a group of immigrants from Italy were starting in Ecuador. (As it turns out, Dow Chemical, the company that I headed years later, bought L.I.F.E in the 1970s.) One of these Italians was instrumental in helping us obtain our visas, and with the visa he offered my father work. Shortly after we arrived, my father turned down the offer because he wanted to start his own company. He had no idea what that company would be.

"Are you worried?" I asked.

He smiled a broad smile at me that seemed to be genuinely free of concern. "This is a great opportunity for us, Paolo. We're on a grand adventure, one that many people back in Italy wish they could be on. We're charting our own course, with a wide open future ahead of us. We can choose what we want to do, and that choice is a great freedom." His eyes glistened in the fading glow of the sun. "Unfortunately that same freedom does not exist right now in Italy. But it will again someday. It won't be long." He spoke of his great desire to find a way to go back and fight the Germans.

He was silent for awhile, staring at the crimson clouds on the horizon before he spoke. "In the meantime, we will enjoy life in Ecuador and make the most of it. This is a great experience, Paolo, one that will serve you well in later years. I feel that in my bones. On the ship to New York, we were fleeing a madman, running for our lives. On this ship, we are heading toward our new lives. And we can make of those lives anything we want. Anything at all."

Those words were like a calming sermon of assurance for me. I rested in his ideals and his optimism, I placed my faith and trust in his guidance and wisdom. I wasn't able to see far beyond the literal: we were on a crowded ship headed to Ecuador, which I knew nothing about. He saw beyond that, saw the possibilities and opportunities stretching as far as his mind could imagine. And what he saw excited him. My fears and anxieties about going to Ecuador vanished with the sun, slipping beneath the ocean.

We sailed for 11 days and 10 nights. About halfway through our trip we came to Barranquilla, a port city in Columbia, and made a brief stop there, though not long enough for us to get off the ship. Soon after that we arrived at Panama and entered Limón Bay, where we dropped anchor and awaited our canal pilot who would steer the ship through the 40-mile waterway that connects the Atlantic to the Pacific. As we entered the first lock at Gatún, line handlers attached steel mooring cables controlled by electric locomotives, called mules. The mules guided the ship through the locks and kept it steady as each successive chamber in the locks fill with water. We proceeded in this fashion through the Gatún Locks, being raised up in three steps until we reached Gatún Lake, which we crossed before going down the Miraflores Locks on the Pacific side. It took about 10 hours to get through the canal, and it was fascinating to traverse the locks.

Our next stop was Buenaventura, a major port city in Columbia, where we were able to get off the ship around midday. Despite my father's optimism and my own excitement at seeing new portions of the world every day, our heart sank as we roamed the streets of Buenaventura, which, near the harbor anyway, were dirt roads that led to broken-down adobe houses and decrepit wooden buildings in an ancient district that looked like it hadn't been repaired since it had been built. We met up with Mom and Sandra, and, along with other passengers, we took in what sights there were and looked for something besides ship fare to eat.

The slight breeze that came off the ocean was soon swallowed up in the hot and humid stillness of the city. As we walked the streets, we passed some elderly Columbians, including one elderly woman whose leathery face was a corrugated mass of wrinkles and crevices criss-crossing each other; she looked as ancient as the dirt we raised by our feet. Two little boys were chasing each other in the street, shouting shrilly and joyously at each other; they were both naked on bottom and had dirty tee-shirts on. A few street vendors had their wares out, and called out to us, beckoning to us to come look. One of the vendors, selling fruit, was blind; she had sunken eyes and a teenage girl who stood silently by, watching us as we approached and continuing to stare at us as we passed. Half a block later I looked back and she was still watching us. A panting dog whose ribs were showing came running up to us, yapping loudly; my father shouted at it and the dog turned tail and limped away, ducking between two adobe houses, one of which had several windows broken.

If Quito turned out to be like Buenaventura, I'd rather we got back on another ship and took our chances in Italy. I was less than enthralled with our first look at a South American city.

We came to the post office, which was the only brick building I saw, and past it there were a few shops and restaurants. We ventured into the restaurant that appeared the cleanest. We sat at a table with rickety and unmatched chairs and were served by a waitress who spoke a stream of Spanish so rapidly that I didn't get a single word of it. When she stopped whatever she was saying and saw the blank looks on our faces, she smiled and slowed down, and my father, partly through words but mainly by pointing to the paper menu, ordered for us. Soon we had some meat and rice in front of us. Dad also ordered some *leche*, some milk, for the ulcers that had been plaguing him since his trouble with the Fascists. As the waitress was beginning to walk away, my father said, "Perdone, tiene burro?"

The waitress looked at him, shocked at first, then, when she saw my father waiting in hopeful expectation, she burst out laughing.

"Dad! What do you want?" Sandra hissed.

"Butter. I just want some butter."

Sandra rolled her eyes and turned, embarrassed, to the waitress.

"Mantequilla, por favor," Sandra said.

"Ah, mantequilla!" the waitress said, and she smiled at my father, as if he had told the greatest joke, and hurried off.

"Of course, mantequilla," my father said to Sandra. "Good for you. You're learning your Spanish." He had slipped into Italian; *burro* means *butter* in our language. "What did I request, then?" he asked Sandra.

"You asked for a donkey!"

The waitress again broke out in laughter as she brought a plate of butter to our table. She put her hand to her mouth to stop herself, and hurried off, pushing through the swinging doors that led to the kitchen. In a moment we heard raucous laughter coming from behind the doors, then muffled voices followed by more laughter. After awhile our waitress checked on us; her eyes were watery and red from laughing so much. My father took it all in good fun, and I was just pleased he didn't try to tell the waitress that her butter was *delicioso*, because who knows what he would have really said.

Finally we arrived at Guayaquil, which is southwest of Quito. We disembarked from the Santa Lucia, and I was glad to be rid of the ship and to be reunited with my mother and sister again. (The Santa Lucia would soon be entered into the war effort, and was sunk off North Africa by torpedo bombers.) I was no more impressed with Guayaquil than I was with Buenaventura, and I began to really worry about what we would find in Quito. It had been very hot and humid in Buenaventura, but the heat and humidity in Guayaquil was nearly unbearable. We stayed at the Grand Hotel, paying a very high price compared to New York, $6.60 a night for two rooms. The beds were small and the mattresses seemed heavy with the sweat of countless previous guests. Everything was damp in Guayaquil; the air hung heavy and everything I touched seemed to hold moisture. We took showers and immediately started sweating again. Three paintings adorned the wall in our hotel room: one of a sweating shrimp fisherman; another of a sweating coffee farmer; the third of a misty rain coming down on a verdant hillside. Everything spoke of moisture. I was continually thirsty and couldn't get enough to drink, though it had to be bottled water. We never drank anything but *Agua de Guitig* while we were in Ecuador. The only highlight was breakfast, where we discovered papaya, pineapple, and other tropical fruits.

We spent six days in Guayaquil and then prepared for our final leg of the journey: a train ride. The only way to Quito in those days was by train. As the crow flies, it's about 250 kilometers from Guayaquil to Quito, and nowadays you can fly to Quito from Guayaquil in an hour, but in 1940 on the Southern Railway, it took 12 hours to traverse the steep terrain between the two cities.

So we boarded the train, and we were glad to be leaving Guayaquil and anxious to get to Quito. We had nothing but the bags with us that we had carried from Italy. I worked up a sweat carrying my bag downstairs, and by the time we boarded the early-morning train, my shirt was soaked. The train made its way east, toward the towering western range of the Andes, and I couldn't wait to get to higher ground, in hopes of cooler breezes.

Our train covered about 130 kilometers before it began to snake its way up a mountain known as *Nariz del Diablo,* the Nose of the Devil. Rather than go around the mountain, the engineers who designed the track decided to go up the mountainside. To do so, they carved a series of tight zigzags into the mountainside, allowing trains to go up, then down, then up, then down, and gradually make their way to the top before descending to the valley on the other side. It made for a scenic, if slow, passage, but we were able to sit back, relax, and enjoy the ride. The cutbacks were fun, the surrounding countryside was beautiful, and every minute brought us closer to our new home.

∞

CHAPTER SEVEN

Port in the Storm

Our new home. Thoughts of our new home elicited excitement in me, along with a little nervousness, because we were not relocating in Venice, or moving to another city in Italy. We were moving halfway across the world, mixing in with a people we didn't know who spoke a language we were only beginning to understand. We were strangers in a strange land, but we were also safe, happy, and, as a popular ad for an airline says, "Free to move about the country." That was not the case in Italy.

And we were, as my mother had put it to Sandra and me in selling the idea of the move, "on a great adventure." We were in Quito, the capital of Ecuador, which was nestled in a valley of the Andes Mountains in the northern portion of the country. Our first impressions of Quito were favorable: it is a beautiful city in a picturesque setting, and I breathed a sigh of relief upon seeing it, despite the good things I had heard about it. I had braced myself for something similar to Barranquilla or Guayaquil—not places I wanted to call home. But Quito was easy to fall in love with, with its numerous parks and fields (finally, a place to play soccer!), its expansive central plaza, the steep and narrow streets that lent charm and distinction to the residential sections, and the Spanish baroque architecture that was evident everywhere.

But before we admired the capital's architecture, we had to find four walls of our own with an attached roof. We were lucky enough to know an Italian family living in Quito who was willing to lend us their house while they were on vacation. They lived about three blocks from the house we eventually rented, which was a modest house with a small yard in an upper-middle class neighborhood on the west side of the city, on a street called Mariscal Sucre.

Our house on Mariscal Sucre was whitewashed with blue shutters. Downstairs were a living room, dining room, and kitchen; upstairs were three bedrooms and two bathrooms. In the back were servants' quarters. The house was modestly furnished; it was nothing like the beautiful antique furniture we had in Venice, but it more than sufficed and we were quite happy in it. My own room was comfortable, with two beds and doors that opened onto a balcony. One night I remember being awakened by shaking; my bed and table were trembling and books were falling off my shelves. I could feel, as I got out of bed, a slight tremor in the hardwood floor. I opened the balcony doors and stepped out, looking out into the night to see the lights of nearby houses shaking. I had never been in an earthquake before. It was a mild one, but it lasted 58 seconds, which is a long time for an earthquake.

A much more mundane new experience for me was to live in a neighborhood with houses. When I lived in Venice in the building my grandfather owned, there was really no neighborhood to speak of, and my friends did not live close by, and we had no fields to play on. In Quito, I quickly became fluent in Spanish, and I had almost instant friends, all living within a block of two of me, all happy to get to know someone from another country, to take me in as one of their own. This made my transition much easier than I had anticipated. Best of all, we could stroll across the street to a grassy, empty lot and play soccer there. Venice seemed a million miles away, and in some ways this wasn't so bad.

Down the street, about a block away, was a house much larger than ours or any of the others in the neighborhood, one with a big yard and a tennis court in the back. The Teran family lived there—Edwin, who was about my age and who would become my best friend in Ecuador; Cecil, his younger brother by two years; and Norita, who was about a year older than Edwin. Norita was beautiful, and I found myself blushing when she'd catch me looking at her, because I was sure she knew I was attracted to her. She was soft-spoken and sweet, with smooth, russet-colored skin and a perfect complexion. She had sparkling white teeth and a smile that illuminated a room, and her eyes were chocolate-colored and almond-shaped. Her eyes and her smile made my stomach flip and turned my knees soft. I'd never been much interested in girls before, but Norita changed that. I was quite happy to hang out at the Teran house, because that meant I got to see Norita more often.

I didn't have many conversations with Norita, because I was too shy to start them, and while she was pleasant around her brothers, she didn't horn in when their friends were around (though I would have been quite happy had she done so). But I do recall one conversation in which she sought my advice, about boyfriends, of all things. She had been dating a guy named Carlos who was a little older.

"Que piensas?" ("What do you think?") she asked me one spring afternoon near their tennis court. I was 17 at the time, and I played tennis regularly with Edwin, who was inside getting his racquet.

"I don't think Carlos is the right man for you," I said, my blood rising at the thought of this older guy, who considered himself quite a lady's man, taking advantage of the pure and sweet Norita. "You shouldn't go out with him."

"But he's nice to me."

She looked seriously at me for several moments with those gorgeous eyes while I slowly melted in her presence. Then she smiled, said "Gracias, Paolo," and walked away. I stayed in my reverie for several minutes, even after Edwin shoved my shoulder, chided me by saying , "Hey, amigo," and handed me a racquet. He had somehow materialized without my knowing it.

"What are you talking to her for? Come on. I thought you came over to play tennis."

It was true I loved tennis. It was also true that the Terans' court was by far my favorite court, for a reason that had nothing to do with tennis.

❦

Mr. Teran was the British consul in Quito, though he was Ecuadorian. His wife was British; that's why their boys were name Edwin and Cecil. Those names were more out of place in Ecuador than mine! The Teran children went to a private school, and two other boys—Raul Iturralde and Choyo Pimentel—went to a different public school than the one I ended up going to, once school began in the fall. It was not the school experience that bound us, but the neighborhood proximity, and our mutual love for playing sports and just being active.

Edwin, Cecil, Raul, Choyo, and I quickly became almost inseparable. We took boxing lessons together, played tennis and ping pong and soccer together. We went to shows together, just hung out together, roamed the streets of Quito, soaking up the sun, constantly challenging each other in contests, always playing hard and laughing harder. We'd go watch soccer and basketball games together, and occasionally on the walk home, Edwin would go up to a house, ring the doorbell, and then peel out, calling out to us, "*Salir corriendo!*" ("Run for it!") Musical laughter streamed from his mouth as he jetted on ahead of us.

As I mentioned, my father had a job offer from some ex-patriot Italians who had started a pharmaceutical company in Quito, but he had turned them down to start his own business. You've heard the phrase, "If life gives you lemons, make lemonade." Well, life—or, to be more precise, Ludovico Foscari—had once given him castor oil. My father, in true entrepreneurial spirit, sniffed the Ecuadorian air like a bloodhound on a scent, and sensed a need—one for purified castor oil. He announced this at the dinner table not long after we had moved into our rented house.

"Ludovico Foscari has given me a great idea," my father said over his steaming plate of veal scaloppine. "I am going to become a manufacturer of castor oil."

"You're joking," my mother said, watching him closely.

"I would never dream of joking about castor oil. Why would I joke about the product I'm going to build a plant for?"

"Castor oil?" Sandra said, unbelieving.

"Not just castor oil. *Purified* castor oil. Castor oil is processed for industrial purposes here, but not for medicinal purposes. And with the war on, it's hard to import purified castor oil. Fruit, I will admit, works wonders, but where fruit can't work, castor oil can. Purified castor oil, that is. That's where Oroil steps in."

"Oroil?" my mother said, trying to keep up.

"Oreffice Oil. Oroil," my father replied.

"I like it!" I said. At first I thought it was crazy that my father would want anything to do with a product that had been used to abuse him. But I could see that he took special pleasure in somehow turning that experience around. He went so far as to call it his "little revenge" on the Fascists. It was a far cry from the work he had done in Italy, but that didn't seem to daunt him. At the end of the conversation, he tipped an imaginary hat in the general direction of Italy. "Thank you, Mr. Foscari."

That was my father: an optimist, an opportunist, a visionary who could see a need and fill it. And so he built his castor oil plant, and began manufacturing Oroil. He hired an Austrian refugee, a chemical engineer, to help him run the plant, which usually had about eight to twelve people working in it. It was hard to say how many employees Oroil had at any one time, because the numbers often dwindled after Saturdays, which was pay day. On Monday, some would return and others wouldn't. Apparently they were satisfied with their week's worth of pay and didn't want to stress themselves by working two weeks in a row. Sometimes these wayward employees would show up on Tuesday or Wednesday; sometimes they would never return. My father took this in stride and just found more workers.

It was, obviously, a small operation. My father cheerfully wore many hats in running Oroil, including that of salesman. He would go door to door to pharmacies in and around Quito, selling a case at a time. He was turned down many times, of course, but some pharmacists took a chance and bought a case, and when my father would return, they would buy more cases, because the customers were buying the product. On the label of the bottles it said, "Oroil: El Aceite Mas Puro" ("The Oil Most Pure"). I accompanied him on a few of these sales excursions.

"What is this?" a pharmacist asked as my father held up a bottle of Oroil.

"It is purified castor oil, a rare commodity in Quito, one that your customers will surely find most useful," my father replied. "Try a case and see how your customers like it."

"What do you mean, 'purified'?"

"I mean you can use it for medicinal purposes."

The pharmacist peered suspiciously at the bottle as if it were a bomb that might blow up. "You can attest that it's approved as a laxative?"

"I can personally assure you it works," my father said dryly. I covered my mouth to hide my smirk. "Take a bottle for yourself. Try it at home. See if it works."

The pharmacist looked at my father as if he were crazy. "Go now! I am too busy for this foolishness!" he said, though his store was empty.

My father shrugged and we left. On the way back to our car, he said, "I think he could have used some Oroil for himself, to get some new ideas flowing." I laughed. We drove on to the next pharmacy, where my father made a sale. Before leaving the store, my father said to the pharmacist, "You should tell the pharmacist on Camino Segundo that he should try some."

"Eduardo Rivera?" the pharmacist laughed. "You'd be lucky to sell him a drink of water in the bowels of hell."

And so it went. Some days were good for Oroil, others were not so good. Some days he sold lots of cases, and other days a few employees would forget to show up. Sometimes meeting Saturday's payroll depended on selling a few cases on Friday. But he began to get repeat orders, and business picked up, and he made a living at it.

In 1943 he began another business to supplement what he made through Oroil. He manufactured tents and tarpaulins for Shell Oil and other companies that were exploring for oil in Brazil. Again, because of the war, it was difficult to import tents and tarps, and my father, realizing this, jumped in. This business actually did better than Oroil. It was really a home business; my mom would stop by and cut cloth or help out in other ways when she had the time. My father had a very simple vulcanization process for the tents and tarps: he would hang them on lines outside and let the sun vulcanize the material.

∞

We had less money in Ecuador, and I couldn't quite understand why we couldn't join the country club or tennis club that Edwin and Cecil belonged to, but we had enough to live on and we really lacked for nothing. Our parents never made us feel that we had less than we did. We just adapted to what we had and made the most of it.

Mom had to adapt as much as any of us. Though we hired a maid once Dad got Oroil going, Mom took over the cooking duties and retained them during our stay in Ecuador. She did this partly, she said, so she could make sure the food was clean and fit for our consumption. She boiled whatever she could in water before we ate it. We drank only bottled water, *Agua de Guitig*. We weren't allowed to touch raw vegetables. She would treat lettuce with chemicals in a pot before allowing us to eat it, and she would make us cut off the ends of bananas to reduce our risks of ingesting any amoebas. To this day I still eat bananas that way.

And it worked: of all the European refugees we knew of in Ecuador, we were the only ones who never got dysentery, which was common in Ecuador in those days.

Shortly before we were to begin school in the fall of 1940, and after we'd been in our house for a few weeks, my father had a set of tools stolen from our garage, which had been left open. He drove to the police station in his 1933 Oldsmobile to report the theft. The lieutenant he talked to gave him a little smile and said, "Just put an ad in the paper and post a reward. They'll bring them back." My dad thought this was a bit preposterous at first: why should he pay to recover his own tools? Why should he reward a thief? And why would a thief respond to an ad? But then he considered the cost of buying a new set of tools. He put an ad in the paper, offering about 15% of the price of a new set. Sure enough, the next day a man returned with the tools and exchanged them for the reward money. He was polite and not nervous at all. If anything, he looked a little disappointed, perhaps because he could have sold the tools himself for more, but he was doing the honorable thing by returning them to their rightful owner. He casually collected the money for returning the tools he stole and strolled away.

We had other people come to our house, too: Indian or mestizo women who sold fruits or vegetables that they carried in baskets on their heads. They would chiefly sell bananas, pineapples, oranges, and potatoes—each one selling only one kind of fruit or vegetable. Some of these women were very old, grandmothers no doubt, and they walked slowly, shooing away dogs as they went. Some carried a thick stick to beat away any persistent dogs, but I had my doubts that most of them could repel a dog that truly meant business.

The first seller I saw was an old woman with her gray hair pulled back from her weather-beaten face. Her eyes, what I could see of them, were dark; her lids were all but shut, like shades drawn in a house to facilitate sleeping in the middle of the afternoon. She seemed not far from sleep herself as she rang the doorbell by our gate. My mom answered the door and I came up also, curious to see what this old lady had to offer.

"Naranjas," the woman said "Tengo naranjas." Her basket was filled with good-sized oranges; my mouth watered at the sight of them. She said this matter-of-factly, neither impolitely nor with any fanfare or sales pitch. My mother gave her a gracious smile and offered her some water, but the woman refused.

"But it's warm out," my mother said. "Aren't you thirsty?"

"No tengo sed," the old woman replied. "Quiere naranjas?"

The old woman was not thirsty; she was asking, of course, if we wanted to buy her oranges. She said this without much hope, and my heart was moved to compassion. The way she said *Quiere naranjas* made it sound, for some reason, like she was offering to sell all she had in this world—and this probably wasn't far from the truth. Her shoulders were hunched forward, as though someone were pushing her from behind. She wore a blouse, a long, full skirt, and a waist sash; the blouse appeared to have been light blue at one point but now was nearly stone white. Over her head she wore a multicolored rebozo, a fringed shawl that kept the direct rays of the sun off her head. I glanced down at her feet and noticed she had no shoes or sandals. Darkened dust had collected between her toes, and the nail of one of her big toes was missing.

But her clothes were clean and she stood at our door patiently, with an unassuming dignity, waiting to hear my mother's verdict. At least she was selling something of her own, and not stealing it and claiming a reward for it.

"Yes, we want some oranges," my mother said. "How much are they?"

"Un sucre cada," the woman said. "Seis sucres para cinco naranjas." *Sucre* was the Ecuadorian unit of money at the time. She was offering one orange for one sucre, or five oranges for six sucres! My mother's charity extended only so far; she bought several oranges from the woman, but one at a time. After the exchange, the woman simply put her basket back on her head, turned and walked back down our walkway, out toward the street, where she would go to the next door. I felt tired just watching her walk.

We bought most of our fruits and vegetables in this manner. Food, clothing, trinkets, pottery, and other works from artisans were sold at tiny stores and markets, and Sandra and I often accompanied our mother to them. As we observed the sellers and buyers, we quickly learned that good-natured haggling and bartering were expected; if you bought something at the initial asking price, you were considered foolish.

As for our meals, they weren't much changed from what we ate in Venice, though we ate even more fruits and vegetables in Quito, if that were possible. We simply were careful with what we ate, but Mom took up the cooking and continued making the Italian veal and chicken and pasta dishes we had always loved.

∞

I was glad we had a few months to adjust to the language and the culture before school began. As my father struggled to get Oroil going, Mom faced a struggle of her own—trying to get a dispensation from the school system to enroll me in eighth grade. I was twelve years old, and by their standards I should be enrolling in fifth grade. My mother visited the Minister of Education and haggled with him quite seriously, unlike the haggling that was expected to take place at the market. The minister demanded to see my education documents, which my mother produced; even so, he was not compelled to enroll me in eighth grade.

"He is only twelve," the minister reasoned. "He would be in with fourteen- and fifteen-year-olds, were he to go into eighth grade."

"He would be bored to tears if he were to have to repeat three grades," my mother countered. "Why should he have to repeat what these documents show he's learned?"

"How well does your son know Spanish?"

"He has picked it up very quickly. It's his fourth language, and he picked the others up quickly as well. Any language barrier will not be a barrier for long, if indeed there's a barrier at all—and it wouldn't be any more of a barrier for him at the eighth grade level, anyway."

The minister considered this. "But part of education is the social aspect," he said. "With your son being new to Ecuador, and being two years younger, it might be very difficult for him. And in our schools, many students skip a year or two to work, to help their families out. So some students will be three or four years older than your son." He assessed my school documents, which showed I had done well academically. "I'm not saying he's not intelligent," the minister continued. "I want the best for your son, and that includes the social aspects of school. Wouldn't he be more comfortable with students his own age?"

"He's always been two years younger than the other students in his class. And he has made many friends already, in our neighborhood." The minister sighed and nodded; my mother smiled in triumph. Any woman who could talk Mussolini's son-in-law into releasing an antifascist from his father-in-law's jails could surely talk her son into eighth grade in Quito's public school system.

And so Sandra and I entered school in September, Sandra in 10th grade in a Catholic school, me in the boys' public school in eighth grade. The boys' and girls' schools were separated back then, and my parents didn't think well enough of the girls' public school to send Sandra there. I was considered to be in high school now, because in Ecuador, high school covers seven years.

None of my neighborhood friends were at my school, which was called Colegio Mejia, so it was a little hard to adjust to in that respect. I had relatively little difficulty in understanding what my teachers and fellow students were saying, and I had had experience in going to a school where my native language was not spoken—or at least was not the principal language. As I said, I picked up the language very quickly, in part because I immediately started mixing with local kids once we arrived in Quito. But, in retrospect, I understand the minister's reluctance to enroll me in eighth grade. The curriculum was tough, harder than it was in Italy, not because of the language it was delivered in, but because of its content. It was not an easy adjustment, but I became comfortable enough with the system after a few months and the move into eighth grade was the right one for me.

I came away from my Ecuador years very impressed with the country's school system. The system was so strong in part because the country realized that high school was going to be the educational stopping-off point for most students, who simply couldn't afford to go to college. Of the seven years in high school, the final three were specialized. You chose among liberal arts, mathematical physical sciences, and medical curriculums. I chose the sciences because I enjoyed math the most. That meant I had three years of chemistry, three years of physics, I went through integral calculus, and I had taken many college-level courses by the time I graduated.

In addition, the school system had some incentives in place that really appealed to me. For example, during the school year you took four tests in each class plus, potentially, a final exam. You received a grade each quarter based on how you had done on those tests and in those classes. Each test was graded on a total of 20 points. If you scored 75 points out of 80 for a class, you didn't have to take the final exam for that class. I never had to take a final exam in math. I naturally did well in those classes, and was greatly motivated to avoid any final exams that I could. I think in several ways Ecuador was ahead of the US in how it approached education and geared its system to motivate students to study and learn.

Another difference in Ecuador's schools was its inclusion of sports. In Italy, sports were not a part of the school system; in Ecuador, they were an integral part, much as they are in the US. If you had asked me when I was in eighth grade what made the Ecuadorian education system stand out, I would have immediately replied, "They play sports in school!" Soccer of course was big there; I played soccer, tennis, polo, and I even played a little baseball in an independent league. I had never played baseball before, but they decreed that and I must know the game because I was a foreigner. I was not destined to reach the major leagues, but I played second base and had fun.

⁂

As you might remember, I had two main dreams as a kid: one was to see the skyscrapers of New York City, which I was able to do when we arrived in America. The other was to play on an organized soccer team. In Italy, chances were few and far between, unless you were an elite player. In

Ecuador, I realized this dream as well. In fact, when I was fifteen, Edwin Teran, Choyo Pimentel, Raul Iturralde and I were all asked to join the Quito Gladiadors' junior team. The Gladiadors were a semiprofessional soccer team, playing teams from Riobamba, Ambato, Guayaquil, Santo Domingo de los Colorados, and as far south as Cuenca, a rugged 300-plus kilometer drive through the Andes from Quito. There were some exceptional players on the Gladiadors, and just a few months before I left Ecuador I was asked to travel with the major league team. I endured the slow and bumpy bus ride to Cuenca and was rewarded by playing center-half (midfielder nowadays) in the match. I also occasionally played goalkeeper. One junior match I was playing center-half when Choyo, our starting goalkeeper, got clobbered. I replaced him as substitute goalie and we won 1-0. I stopped a lot of shots, and a few went just over the goal, and somehow I preserved the shutout. It was a great moment for me, and the whole experience of playing soccer was great—and one I probably wouldn't have gotten, had we remained in Italy.

When we first moved to Quito it was a little hard to adjust to the altitude, as we were 10,000 feet above sea level. When I did any running for the first few weeks, I got easily winded. I noticed it even when walking. They excused me from PE for my first month in school, but once I adapted, I had no difficulties playing soccer or anything else. It was always an advantage for us to play a coastal team, because they would have the same difficulty with the altitude that I first did.

While playing soccer for a major league club was a huge thrill, and it was the highlight of reaching that particular dream, I also did something in Ecuador that I never could have dreamed of doing: I played the great Pancho Segura in a tennis match. This was in the summer of 1944, when I was 16 and Pancho was 23. Pancho was born in Ecuador but had moved to the US in the late 1930s. He was the No. 3-ranked American and had just finished as runner-up in the US Open when he returned to Ecuador to play in the Ecuadorian Open (a tournament he had won six years earlier, before moving to the United States). Pancho was always a crowd favorite with his smile and his humor and pleasant demeanor. I still remember him walking in that bow-legged style of his, which he had as a result of suffering from rickets as a child. He was short, and bowlegged, and disarming, and he also had the most devastating two-handed forehand known to man.

I had somehow won a junior tournament to qualify for the Open. For me to win that tournament was a huge upset; I was a scrappy player with a game that was long on hustle and short on style. As a reward for winning the tournament, I was pitted against Pancho in the first round of the Open. When I found out, I was both excited and nervous. It made me recall the jumping competition at Padua with Pasquina and Vespa. I had been nervous and excited then, too, but as a youth competing in an adult competition, no one really expected anything of me. Here, playing against Pancho Segura, surely no one would expect me to do well, but the spotlight would be at least partially on me, because Pancho was well-loved in Ecuador, and everyone was thrilled to see him return to play in the tournament.

The night before the tournament, I was at the Teran's house, playing cards with Edwin and Cecil; Choyo and Raul were there as well.

"Hey, you can take him, Paolo, no sweat," Edwin said.

"Yeah, just because he took second in the US Open doesn't mean he's any good," offered Choyo.

"He's probably peaked. He can't hope to compete against the up-and-coming Paolo Oreffice," chimed in Cecil.

"He's so weak he has to hit his forehand with two hands," Raul said. (That two-handed forehand came directly from his case of rickets; it weakened him so that he had to grip his racket with both hands. Not a bad example of making lemonade of lemons.)

"He's so bowlegged all you have to do is hit it straight at his legs. He can't move," Edwin advised. (Which was perhaps the biggest lie of all; we all knew that Pancho was lightning-quick on his feet, very nimble and agile.)

My friends continued to offer me sage advice and sound encouragement throughout the evening, all of which served its dual purpose: to help me relax a bit and to make for an entertaining evening (either with me or at my expense; it was going to happen either way).

"Thanks, guys," I said. "With friends like you, how can I lose?"

Do you really want me to tell you?" Edwin asked.

"We'll be pulling for you all the way," Raul said.

"Unless you lose," Choyo added. "Then we were pulling for Pancho all the way."

∞

I played Pancho in the first round and lost 6-1, 6-0—which also meant I was the only player in the first three rounds to capture a game from him. I'm not sure if he fell asleep during the game I won, but Pancho was gracious, he was funny, and he was very, very good. He swept through the tournament, winning it easily, to the delight of the fans. I had no business being on the

At right: Parents' wedding, 1922

Below: Family in Chirignago, 1936

At right: Learning to jump, 1936

At left: Forced members of the "Young Fascist's Organization" gather in St. Mark's Square to spell out the word *Duce* in honor of Mussolini, 1937

Below left: Paul dressed in "Balilla" uniform, 1937

Below right: With Nonno and Papa in Venice, 1937

Beauty
1937

Top: Father jumping, 1937

At left: With Uncle Mario shortly before boarding the ship "Manhattan," 1940

At right: Arriving in New York with mother and sister, Sandra, with the Statue of Liberty in the background, 1940

Above: High school graduation in Quito, Ecuador, 1944

At right: With parents in Larchmont, N.Y., 1947

Below: With father in Lido, Venice's beach, 1962

Above: Carl Gerstacker, Ben Branch, Earl Barnes and Dow CFO, 1974

At left: Chiding Carl Gerstacker, 1976

At right: Ad-libbing to shareholders, 1986

Above: With President Ronald Reagan, 1988

At left: With Senator Claude Pepper, 1989

At right: Boating with former President George H.W. Bush, 2005

Above: With JoAnn, 1995

At right: With the grandchildren, 2005

Below: With Andy, Jamie, Laura, and Jon in St. Mark's Square, 2003

Above: Leading Storm Song with Cot Campbell after the Breeder's Cup victory, 1996

At right: Dick Clark, Nat Slewett, and Bob Hope, 1986

Below: Playing tennis, 1986

court with him—yet I was proud to be there, and I can always say I won a game against Pancho Segura, who is enshrined in the International Tennis Hall of Fame.

Many years later, I had another brief connection with Pancho. In the mid 1970s, my son Andy took lessons from Pancho in La Costa, California, where Pancho was a teaching professional. As we made the connection, I shook hands with Pancho and said, "You probably don't remember me, but I played you a long time ago in the Ecuadorian Open."

Pancho smiled disarmingly and said, "Did I win?"

"Yes, as I recall, you had no trouble beating me."

Pancho looked at my young son, who was eager-eyed and soaking this all in. I had told Andy beforehand, of course, how famous Pancho was and how I had actually played him once. After looking at Andy for a moment, Pancho returned his gaze to me.

"And so, all these years later, you are returning with your son, in hopes that *he* can beat me?"

We laughed. "Not exactly," I said, "but if you can make that happen, I'm happy to pay you a bonus."

Pancho looked with mock seriousness at my son, then put his hand on Andy's shoulder. "Let's get to work, son," he said. "We have plenty to do."

Suffice it to say that no Oreffice has beaten Pancho Segura on the tennis court. Yet.

∞

Ecuador had quickly become our port in the storm, but in the outside world, the storm raged on. The pact between Mussolini and Hitler grew tighter, and Italy bombed Malta in June 1940 and attacked Greece four months later. Winston Churchill sent British troops to aid Greece, and the Italians were driven back from northern Greece and Albania. Just prior to attacking Greece, the Tripartite Pact between Rome, Berlin, and Tokyo was signed, and Hitler continued to pressure other nations to join the pact. Eventually, Bulgaria, Hungary, Romania, and Slovakia were coerced into signing the pact. More and more countries were drawn into the war as the Rome-Berlin-Tokyo Axis moved aggressively forward. In May 1941, Italy annexed the Yugoslavian territory of Dalmatia, and two months later Hitler and Mussolini announced the dissolution of Yugoslavia, with much of it annexed to Italy.

Meanwhile, in March 1941, American President Franklin D. Roosevelt signed an agreement with Winston Churchill outlining US-British cooperation, should the United States be drawn into the war. Foremost in the agreement was this: Germany must be defeated first.

In May 1941, Japan demanded that the US stop supplying war materials to China; the US refused to do so. Soon after, Roosevelt froze all German, Italian, and Japanese assets, as well as those of occupied countries, and closed the German consular offices in the US. The US continued to offer assistance to Britain, China, and the Soviet Union, and the confrontation between Japan and the US heated up. In early December 1941, the Japan Embassy began to leave, destroying codebooks and files as their personnel left. On the 6th of December, Roosevelt sent a last-minute plea to Japan for peace. However, on December 7, 1941, the Japanese Navy carried out a surprise attack on the American Navy base and Army air field at Pearl Harbor in Oahu, Hawaii. More than 2,400 Americans were killed, and Japan had control of the Pacific and was free to conquer southeast Asia and the entire southwest Pacific.

On December 8, the US Congress declared war on Japan and intensified its military mobilization. Three days later, both Germany and Italy declared war on the United States. Its days in a supporting role were abruptly over; now the US entered the war theater and proceeded directly to center stage.

I learned about Pearl Harbor on the first tee of our golf course, where I had just recently learned to play the game. I was playing with, among others, the commercial attaché to the American Embassy. Someone from the clubhouse shouted to us on the green that the Japanese had attacked the US, and that some huge announcement was about to take place. We rushed inside the clubhouse and clustered around a radio that had been set on a counter. I didn't understand much English, but the attaché translated Roosevelt's speech for me:

> Yesterday, December 7, 1941—a date which will live in infamy—the United States of America was suddenly and deliberately attacked by naval and air forces of the Empire of Japan. . . . As Commander-in-Chief of the Army and Navy, I have directed that all measures be taken for our defense. . . . With confidence in our armed forces, with the unbounded determination of our people, we will gain the inevitable triumph, so help us God.

I was only 14 years old, but I knew something momentous had happened. When I got home, one look at my father told me he had heard the news. He slowly shook his head and said, in reference to the Japanese, "They don't know what they've awakened."

CHAPTER EIGHT

∞

Voice of the Andes

Not long ago I came across a letter, written on the stationary of the Republic of Ecuador from the Ministry of National Defense:

16 July 1941
To: Captain of Artillery
Max Oreffice
Subject: Thanking for Patriotism

> *This ministry, in its own name and in the name of the Armed Forces, acknowledges your communication of July 8. We sincerely thank you for the outstanding offer of your services in the defense of the Ecuadorian borders, grievously under the aggression of Peruvian troops, and will consider this offer at the opportune time.*

Honor and Country
For the Minister of National Defense
The Undersecretary
H.A. Saens R.
Colonel

Peru had invaded and partly occupied Ecuador in 1941, based on a border dispute that had been simmering since the 1830 breakup of Gran

Columbia. My father had offered to fight for Ecuador because that country had taken us in; he felt he owed something to Ecuador.

Ecuador was not the only country to whom my father offered his military services. From 1941 to 1945 he pestered numerous military and political officials, from the American ambassador in Quito to a visiting US Army general to other contacts in Ecuador and New York and Italy. His motive was singular and undiluted: he wanted to return to Italy to fight the Germans. His consistent efforts to enlist were met with appreciation, but nothing ever gelled. Of course, he was in his late 40s and early 50s when he was offering his services, so age might have had something to do with it.

When he was unable to enlist, he turned to other means to aid in the efforts against Hitler and Mussolini and to help his country be free. He founded a group called *Italia Libera,* the Free Italian Society, and he was president of the *Societá Mazzini,* a group dedicated to the ideals of Giuseppe Mazzini, a 19th-century Italian writer and politician. Mazzini organized a political society in Italy to unify the modern Italian state, rather than having a number of separate states, many dominated by foreign powers, operating on their own. Essentially, Mazzini preached a unified republic—something my father was deeply committed to as well.

As he could not be in Italy to help this happen, he had to content himself with his efforts from afar. He published a four- to six-page newspaper, *"La Fiamma"* ("The Flame"), which provided all the news he could gather about Italy and the fight against Fascism. My mother aided him greatly in these efforts. My father was recognized as the unofficial Italian ambassador, the ambassador of the free Italians, those Italians who opposed Mussolini and Hitler, not those who believed in and fought for the Axis Powers. While the position was unofficial, the time and effort he spent was taxing and real. He worked long hours in that capacity on top of trying to get his own businesses going. He never begrudged the hours, because it was all pointed toward one ideal that he knew without questions was worth dying for: freedom. If he could not fight in the front lines, he would contribute from the back lines.

Indeed, from nearly the moment we arrived in Quito until the time we left, my father was recognized as a hero, because he had stood up to Mussolini, he had not been afraid to speak his mind and oppose fascism, and he had escaped the clutches of the fascists. As such, he was welcomed in Quito with open arms, and he and my mother were regularly invited to the Allied embassies for both official and unofficial events. I find it amazing, thinking back, that here were a man and a woman who were refugees, who had fled for their lives to another country, and they not only found shelter in their new country, but they attended embassy parties in tails and long dresses, absorbed so naturally into the political circles that you'd have sworn they were born into those circles.

Two of the friends my father made through his embassy connections were Galo and Leonidas Plaza Lasso. When Galo Plaza Lasso became president of Ecuador in 1948, he became that country's thirteenth president in the past 12 years—and its fifth in the past year! Most were knocked out by bloodless revolutions. One time Leonidas was jailed, before his brother became president, because Leonidas was considered by those in power to be a political threat to Ecuador. Leonidas was quite thin, and Galos was much heavier. To get Leonidas released from jail, Galo went to visit him and smuggled in cotton, with which Leonidas stuffed his cheeks so that he could look like his fuller-faced brother. When it was time to leave, it was Leonidas that walked out, and Galo stayed. After an appropriate wait, Galo called the jailers and said, "You have the wrong man." The confused guards released him and both brothers were out.

There was another way my father contributed to the war efforts in his unofficial role as ambassador of the free Italians: he broadcast reports—real news, not propaganda—back to Italy through a shortwave radio station. The station was run by Protestant missionaries; they agreed to let my father do the broadcasts and helped in the setup and operation.

The news he broadcast was significantly different from the news Italians were fed by the Axis Powers' propaganda machine. Most of the news came from Allied sources or from neutral countries such as Switzerland. My mother took an active role in this broadcasting as well. They both wrote, edited, and produced the half-hour broadcasts, which aired on Tuesdays at one or two in the morning, so Italians could have the news as they awoke (there was a seven or eight hour time difference). They aired on other days as well if the news was of special significance. They began the radio reports in 1942, continuing until the end of the war. Each time my father would open with, "This is Max Oreffice, the Voice of the Andes, bringing you news of the war." He would sign off saying, "Until next time, this is the Voice of the Andes." He had no idea if anyone was listening, but he never thought of abandoning the broadcasts. Simply to report the truth, to make the truth of the war available to his countrymen overseas, was reason enough to keep going.

Years later, when my parents returned to Italy after the war, my father was stopped many times on the street. "Max Oreffice! The 'Voice of the Andes'!" his greeter would say, smiling and pumping my father's hand. "We listened to your broadcasts all the time!" My father lost track of the times he was stopped and thanked, and told how he provided hope in a time when hope was a rare commodity.

❧

One August night in 1943 I was awakened by a short, sharp scream. I sat up in bed and rapidly blinked, trying to focus my eyes on my surroundings. Then I heard a distant, muffled sob, and I realized it was my mother. I got out of bed and ran down the hallway to my parents' bedroom, nearly bumping into Sandra as I did. Through the closed door we could hear the soothing tone of my father's voice, but it was drowned out by my mother's cries. We knocked and entered and went to the bed, sitting on the edge. My parents were sitting up; my father was holding my mother in his arms and gently stroking her head, trying to calm her. She looked at us and tried to calm herself. In the pale light her tear-streaked face looked ashen.

"Nonno Vittorio, Nonno Vittorio!" she kept saying.

"Everything will be all right," my father said.

"What about Nonno?" I asked.

"He's calling me!" Mom said. "I heard him calling me, and, and . . . something was wrong."

Whatever that something was, either she didn't know or wouldn't say.

"You heard his voice?" Sandra asked.

"As clear is if he were in this room."

Talking calmed her some. She took a deep breath and smiled, if wanly. "You children get to bed now," she said, returning to her motherly ways. "It's late." I refrained from mentioning the reason we got *out* of bed was her screaming, and gave her a hug before returning to my bed.

Because of the war, personal news was hard to come by from occupied Italy. On occasion we would receive letters through the Red Cross or through relatives in Switzerland or Argentina, both neutral countries.

And so it was nearly six months later that we received word, through Argentina, that Nonno Vittorio had indeed died—the very night that Mom had dreamed of his death and heard him calling her. He died at age 84 after being ill for a few days, and just a few weeks before the Nazis arrived to occupy Venice. His last words, according to the letter from Nonna Emma, were "Elena, Elena!" My mother was always her father's favorite; whenever he went on a walk or had an errand to run, he would ask her if she wanted to go, and she would gladly accompany him. Now, on his death bed, he called her one last time to accompany him, at least in thought. He died peacefully in his own bed with his Elena in mind, even as he jolted my mother awake in hers.

He was not the only grandparent I was to lose during the war years. Nonna Alice, my father's mother, had remained in Venice and had gone to the family summer home in 1943 when word of the imminent Nazi occupation reached Venetians. Many of my relatives fled to Switzerland (among them my Nonna Emma, Vittorio's widow) and stayed in refugee camps there until the war ended, but Nonna Alice stayed at the Villa in Bosco di Nanto, along with a farmer's family and our old family friend, Bepi Rosini. Nonna had diabetes and was nearly blind by this time; she was not healthy enough to flee. When word came that the Nazis were closing in on the villa, Nonna became distressed. She had a horrible fear of the Nazis. Bepi tried to calm her but couldn't, so he took the action he knew would give her the greatest peace of mind: he hid her, at her request, in the hayloft on the farm.

"Don't leave me," Nonna Alice quailed, clutching Bepi's arms as he gently helped her to a comfortable position in the hay.

"Of course I won't leave you. Why would I leave you?" Bepi responded. His voice was calm and smooth, and meant to be reassuring.

"Shut that door," she said, pointing to an open door through which they could be seen from the road. "I don't want them finding us here."

"No one will find us, I assure you," Bepi said. He rose to shut the door, which was split so the top and the bottom could open and close separately. He left the top part open to allow some air movement.

"Do you think it's okay to leave that part open?" Nonna asked, doubtfully.

"No one can see us in here unless they fly by, or climb those trees by the roadside."

"But they fly planes! They can see us in their planes!"

"No one is flying around looking for small openings in barns to see if people are hiding in them."

"But it's true, those trees, they could climb them."

Nonna paused, and looked at Bepi smiling kindly at her, and she relaxed and smiled back. "I guess Nazis wouldn't waste their time climbing trees, would they?" she said.

Bepi nodded and patted her hand. "Just relax. The worrying does you no good. Why don't you try to nap for a bit? It's a little warm, but there's a breeze coming through."

Nonna nodded and grumbled about what was this world coming to when old ladies were forced to hide in barns, but the afternoon heat and the worrying had made her drowsy, so she did nap, with Bepi sitting right next to her. An hour later, when Bepi gently touched her shoulder to suggest that they could return to the house, the shoulder was cold. Bepi wept. He had worked for my father for a long time, and he loved my family like he loved his own. Now my father's mother had passed away, and her son was half a world away. It should have been Max that was with her, Bepi thought. But Max was forced to flee, and I am here in his stead. He looked at Nonna Alice, who looked peaceful now; the worry had vanished from her face. Yes, Signora Alice, what has this world come to?

Nonna Alice was not worrying needlessly. Not long after she died, the Nazis occupied the area and as one of their countless thousands of senseless, brutal acts, they burned down the villa where my grandmother had been staying. All had fled the villa by then; the Nazis did it not to destroy human life, but simply to destroy.

∞

There are three others whose stories I must recount. The first is of Bruno Finzi, a first cousin of mine; the second is of Giorgio Cavaglieri, another relative; and the third is of Grete Grossman, my nursemaid from Czechoslovakia.

Bruno Finzi was born in 1918 in Bologna, a son of my Zia (Aunt) Olga, on my mother's side. He studied medicine at the University of Padua and became a doctor, living and practicing in Venice. When the war swept over Europe, he joined the Italian partisans, made up of people of varying political parties or ideologies who were all united in their desire to fight fascism and Nazism and to keep Italy free from German occupation. Indeed, the partisans provided fierce resistance against German troops during the occupation of Italy in 1943. They were in some respects a rag-tag group of citizens and soldiers, some who had come from the dissolved Italian army, some who were former prisoners of other countries, some who were too young or too old to be in the regular army. They hid in the mountains and surprised the much-larger enemy forces in ambushes. Only when forced to (such as in Emilia-Romagna in the north) did they fight in and around cities, on plains, or along the coast. It was in Venezia Giulia, at the head of the Adriatic Sea (much of this region was awarded to Yugoslavia shortly after the war), that German troops first faced a partisan uprising. This occurred in September 1943, and the resistance surprised and dismayed the Germans, who called for reinforcements. While the Germans eventually overcame the resistance there, it was the first taste of serious partisan resistance, something that Hitler had not anticipated and that his generals had not concerned themselves with.

Partisan uprisings sprang up throughout the country, in Colle San Marco, near Bosco Matese, and in Naples, where the partisans fought on the streets, for four days in September 1943, soldiers, patriots, men, women, and boys fighting side by side and forcing the Germans to surrender and leave the city in defeat. A few days later, Allied troops arrived to take back Naples from the Germans, only to find it had never been relinquished. Other partisan uprisings took place in Lanciano and in Villadossola. The partisans won some battles and lost others. But they never stopped fighting, and they proved to be a deterrent to Hitler's occupation forces.

My cousin Bruno was in the midst of this. He was the only doctor the partisans had in the north. As such, he was quite valuable to the partisan effort—not that the others weren't. But he was the one who could mend wounds, perform surgeries, give medications, set bones, and help heal the wounded. His life calling, he said, was to heal people. He was used to making house calls to those who could not come to his office in downtown Venice; it was, for Bruno, a simple transition to making those calls in the wooded hills of northern Italy. It was all the same to him. In fact, he was serving a dual purpose: on a smaller level, he was healing people, as he had always done; and he was doing it within the context of helping to heal his country. He abhorred violence, because he believed it to be morally wrong and because it damaged the body as well as the soul. But he did not fear the violence that surrounded the partisans. He worked calmly in the midst of chaos. He was a one-man M*A*S*H unit, extracting bullets and treating wounds under cover of trees, behind barns, in alleyways, in the houses of people who took them in, wherever he came upon the wounded. When he joined the partisans in the north he simply said, "Send me where you need me." And they did.

Bruno did not directly engage in combat, but he was directly imperiled. He was captured by the Germans near Vicenza, along with some other partisans; they were on their way to join another group of partisans who needed help. Bruno was not so much upset about being captured as he was about not being able to provide the medical services that he knew his fellow partisans needed.

Bruno and some fellow partisans were forced into the back of a truck, where they sat, hands tied, on benches on either side of the truck's interior, under the watchful eyes of two guards.

"Where are you taking us?" one of the partisans demanded.

One of the guards looked spitefully at him without speaking. The truck bounced along the uneven road, jostling everyone inside.

"I said where are we going?" the partisan said. He said this in crisp, clear, German, biting off each word and spitting it out.

The first guard refused to even look at his captive this time, but the other guard sneered and said, "You are going where you belong. To one of your Italian jails."

"You cannot keep us in jail."

"Maybe you're right. Maybe we should just kill you instead."

The partisan became so enraged that he lunged at the guard, using his tied-up hands to hit him with a glancing blow to the head. The guard reared up and hit him hard in the head with the butt of his rifle. The partisan crumpled to the floor of the truck, unconscious, blood pouring from his temple.

Bruno sprang up swiftly, and the guard turned to him, ready to beat him senseless too, but he saw that Bruno was moving toward his crumpled compatriot. He could do nothing, of course, because his hands were tied. But his instincts brought him to his friend's side.

As Bruno knelt by the man's side, the guard peered fiercely at the other prisoners. "Anyone else?" he barked, his eyes wide and blazing.

Before anyone could answer, several sharp thuds pounded the truck. Bruno heard glass breaking. The truck lurched to an uneven stop, and the prisoners in the back all toppled over each other, some spilling into the startled guards. Shouts came from outside the truck and from inside the cab. Gunfire sounded. The two guards scrambled out of the back of the truck. More gunfire. The one that had knocked out the partisan stepped around the back of the truck on the driver's side and was immediately shot. His rifle skidded down the road as he was flung, lifeless, to the ground. The other guard went around the other side of the truck. The partisans stayed low in the back end. More gunfire. The gunfire was coming from both sides of the truck. More shouts. One more blast of gunfire. Then silence.

In a few moments, a group of partisans appeared. They untied the hands of their fellow partisans. Bruno treated the partisan who, by this time, was regaining consciousness. He cleaned the wound and wrapped the man's head in gauze and bandages. In a matter of moments, the partisans had disappeared, leaving behind several dead German soldiers and a battered army truck.

Another time, the Germans were successful in putting Bruno in jail. He and a few other partisans were captured near Udine. The Germans had occupied Udine and were using its jails to hold the resisters. (This was better than their response in some cities, such as Lanciano, where the Germans shot those taking part in the uprising.)

"Don't worry," a partisan named Alessandro told Bruno in their holding cell. Six to eight partisans were in each of several different cells. Alessandro, short and squat and in his sixties, with a short, grizzled beard, spoke low enough that the German guards watching the cells could not hear him. "They won't let us stay in here."

"Do you know something I don't?" asked Bruno.

Alessandro smiled widely, revealing a golden tooth. "I know you're my ticket out of here."

Bruno's eyebrows rose. "I am? How so?"

"Because you're our medic. We can't fight if we can't get patched up."

Alessandro knew what he was talking about. That night, a band of partisans stormed the jail, overtook the guards, and freed the thirty or so partisans that had been held.

Not long after this, Bruno was captured a third time. And for a third time, another band of partisans freed Bruno. Each time he was freed, he went about his business of healing people, serene and unperturbed as ever. He was following his calling, and his calling had him treating partisans. He took care of the partisans, and the partisans took care of him.

∞

Giorgio Cavaglieri was a relative of my father's, born in Padua in, I believe, 1910. Giorgio was not the altruistic soul that Bruno was. In fact, Giorgio was obsessed with . . . how shall I say this? With Giorgio. Giorgio came from a family with lots of money, and Giorgio never sank so low as to actually work. Why work, Giorgio reasoned, when you could play? Giorgio's chief toys were fast cars and faster women. He loved convertibles, and had more than a few expensive cars. He was six-foot-three, 180 pounds, with a supple, athletic body and the good looks associated today with movie stars. He had sleek black hair and an engaging smile emanating from his always-tanned face, and he preened himself so that attractive young women would flock to him like moths to a flame. As Bruno made the rounds in hospitals and the homes of his patients in Venice, Giorgio made the rounds as well, visiting nightclub after nightclub in Padua, in Venice, in Rome, and Paris; in short, anywhere his heart and his wheels took him. Giorgio had a rigorous schedule; not many could attend so many parties and social engagements and be seen in so many clubs with so many women in so short a time, but Giorgio valiantly—even cheerfully—put up with this demanding timetable.

So when the Germans began their occupation of Italy, no one in our family was surprised when Bruno Finzi joined the partisans and did what he could to stem the tide. And *everyone* in our family was surprised when Giorgio Cavaglieri did the same thing. In fact, this was the *last* thing we thought Giorgio would do. Giorgio was the epitome of selfishness, and joining the partisans was about as selfless an act as anyone could do.

Yet Giorgio did just that, and without a moment's hesitation. He joined a partisan group in northern Italy, a different one from Bruno's, though they ran across each other on occasion.

In the summer of 1944, Giorgio's group was planning a resistance against German forces in Vicenza. A newcomer named Giuseppe was keenly interested in the plan and ingratiated himself to the leaders. Giorgio was a little suspicious of Giuseppe, wondering why he was joining the partisans so late. Giorgio questioned Giuseppe about where he had been since the resistance had begun the previous year. Giuseppe replied that he had been with partisan groups in the south, but he was vague about who they were and where they operated.

Giorgio drew Filippo, one of the leaders, aside during a meeting. "Filippo, I don't know about this Giuseppe."

Filippo studied Giuseppe for a few moments, then shrugged. "I guess we can't know, can we? Time will tell."

Time told in less than 24 hours. The next day, German forces, on the offensive, overwhelmed the partisans outside of Vicenza, killing dozens and rounding up the rest before the partisans could begin their own attack. Giuseppe was nowhere to be seen that day. Giorgio was transported by truck to a jail in Vicenza, where he and the other partisans were held for a couple of weeks. Then one morning they were transported to the train station. They joined a few thousand other prisoners who were being shipped out of the country, to a "labor camp," or so Giorgio heard.

As he boarded the train, Giorgio saw Filippo for the first time since their group had been jailed. "I guess now we know about Giuseppe," Giorgio said.

"Keep strong," Filippo replied. "Keep your eyes about you."

Giorgio nodded as they both climbed into their train car. It was just an empty boxcar, no seats, made to transport goods. There were dozens of such cars, most of them already overloaded with grim-faced men, women, and children. It was August, and the sun beat down on the cars. The heat inside was stifling, and the stench was nearly unbearable. Dozens of guards supervised the boarding of the train. Once everyone was in, the guards rolled the doors shut and locked them. It was dark inside the cars. Giorgio felt entombed, but with nearly a hundred other people. A panic rose in his throat; he fought to quell it, to maintain control.

The train lurched forward, then began its slow, steady push. Though Giorgio did not know it at the time, its final destination was about 900 kilometers to the east: through Austria, through Czechoslovakia, into Poland, and to Auschwitz.

The train would stop at various times along the way and the guards would let the prisoners out to relieve themselves along the tracks. There was no privacy; everyone was humiliated, and many of the guards took great pleasure in increasing that humiliation. Some prisoners were forced to relieve themselves in plain view of others, or not to relieve themselves at all. Sometimes people would choose not to relieve themselves, hoping they could hold it until the next stop, and they'd end up humiliating themselves—and adding to the stench in the box cars—not far down the tracks. Some who were old, or weak, or who were emotionally unable to handle the stress and were making a commotion were taken to the side of the track and shot. Their bodies were left there as the train was slowly reloaded, the doors shut and locked, and the procession continued its trek eastward.

On one such stop, Giorgio overheard two guards talking quietly about how many days it took to reach Auschwitz. The other had replied they should be there in two days. This confirmed what Giorgio felt sure was true. Without drawing attention to himself, he walked slowly over to Filippo and quietly said, "You know where this is headed."

Filippo nodded.

"We need to make a break for it," Giorgio said.

"I think we can break the lock from the inside. I found a piece of wood that we can use."

Giorgio nodded, then looked straight ahead at nothing as a guard glanced over at them.

The boxcars were made of wood, and a few broken pieces lay on the floor of their car. Once they were back inside, Filippo and Giorgio took turns working on the lock.

It took them nearly two full days. Some other men pitched in as well, and for many, the effort was the first ray of hope they'd had in weeks. Many saw it as their last ray of hope as well. Others were nervous about the attempt to break out.

"Are you crazy?" a middle-aged woman shouted. "You're going to get us all killed!"

Giorgio, who was working at the lock at the time, turned to her, sweat coursing down his face. None of the young female beauties in Padua would have recognized Giorgio at this moment. He was about to retort that if they *didn't* attempt to escape, they would surely all be killed, but when he recognized the look of terror on the woman's face, even in the darkness of the car, he took a deep breath and said, "God bless you, Signora." Giorgio was not a religious man; he had no idea why those words had come out of his mouth. But then he had no idea how he had gone so quickly from a playboy to a partisan, and from a partisan to a prisoner, one headed for a death camp in a godforsaken land.

His statement disarmed the woman and seemed to somehow calm her. Giorgio continued trying to break the lock.

They were in Poland now. Less than 100 kilometers to go. The train stopped outside of Jastrzebie Zdrój, 50 kilometers to go.

"Maybe we go now," Giorgio said quietly to Filippo as they urinated on the side of the tracks.

"No, we've almost got it."

"But if we don't get it, we're not going to get a chance."

Do you call this a chance?" Filippo nodded toward two guards standing twenty yards away, rifles at the ready. Dozens of other guards were stationed all around the prisoners, watching. As the train had moved into Poland, the tension felt by prisoners and guards alike had increased. Perhaps the guards felt the chances were greater that some would try to escape. Whatever it was, they were keenly alert, and uniformly sour-faced and meaner than usual. When the guards were in a good mood, they humiliated the prisoners. When they were in a dour mood, they hustled them off and on the train and watched their every move, ready to punish them severely when the slightest resistance was shown.

Giorgio glumly agreed that there was little chance of escape at that moment. To run now would surely be to die with bullets sprayed in your back. But to board the train again? Wasn't that surely death, too?

Less than 10 kilometers outside of Auschwitz, Filippo and Giorgio succeeded in breaking the lock. Filippo turned immediately to the others. "There are only a few kilometers to go. We're going to push open the car door and jump out. Are you coming?"

There was a mix of replies, but most were in the positive. "Let's go now, no more talk!" one said. "No time to waste!"

Filippo looked at Giorgio and nodded. Giorgio pulled open the door, needing help from Filippo and another man because the train's motion made the door harder to open than if it were standing still. They managed to get it open and looked out to see a wooded area immediately in front of them, and to their left, toward Auschwitz, the beginning of an industrial area.

"Take to the woods!" Filippo shouted to the others, and then he and Giorgio jumped and rolled along the side of the tracks, receiving cuts and abrasions from the rocks along the side before rolling onto grass farther out. Two others jumped, then three, then two more, then four, and they kept on coming. Giorgio watched a few others jump; they looked to be, for a moment, suspended in midair between the train and the ground, before landing abruptly and rolling. A few landed awkwardly, twisting their ankles or spraining their shoulders.

"Let's go!" Filippo said to Giorgio and several others who had jumped right after them. Even before they picked themselves up, though, the sound that Giorgio feared the most rang in his ears: the screech of train brakes. Forty or fifty prisoners had leapt from the train before the first guards jumped off as the train was rolling to a halt. Another twenty prisoners leapt from the open car, but even as they leapt they were being shot at. The guards had no intention of rounding them up and getting them alive to Auschwitz, less than five kilometers away now. The majority of the men, women, and children who poured from that open car had no chance. They were gunned down, either in the back as they ran, terrified, for the woods, or they were shot in the chest as they stopped and faced the approaching guards, their hands held high above their heads. Pleas of "Don't shoot!" were answered with gunfire, and soon the only sounds were of the cawing of crows, stirred from the nearby woods by the shooting, and the crackling of the guards' boots on the cinders and rocks along the tracks as they surveyed their carnage. When they came to the open box car, they found twelve people huddled inside; they were holding each other and several were crying. Among them was the woman who had called Giorgio crazy, who had said he was going to get them all killed. Two guards conferred for a moment; one nodded and shrugged. They then faced the door again and opened fire on the people huddled inside, killing them all.

All but seven people from that car were killed, whether they tried to escape or not. The first seven who jumped off the train made it to the woods before the guards could get them in their sights. That's seven more people with a chance to live than if they had all remained inside the locked car and been escorted into Auschwitz.

The seven who escaped ran together through the woods for awhile, intent on putting as much distance between them and the guards as possible. Several guards had taken off after them. The woods were not thick enough for Giorgio's liking; there was too much space between trees. On the other hand, it allowed them to move quickly, which they did for a couple of kilometers before pausing to rest for a moment. They had heard, a few different times, guards calling out to each other, and the distant crashing of boots on dead leaves and sticks.

Sweat ran in rivulets down the faces of the seven men. Their shirts were soaked, and it would not be long before they would be dehydrated, because they had not been given enough water in the last several days. A couple of the men, much older than Giorgio, were panting hard, and one was pale and had stopped sweating, a sure sign of heat exhaustion.

"We can't outrun them, but we can outsmart them," Filippo said. He looked at each man, then looked ahead, toward the trees that he hoped would continue to cover their escape. "We need to split up. If they capture us as a group, we're all dead. If we split up, some have a chance of making it."

Everyone agreed. The groups had already been formed by the bonds made when the men jumped out with each other. Filippo and Giorgio would go together, the next two who followed them would be a second group, and the three that jumped after that would comprise the third group. Filippo suggested three different routes, all headed west, toward Czechoslovakia, which was a good 70 kilometers away. He had no immediate plans beyond that; they all just wanted to put distance between themselves and the German guards pursuing them, and to get out of German-occupied Poland.

So they split up. Filippo and Giorgio took off, and the other two groups did as well, each wishing the other luck before leaving. But the group of three was caught within half an hour, and the two men who jumped the train right after Filippo and Giorgio were caught later that afternoon. Whether any of them lived to see the light of another day is unknown.

Filippo and Giorgio kept going. They were both in their early thirties, both in good shape, both fueled by a tremendous hatred for the Germans and an equally tremendous desire to see Italy again. Even before they had been captured, many Italian cities were being liberated by Allied forces, and Mussolini had been forced to resign the previous summer, restoring hope and pride in Italians even as they fought to repel their former ally, Germany. Rome had been liberated only a few months before. But none of that mattered now. Only their survival mattered.

After traveling west for several more kilometers, Filippo and Giorgio paused by a stream. They knelt in the streambed, cupping the cold water in their hands and drinking deeply. After drinking their fill, they immersed their heads and came up shaking, like big dogs, the water spraying off their hair and faces. They allowed themselves a brief smile as they leaned their backs against a tree. They had heard no pursuit for some time.

Water still dripping off his chin, Filippo turned to Giorgio and said, "I think we circle back to the tracks. We follow those all the way back."

"Do you think that's safe?"

Filippo looked straight-faced at Giorgio for a moment and then laughed. "Of course it's not safe! But it's no less safe than this." He gestured vaguely at the woods surrounding them.

Giorgio shrugged. "Anything to get us back to Italy."

They rose and began walking northwest, knowing they would eventually make their way back to the train tracks, and hopefully through Poland, Czechoslovakia, and Austria before reaching Italy. To do so, they would have to pass through the Alps in Austria and northern Italy. But that was the least of their concerns at the moment.

It didn't take them long to find the tracks. They kept out of view of passing trains, and were guided by the silvery rails that made their way west. They traveled by night, slept in the woods during the day, scrounged for whatever food they could find. They drank from streams, ate roots and berries, caught an occasional rabbit or squirrel, going deep into the woods to roast it over a small fire. They would eat ravenously, looking nervously over their shoulders and putting out the fire as quickly as possible. As they passed by towns, they would find, under cover of night, stale bread and other edible food thrown out by bakeries and restaurants. In short time they looked like bums, their clothes dirty, their faces bearded. As long as their progress was unimpeded, they didn't care about their appearance. Like salmon struggling upstream, their focus was singular, their every move directed by their effort to accomplish the one thing they had to accomplish: reaching Italy. No energy was wasted on anything that was not directly related to that purpose. As they trudged on toward the west, train after train rolled by them, heading east, toward Auschwitz, carrying thousands of people to the fate they had so narrowly escaped.

As miraculous as it seems, their first meeting of significance with another person happened in Austria, after they had passed through Poland and Czechoslovakia. They had passed by Vienna, and were in a wooded area outside of the town of Mödling, sleeping, as usual, during the day, when Giorgio awoke to see the blue-gray barrel of a rifle pointed at his face. At the end of the rifle, to his relief, was not a German soldier, but an Austrian farmer with a long, angular face and a slouch hat shading his eyes.

"What are you doing here?" the farmer asked.

Giorgio sat up slowly, making no sudden movements. Filippo sat up as well. Giorgio smiled weakly, calling on his old charm to win people over. They had been traveling for nearly two months now, and in his condition he felt less charming than normal.

"We're just passing through. We got tired and took a nap," Giorgio said, watching the farmer closely to see what effect that explanation would have on him.

"You're on my property."

"We can move on," Giorgio suggested.

"You're Italian."

Giorgio smiled, a more genuine smile this time. "Yes, yes, Italiano. We are headed back to Italy."

"Walking?"

Giorgio looked at Filippo, who looked closely at the farmer and then, after a moment, nodded.

"We were captured by Germans in Italy and shipped to Auschwitz. We escaped," said Giorgio. He was taking a chance in saying this, but it was a calculated one. Nearly a million Austrians had served in either the German army (the Wehrmacht) or the elite Nazi military unit known as the Waffen SS. But after Germany lost the Battle of Stalingrad in early 1943, Austrian support for Germany began to crumble, and Austrians saw themselves for what they were: victims of Hitler's aggression. Still, Austria was known as enemy territory, and on which side this Austrian farmer fell was anyone's guess.

The Austrian seemed to be trying to decide this for himself as well. He kept his rifle trained on Giorgio for about ten seconds, not indicating either way how their confession struck him. Finally, he lowered his rifle and allowed a slight smile to register.

"You should have said so in the first place," he said. Giorgio took a deep breath.

"We haven't been saying much of anything for awhile," Filippo said. They rose. "We'll move on, if you want."

"Without food? Sleeping under a tree? My wife would never hear of it." The farmer led them to his house, walking with a pronounced limp. "Bad knee," he said. "It's probably why I'm alive today." Giorgio and Filippo exchanged glances.

At the house his wife, Marta, greeted them first with suspicion, then warmly once her husband explained who they were. Her husband—who introduced himself as Franz—told them that Marta had lost a brother in the war. He was serving in the German Wehrmacht, and had died at Stalingrad. She had been against him entering the war in the first place, and despised the Germans as much as most Italians did. Franz had initially been in support of the German war effort, but he thought differently now. His knee kept him out of the service, out of Stalingrad, and in his fields.

In the living room, after the introductions, Marta told Giorgio and Filippo to sit and she would prepare them some food. "It looks like you haven't eaten in weeks!" she said.

"No, no, just the other day we had our fill of roots," Giorgio smiled.

"There's an endless supply of roots out there," Filippo agreed. "Not," he was quick to add, "that we couldn't try a change in our diet."

"Roots! Roots are for bugs, for small animals!" Marta said. "Roots are not food. If you want food, don't delay me a moment longer. I will prepare you some real food."

That was the best news Giorgio had heard in weeks. He was about to thank her, but she held up her hand, staying him, and called out, "Franz! Come here!" Franz had wandered off to the kitchen. As he came back to the living room and husband and wife conferred, Giorgio leaned over in his chair and said, so that only Filippo could hear, "I think we know who runs the house."

Franz nodded to his wife and began shutting the curtains in all the rooms of the house. "No one needs to know we have guests. You understand," he said to Giorgio.

"Of course."

"Especially those in the Wehrmacht," Franz said. "They might be very interested in meeting you."

Giorgio noticed that Franz kept his rifle by the front door. When they moved into the kitchen to eat at the long wooden table, Franz brought his rifle with him.

"If I'd have found you a year ago on my property, I would have shot you or turned you in," Franz said matter-of-factly. Giorgio and Filippo were too famished to even comment. They had not seen food like this for a few months. They said essentially nothing during the entire meal, eating to make up for lost meals as Marta kept filling their plates. Giorgio and Filippo knew what war rationings meant and expressed their thanks multiple times to the couple.

As they were finishing, Franz appeared uncomfortable and cleared his throat. "I think it would be better if you stayed in my barn today. Not in the house. You understand."

Giorgio and Filippo had no problem with that. The barn was a bit musty, but offered good shelter and was relatively cool even in midday, as it was mid-October now.

"I'll come get you at nightfall, and you can have a meal before leaving," Franz said. And so Giorgio and Filippo slept the best they had slept in two months, and awoke to a meal of bread and ham. They ate by candlelight, not for the romance but for safety, with all the curtains still drawn. When they were finished, they had a strong Viennese coffee that would be sure to keep them awake during their night march. A quarter moon had risen, shining pale light on the surrounding wheat and maize and sugar beet fields as they bade their hosts goodbye. They left with a small portion of ham and bread and a bottle of pear schnapps that would help keep them warm during their nights. Marta gave them each a blanket as well. Their hosts wished them safe travel. During the dinner Franz had told them the best pass to take through the Alps. It was not necessarily the easiest, or even the most direct, but it was passable by foot, and had towns along the way, and was least likely to be clogged with German soldiers.

And so they made their slow way southwest, passing like ghosts around towns like Wiener Neustadt, Semmering, Judenburg, and Villach. Marta had given them enough to subsist on for a couple of days, and they were energized by both the food and the kindness showed them. But they had a long ways to go yet, and Italy was still occupied, so if and when they returned, they would still have to slink around like thieves.

∞

On a cool evening in November 1944, a knock sounded on the front door of the Cavaglieri house in Padua. No one answered, and the knock sounded again, this time louder. Finally a maid peeked out from behind a front room curtain, straining to see who might be knocking. The knock sounded again, louder and more insistent yet. The maid hesitated, then finally went to the door and opened it a crack.

"Who are you? What do you want?" she said.

"Who am I? Is that you, Emilia?"

"How do you know my name?" She had not opened the door further, and was ready to slam it shut at once.

"And how do you *not* know mine?"

"What do you want? Bread? Drink, more likely. We have nothing here. Go."

"But I live here. I have been on the go for more than three months. I want to sleep in my bed for once. Now, let me in."

"You are a lunatic. Go! I am calling the police at once." She tried to slam the door, but Giorgio stuck his foot in.

"I am Giorgio. Do I look that bad?"

Stunned silence. Emilia opened her eyes wide and looked for a moment like she might faint. She peered closely through the crack at this filthy, ragged, thin man—this specter on her doorstep. The Giorgio she knew was much bigger, stronger, handsomer, cleaner. Giorgio in rags? Never. Giorgio unkempt? Not on your life, or anyone else's. Giorgio home? After nearly three months missing, after the rest of his family had gone in hiding, after she and two other servants were left on their own?

She flung the door open, dragged him inside, hugged him tightly— clearly overstepping the normal bounds between them. Neither of them cared. Giorgio closed his eyes and smiled as he hugged Emilia, who bawled unashamedly as she ushered him in and bade him sit. He had, indeed, become a phantom of his former self; he had lost 70 pounds, his hair was long and stringy, and he smelled and looked horrible. But he was home. He had made it, and Filippo had made it to his hometown of Vicenza. Emilia nursed Giorgio back to health, and as soon as he hard regained his strength, he rejoined the partisans, fighting with them until Italy was liberated. After the liberation he was reunited with his family.

∞

Grete Grossman's story is not so happy. Grete had left Venice to return to Czechoslovakia in the fall of 1939; she was worried about her mother as the war began. My parents heard from her early on. Grete did not intend to stay in Czechoslovakia, but with the war in its early stages, travel was perilous, especially in eastern Europe. She began to date a man back home. That was the last we heard of her before we left Italy for South America.

After the war was over, my father tried to contact her, but couldn't. He couldn't locate any of her family. It was possible that she had gotten married and, with her new surname, was just difficult to find. At least that's what my parents said.

A year or so after the war ended, my father learned otherwise. He had returned to New York, and he found her name listed in a registry among those who died at Auschwitz. Her mother perished with her, as did other family members. She was unable to escape, as Giorgio had, as we had. She was a great influence in my early life, one I will always be grateful for.

∞

Life went on for us in Ecuador. Not much of it was similar to our life in Italy, and that was okay, even though we had to abruptly adjust to a lower standard of living. After awhile, my father did manage to renew one familiar passion of mine: he bought me a horse, Gitano, which we kept at a stable about 15 minutes from our house, and I was able to do some riding. I rode several other horses as well, including one owned by the Danish ambassador. This horse would let no one ride but me—anyone else, he threw off. I had soft hands with horses; I didn't abuse their mouths with the bits. The ambassador saw this, saw how I handled his difficult horse, and he asked me to ride his others as well, to give them exercise, so I got to ride a lot in Ecuador.

In Quito, I not only rode; I learned to play polo. I had the good fortune of falling under the aegis of Colonel Proctor, the military attaché to the American Embassy, and his wife. They were both fine polo players, and they helped me pick up and enjoy the game. The horses were unbelievable. They learned how to follow the ball and they turned on a dime. I thought it was great fun to play and ride. I enjoyed it all, except for the time my helmet strap broke, my helmet tumbled off, and not long after, a high shot hit me in the head, where my helmet should have been. I was knocked off the horse and nearly knocked out. I eventually became pretty decent at polo, but mainly I simply enjoyed riding and playing.

I was quite active in Ecuador: soccer, tennis, baseball, horse riding and jumping, golf, polo. I did well in school. I made great friends in Quito. I learned how to play bridge there, and this is still a passion of mine. My life blossomed. I even went on my first date, though it was the girl who set up the date—Norita Teran, Edwin and Cecil's sister—whom I would have preferred to go out with.

The date was more or less a dare from Edwin, who had gone out with several girls. "Hey, man, how come you don't go out with anyone?" he said one summer evening when we were playing cards at their house. Norita was getting ready to go out with some friends and she heard her brother.

"I'm just not interested in anyone, that's all," I lied, not able to look at Norita and hoping if someone noticed my blushing they would take it for sunburn.

Norita, combing her hair in a mirror, looked at me in the mirror and smiled. "I know someone who's interested in *you*."

My heart skipped a beat; I thought for a moment she was talking for herself. But of course she wasn't. She had no idea I was crazy about her, and she never would. Her friend, Vituca, was the one who was interested. Vituca was pretty, I guess, but at that point I only had eyes for Norita. But to her I was just like Edwin or Cecil: a kid brother.

I took Vituca to a movie. I didn't really know what to say or do. I kept my hands in my pockets and my eyes glued to the screen, though I don't recall the movie being that great. Vituca was a little shy as well, so our first date consisted of a few embarrassed smiles (mine might have been grimaces), several uncomfortable pauses after the movie was over and we were walking down the street, and great relief upon saying goodbye.

I dated Vituca again, took her to a dance at the tennis club, but it didn't progress beyond that. I just wasn't ready to date yet. I wasn't ready to drink yet, either, but friends coaxed me into drinking beer when I was 17 and attending a party for an Ecuadorian friend who was leaving to go to college in the United States. Edwin and I had stuck to beer most of the night, and that was novel enough, but on a dare from someone I drank a good part (or perhaps it was the bad part) of a bottle of cognac, and that was one mistake too many for that night. After awhile Edwin looked at me and said, "What are you doing, Paolo? You can't even stand up!" I not only couldn't stand up, I couldn't sit without sliding off a chair, I couldn't speak and make any sense, and I was so dizzy I thought I was going to pass out.

"I think I drank too mush," I slurred.

"No kidding. Let's get you home."

"No, no," I said, waving my arms in slow motion in front of me. It reminded me of a conductor, and that struck me as hilarious. I found myself laughing on the floor, holding my sides. I closed my eyes to stop the room from spinning, but my head continued to reel. I wondered if this was what it felt like to be seasick. Then I wondered what it would be like to be drunk *and* seasick. At least I wasn't on a boat, though it felt like I was.

"I can't go home."

"What do you mean? Come on, get up." Edwin somehow helped me up. He got me out the door, my arm slung around his back, and we wobbled in the direction of my house, though I didn't want to show up drunk there. I had never been drunk in my life—and I never have been since that night in Quito. I became violently ill on the way home, threw up again in bed during the night, and woke up feeling terrible. I vowed that would never happen again, and it hasn't. I'll have a beer or a glass of wine, and on rare occasion, two, but never more.

My parents, by the way, handled this very well. When they saw how chagrined I was, they understood my self-disgust was more punishment than they could dole out, so they didn't add to it. One of the many things they taught me is sometimes you have to be tough, sometimes you have to go easy, and the balance of knowing when to do which is something they had in abundance. I've tried to emulate that quality in my own life.

I mentioned I learned to play bridge in Ecuador. My parents were excellent players (in fact, they played with Eli Culbertson and his wife, in New York, just before coming to Ecuador; the Culbertsons were world-renowned players and teachers of bridge). I learned a lot just by watching my parents play with friends. I'd sit quietly and not bother anyone, but watch the cards being played and pick up on the strategies involved. Later I'd ask my dad why he played a card at a certain juncture, and he'd explain. He had a tremendous memory and could recall each hand in minute detail.

Mrs. Hughes Hallet, the wife of the British Ambassador, played regularly in my mother's group. Now, Mrs. Hallet was undoubtedly a wonderful woman, with many fine qualities, but honesty in card playing wasn't one of them. She dealt off the bottom of the deck and she did some other dishonest things that my mother caught. (Mrs. Hallet refused to let me watch their games, perhaps because she was afraid an observer might catch her at her tricks.) Another friend brought up Mrs. Hallet's cheating to my mother after a game at our house one afternoon. Mrs. Hallet had been picked up by her chauffeur already, and my mom and her other two friends discussed the problem. One lady said she didn't want to play with a cheat, but Mrs. Hallet was, after all, an ambassador's wife, and it would be embarrassing to confront her. This lady didn't know what to do.

My mother did. "Let me handle this," she said, putting a hand on her friend's arm.

The next week, the same foursome gathered at the embassy for a game. In private, my mother confronted Mrs. Hallet before the game began.

"Leticia," my mother said. "We know what you've been doing."

Mrs. Hallet looked puzzled. "What I've been doing? Whatever do you mean?"

"Well, for one thing, you've been dealing off the bottom of the deck." My mother mentioned a few other things as well.

Mrs. Hallet's cheeks turned pink. She drew back, as if she were alarmed at the accusation. "You're accusing me of cheating."

"Leticia, we know you're doing it and *you* know you're doing it. If you do it again, you'll have to find another game. Now, please. We enjoy your company and want to continue playing with you—so long as we all have the same chance of winning."

Mrs. Hallet considered this. Finally, she sighed and attempted a wry smile. "Well, Elena, no one will ever have the same chance of winning when I'm in the game, but I can assure you my play will be above board." Her joking boast was an attempt to save a little face, and my mother allowed her to do so. My mom took Mrs. Hallet arm in arm and they walked to the bridge table together. Mom winked at their two friends as they sat down, letting them know that all had been taken care of.

Mrs. Hallet never cheated again—at least in a game involving my mother.

✑

On July 10, 1943, Allied troops landed in Sicily and quickly gained control of that island. Two weeks later, Mussolini's fascist government was overthrown. King Victor Emmanuel assumed control of the Italian army and promised that the nation would find recovery "in the respect of her old institutions." The tide was turning. Many felt that with Mussolini gone, Italy would pull out of the war, though Germany refuted that and tried to minimize the change in power.

The Germans were again wrong. Italy signed an armistice in September 1943 with the Allies. Germany occupied most of Italy at that time, except for portions in the far south. This gave rise to the partisans, including Bruno and Giorgio, who wanted to free Italy from the Germans. In October 1943, the official Italian government declared war on Germany.

As for Mussolini, he was arrested by the king, but rescued from prison by the Germans. He holed up on Lake Garda in northern Italy and declared a Republican Fascist state there, but he was little more than a mad despot muttering inanities to himself. He did manage to execute some of the Fascists who had turned against him, including his son-in-law, Galeazzo Ciano, who had granted my father's release several years earlier at the bequest of my mother. He blamed Italy's woes on those citizens who did not have the foresight to follow him, to bring his imperialistic ideals to reality.

He was reduced to what he had chosen to become: a puppet of the German state. As Allied troops approached, he tried to escape to Switzerland in April 1945 with his mistress, Clara Petacci. Italian partisans seized them at Lake Como on April 27 and executed them the next day, putting their bodies on public display in Milan.

Just one day after Mussolini's execution, Adolph Hitler married his own mistress, Eva Braun. The day after that, as the Russians closed in on Berlin, Hitler and Braun committed suicide. One week later, Germany unconditionally surrendered. Three months later, Japan followed suit. The war was over, at a horrific cost: an estimated 55.5 million people lost their lives. Nearly half of those killed were not even in the military. We were among the lucky ones. I knew that.

On the day Rome fell to the Allied troops, the American ambassador sent my father four bottles of champagne, along with a note, "Soon, very soon, I will have your visa." That news thrilled me, because it meant I could return to America, go to college there.

I had a bit of "senioritis" when I was nearing high school graduation. A friend of mine named Angel was stricken with the same disease. "I'd give anything to be out of here," I said to him as we walked down a hall between classes.

"Are you chicken?" Angel asked.

"What are you talking about?"

"You want to leave, you just leave."

"They'll stop you."

"Watch and learn."

I watched Angel walk to the end of the hall, past two school administrators, and out the door. He walked like it was his business to leave, like it was nothing out of the ordinary. And the administrators didn't bat an eye.

I learned a valuable lesson that day: you act like you know what you're doing, and people will, by and large, let you do it. You act like you belong and people will let you in. It's in your attitude, how you carry yourself, what you expect of yourself and others. Angel expected to encounter no problems in leaving, and he didn't.

I learned some other nonacademic lessons in school, too. Because I was two or three years younger than my classmates, and perhaps because of my own shyness and upbringing, I was pretty naïve about sexual matters. I remember when I was a junior, I was standing next to a guy as we both looked for our test scores, posted on a board outside our classroom. Out of the corner of my eye I noticed the guy was looking more at me than at the board, and he moved very close to me. After I found my score I moved away and rejoined a friend, Fernando, as we walked to our next class.

"Hey, Paolo, don't you know what that guy was trying to do?" Fernando asked.

"What guy?"

"The guy who was moving in on you at the board."

"What?"

"Moving in on you. He likes you."

"What do you mean, he likes me. I don't even know him."

Fernando sighed in frustration. "No, I mean he *likes* you. You know, like a boy likes a girl."

I figured I was pretty smart, but I had no clue what he was talking about. "But he's a guy, just like me."

Fernando laughed. "I don't think so, man. He's a guy, but he isn't just like you." He then explained what a homosexual was. I had never even heard of that concept before. Fernando had a good laugh over my naiveté.

But I was no less naïve than the government official who visited our school during my senior year and told us, during a school-wide announcement, "If there are any student demonstrations against the government, we will have to shut down the school." This official was warning us in light of the political unrest across the country; as I mentioned earlier, Ecuador changed presidents back then about as often as I change shirts. No doubt this official thought he was pretty smart in quelling any potential uprisings at Colegio Mejia.

In reality, he gave a group of seniors a splendid idea, one aimed at earning a little extra vacation.

The next day, I was among a group of seniors who organized a student march on the President's Palace in Quito, which wasn't that far from the high school, shouting as we arrived, "Down with the government! Down with Velasco! Down with the government! Down with Velasco!" Velasco was Dr. Jose Maria Velasco, the president at the time.

Mounted police started chasing us. Thankfully, they didn't open fire on us. We didn't care about the government and we didn't care about President Velasco. We cared about getting some extra time off.

And we got it. The next day our school was shut down for two weeks because of the demonstration. No students got in trouble; school was just shut down. The government official who felt it wise to issue the warning about demonstrations obviously wasn't the father of a teenager, or he would have known better than to tell a bunch of students how to shut down the school.

∽

I was 16 years old when I graduated from high school in 1944. To graduate, I had to pass both written tests and an oral exam. Five professors would be present at the oral exam, and they could ask you questions on any of your subjects that was covered during your high school years.

I began sweating as soon as I learned about the orals. Typically, 250 or more people, including, of course, your family, would attend the exam; you had to perform in front of an audience. I had never been so nervous. I lost more than a little sleep in the nights leading up to the exam. I tried to keep the date secret, but my parents found out and attended.

The auditorium was packed as I walked on stage. Five professors sat at a long table, facing the audience, whose seats sloped upward—the better that each person could see me sweat. Thankfully, I faced the professors, not the audience, but I was no more assured by looking at them than I would have been by looking at the sea of expectant faces behind me. As it was, I felt their eyes bore into my back. I hated being on display, having to answer in front of all these people. This was one aspect of Ecuadorian education that I definitely did *not* appreciate.

Thankfully, my first questions were on math. I loved math and was given a few problems that I could solve quickly. I ended up with a score of 9 out of 10 on my high school diploma and breathed a huge sigh of relief when it was over.

But, because of the war, it was another year before my visa came through and I was permitted entry into the US. I attended the University of Quito during that year; the university was as bad as the high school was good. With the help of the commercial attaché to the American embassy, I had looked into American colleges and narrowed my choices to Purdue University in West Lafayette, Indiana and Cornell University in Ithaca, New York. I finally chose Purdue over Cornell. Purdue was one of the top engineering schools in the country, and I was interested in engineering. I felt that Purdue was a slightly better chemical engineering school than Cornell, but what clinched my decision was that my cousins Alberta and Marina were attending Cornell, and their pitch to get me to go there was that I would be able to mix in with them and their Italian friends on campus. They figured that would reassure me, because they knew I barely spoke English.

Instead, I resolved to go where I knew no one, because the best way to become Americanized and learn the language properly was to be where I couldn't get by on my Italian. Looking back, that was a very sage decision for a 17-year-old.

❦

PART III
LAND OF THE FREE

∞

CHAPTER NINE

America Revisited

Two days before I was to depart for the US, my father and I had a talk. He and I were alone, in the living room; Mom and Sandra had gone for an after-dinner walk, which I believe my father orchestrated so we could be alone. He had noticed an unsure look in my eyes as my travel date neared.

"Do you remember what your mother said to you when she told you we were going to leave Italy?" he said.

I struggled to remember; that had been so long ago. "I remember she told us about Ecuador," I said, though I knew that wasn't the answer he was looking for.

"She said, 'You are embarking on a great adventure.' And it has been quite an adventure these past five years, hasn't it?"

Like a flickering reel in a movie theater, I saw snippets of scenes: leaving Venice; first seeing the SS Manhattan in dock at Genoa; seeing the Statue of Liberty as the announcement of Italy entering the war was broadcast on the Manhattan; seeing New York's magnificent skyscrapers; being handed food from Mom and Sandra over the fence on the Ship from Hell to Ecuador; taking the bumpy bus ride to Cuenca to play soccer with the Gladiadors; making friends with Edwin and Cecil. It had been quite a ride.

"It's been great, all of it," I agreed.

"Even the ship to Ecuador?"

I smiled. "I wouldn't want to repeat that trip, but it was all part of a great adventure."

"The last five years have made you grow up in a hurry, haven't they?"

I shrugged. I hadn't envisioned this sort of life, but I wasn't sorry for it in the least. "That's not a bad thing," I said.

"Maybe not, but I do apologize for putting you and your mother and sister through all this. Yet, I'm sure it has made you stronger, prepared you better for the rest of your life."

I agreed with that; I was just a little uncertain I wanted the rest of my life to begin in two days. "You don't have to apologize for anything, Papá."

He smiled. "And neither do you. I want you to have total confidence in your ability to succeed in this next phase of your life, in America, and in whatever you do beyond school. You are a very intelligent and well-balanced young man. All you lack is confidence. You think other people are better than you. I'm here to tell you that you are better than you think you are. Much better."

I smiled in a way that deflected the praise.

"I mean it, Paolo. Don't be afraid to dream. Don't be afraid to aim high. So what if you don't get exactly what you aim for? You will get something else just as good, maybe even better. The point is, you have great ability, and you need to have the confidence to use it. Remember what I said about the Black Shirts when they first came to our house? That they wanted us to live in fear? Don't live in fear, Paolo. The only person who can hold you back is yourself. And you don't want to do that. Don't shortchange yourself."

I nodded. "Okay, Papá."

"I want you to remember one other thing. "Intelligence and wisdom are great gifts, but if they aren't governed by honesty, they're wasted. That's another way you can shortchange yourself, by cutting corners, being dishonest with yourself or others. Honesty isn't always easy, and it can hurt at times. But it's the best route."

He should know. Because of his honesty about Fascism, he had suffered. And look at the route we had taken as a result. Was Venice to New York to Quito to West Lafayette, Indiana, where Purdue University was located, the best route for me? Absolutely. I nodded. It was easier for me to agree to be honest than to assert that I would have the self confidence he wanted me to have.

"It's time for you to take yet another step forward, and this time on your own. But you're ready to do it. You have a great opportunity ahead of you. You, Paolo, are headed toward great things in America."

His strength and conviction washed over me like the waves of the ocean upon a shore. Even as the waves receded, some of the water soaked into the sand. I hoped the same would happen with his belief in me—that it would sink into me, that I would take it on for my own.

"Above all else," my father said, "always remember that your father and mother love you and will always be there for you. God bless you, Paolo." He hugged me, and I had none of the usual teenager's aversion to being hugged by a parent. I felt his love and belief in me flow through his arms, and suddenly everything was all right.

∽

September 14, 1945 dawned clear and mild, just like any other late summer day in Quito. But the butterflies in my stomach let me know this was not like any other day. I was on the way to Quito International Airport, bound for Miami. From there I would catch a train to New York, spend a few days with my aunt and uncle and cousins, and then catch another train and head into the heartland of America: to West Lafayette, and to Purdue University, where I would study chemical engineering.

"Paolo," my mother said as we waited in the terminal. "You study hard. And don't be shy to ask for help if you need it." The former reference was to my lackadaisical approach to my studies at Quito University, an approach that mimicked that of my fellow students—and most of my professors. The university work had been easier than my high school studies. The latter was a reference to my reluctance to learn English before I returned to America. My approach there had been *Mañana:* tomorrow. Well, *mañana* had arrived. Now, I wished that I had picked up a little of the language, but I didn't want to let on that my mother's concern might be warranted.

"Don't worry about me," I said, though the thought of being so far away from my family caused those butterflies to flutter and fly wildly against my rib cage. I was only 17, and my lone trip to America had come five years earlier, under the protective wings of my parents. Now Mussolini and Hitler were both dead, the war was over, and, through the help of the same American ambassador who had sent champagne to my father on the day that Allied troops reclaimed Rome, a young Italian expatriate was allowed to enter America and study at one of her most prestigious engineering universities. Passage was still hard to come by, and the ambassador had pulled some strings in getting me flight priority. Anything, he had said, to help the son of Max and Elena Oreffice.

"You'll do fine," my father said. "Tell Uncle Alberto we won't be too long after you."

"I'll tell him," I said. I held tightly to the conversation we'd had two days ago, knowing I would need to remember his words and believe in them in the days ahead.

"Lucky stiff," Sandra said, but she was smiling. She would remain in Quito with my parents, coming with them a few months later, as soon as Dad was able to wrap up his businesses.

I hugged them all, boarded the plane, listened to the powerful whine of the engines as we taxied down the runway, and in moments I was lifted in the air, above the few puffy white clouds that hung over Quito, looking as if they'd been hung as decorations to break up the brilliant blue of the sky. My throat constricted and I concentrated on not crying. Even though we had gone from Italy to America to Ecuador, I had always felt moored. Now I was loosed, floating on the wind currents, being blown to who knows where. I felt very small on that plane, and already missed my family and friends, especially Edwin and Cecil. Quito was quickly lost in the Andes, and then the Andes gave way to the coastal region of Columbia, and then we were over the Atlantic, continuing north toward Miami, where I knew no one and no one knew me. I could not help the tears from welling up as I said my goodbyes to Quito, to Ecuador, to our refuge for the past five years. In many ways it was harder to leave Quito than it was Venice.

But I *was* looking forward to college in the states, I *was* looking forward to seeing Uncle Alberto and Aunt Xenia and my two cousins, Marina and Alberta. I didn't know what the future held for me, but I had no doubts that it would be good.

❧

"Paolo! You look wonderful!"

My Uncle Alberto was probably a bit generous in his assessment; after a long flight and a longer train ride, I had arrived in New York City anxious, excited, and tired. My clothes were rumpled from sleeping—or trying to sleep—on the train. I was reminded of the words inscribed beneath the Statue of Liberty: *Give me your tired, your poor, Your huddled masses yearning to breathe free.* Five years ago, I had not felt like these words fit me, though I appreciated them, especially the part about yearning to breathe free. But I was on a grand and exciting adventure then, and America was a stopping off point. Now, it was my new home, and I fit Lady Liberty's description well, like slipping into a comfortable, well-worn shirt. I was no longer passing through. I was truly an immigrant, and I felt more like I imagined an immigrant should feel: tired, poor, grateful, excited, anxious, ready for a new life to begin.

Just as I had hugged my parents and my sister upon departing Quito, I shook hands with Uncle Alberto and hugged Marina and Alberta. Marina was my age and Alberta was two years older.

"I don't know about how I look," I said, "but I'm glad to be here." Of course, we were speaking in Italian, as our conversation in English would have been quite restricted. I hadn't seen Marina and Alberta since 1939, but we renewed our friendships as if we'd only been apart a few days. They were like sisters to me and Marina especially reminded me of my mother because of her size. They had lived in New York for four years and they were completely comfortable in their surroundings and with the language. Just being around them comforted me, because I could see myself adapting quickly, as they had.

"How much time do you have before you leave for school?" Marina asked as we walked from Pennsylvania Station to Uncle Alberto's car.

"About ten days."

"Ten days!" Alberta said. "That's great."

"Plenty of time to show you around," Uncle Alberto said. "And to learn more of the language." He sounded like his sister, my mother—though I had to admit I was happy for the time to expand my vocabulary, which fizzled out after about fifty words or so. I could order off a menu, but that wouldn't do me a lot of good once I cracked my engineering books.

Uncle Alberto and Aunt Xenia lived in Riverdale, the nicest part of the Bronx. Their neighbor was Fiorello LaGuardia, mayor of New York City from 1934 to 1945, and the man for whom LaGuardia International Airport was named. My relatives made me feel special during my stay with them, and they showed me all the sights. The pace of life in New York City is, of course, quicker than that in Quito, but I fell easily in step with that pace, guided by my cousins, feasting on the wonderful meals made by Aunt Xenia, reveling in the stories told by Uncle Alberto, some of the old country, but much more of the new. Uncle Alberto had had no trouble adapting to life in the US, and while he intended to return to Italy to visit, it would be as an American citizen.

What I remember most from that visit, however, is a girl named Mignon. She was Marina's friend, half-French and all beautiful. I went out with her almost every night for a week, and I fell for her like free-falling out of a plane. I had never experienced feelings like that before, though they had been stirred by Norita in Quito; by the time I had to leave for Indiana, I wanted to continue the relationship long distance, but Mignon knew better. Deep down, I knew so too, but I couldn't imagine meeting anyone like her on campus. The night before I was to board the train headed west, I stayed out until well past 3 A.M., unable to tear myself away from Mignon, unable to stop looking into her deep blue eyes, her pretty face, her sweet smile.

Mignon was the first girl I kissed, and I experienced a kind of heartbreak that I had never felt before when at last we parted. For her, I was just a nice guy to date for a few times. For me, she was a blonde-haired angel that made even Norita seem like some childhood ideal conjured up from my distant past. Mignon was alive and real in the here and now, and she filled my heart with immense longing and joy, and even more immense sadness upon departing. Now I realize she was kind not to allow any relationship to linger, because it couldn't have survived, but on the train to West Lafayette I licked my wounds, lamenting my loss, wishing that somehow we could have stayed together.

But Mignon was destined to fade from memory as I quickly became preoccupied with registering for my first semester at Purdue, finding a place to live, and buckling down to what I knew was the biggest challenge of my life. I was given 20 hours of credit for my high school classes in Quito because, as one Purdue administrator said, "You're years ahead in math, chemistry, and physics." That certainly got me off to a good start—though the same administrator warned, "Understand, we believe you can do this. But if you don't pass your courses this semester, you'll have to go back and pick up all of these courses that we're giving you credit for." This deal appealed to the gambler side of me. I liked the odds and the challenge involved, knowing I'd have to start all over if I didn't do well. I eagerly accepted that challenge.

This was a mixed blessing—I was glad for the credit going in, but it also meant I would immediately enroll in more advanced classes, without the slightest command of the language. Chemical engineering was tough enough if you knew the language. It was nearly murder without it.

My 3 A.M. farewell to Mignon was quickly replaced by 3 A.M. study sessions in the room that I rented in a house on the edge of campus. I rented from a family, but I didn't really get to know them because I had to immerse myself in my work, studying with two books open at all times: the textbook I was reading and a dictionary.

Those first two months at Purdue were extremely intense. For some reason my academic advisor thought it wise to have me sign up for 21 credit hours while taking courses in a language I didn't understand! I knew no one, couldn't take the time to get to know anyone, and frantically tried to stay up with my courses. I could barely understand the professors in the daytime and in the nighttime the books weren't any easier to comprehend. Though all my classes were hard, my experience in qualitative chemistry was most disastrous.

Qualitative chemistry was taught by Professor Dennis Pearce, a southerner. I had enough trouble with the language; Professor Pearce's southern drawl was, to me, like another language unto itself. So there I was, a freshman in a sophomore chemistry class, an Italian from Ecuador who knew plenty of languages, but none of them English. And I was in a class with a professor who liked to put people on the spot. In the first class he looked at us with a droll expression and said something like, "Ah'm going to find out what y'all know." He proceeded to shoot questions at us. Most of them I couldn't understand, but luckily he didn't call on me. Then he asked, "What's a redox equation?" I heard the syllables to that one, but didn't know what they meant.

No one proffered an answer (or hazarded a guess). Professor Pearce looked at us with little hope or expectation. He sighed, then looked at a class roster he was holding. He scrolled a finger down the roster and stopped.

"Nyberg?" he said.

Nyberg, sitting one row ahead of me, squirmed in his seat before admitting he didn't know. Professor Pearce looked as if he didn't expect Nyberg to know how to work a door handle all by himself. He finally dropped his gaze to the dreaded roster sheet and scrolled down a little further.

"Aurahfice?" he drawled in a way I'd never heard my name pronounced before.

I froze. *Redox equation?* Now, if he had asked about a *reduction oxidation* equation, I would have fared a little better. I wouldn't have hit a home run, but I wouldn't have struck out, either.

I said nothing. Not a thing came to mind. I was a deer frozen in headlights under the weary gaze of Professor Pearce.

"Way-uhl, Aurahfice?" he said quietly. I had no idea at the time that "Way-uhl" meant "Well"—not that it would have mattered. I still had nothing to say.

He finally moved on, but not before he registered his disgust with my lack of response. At the end of class I mustered my courage and approached him.

"Professor Pearce?" I said, getting his name better than he got mine. He looked up from his desk with a show of tremendous effort. I got the idea that students really bothered him. "I . . . I didn't know what you meant, *redox equation*. I didn't know how to, to translate it."

"Way-uhl, there wasn't any *translatin'* to do. It was a simple question, one aimed at seein' what you know." And from his look, it was evident he believed I knew nothing.

"I am learning the language."

"Where y'all from, Aurahfice?"

"From Italy. But I lived the last five years in Ecuador."

"Whyn't ya go to school where ya know the language?"

I didn't have an answer to that, at least not one that he wanted to hear. So I walked out.

Not long after that, I decided to drop Professor Pearce's course. Unfortunately, I didn't understand the method for dropping a course; I thought you could do so by just not showing up anymore. At the end of the term, much to my surprise and chagrin, I was given an "F" in the class.

Things did get a little easier the following year when I joined Tau Kappa Epsilon fraternity. That brought me out of my shell and provided some experience that I found useful in my business career. I was one of the organizers of the Purdue Soccer Club, I went out for the varsity golf and tennis teams, and I became involved in a number of inter-fraternity sports. In fact, I participated in 13 different sports in one year, including cross country, which I had never run before. There were 35 teams in this competition. Each team ran four men, three of whom scored. Our fourth guy was ill, so my fraternity brothers asked me to run. "Are you kidding?" I said. "I'm not a runner."

"Neither are we. And you're in good shape at least, with all that soccer and tennis you play."

I shrugged and agreed to run. I figured I'd be our fourth guy, anyway, so it didn't matter too much. We just wanted a fourth runner in there in case one of our top three—who all were pretty good—had to drop out.

The race was a hilly 2.5 miles on a golf course. As the gun went off, everyone seemed to sprint like it was a half-mile race. I took off at a more leisurely pace and soon found only two runners out of the pack of 140 behind me. But I felt strong as the race went along, and started picking runners off. In fact, I spent most of the race passing runners. I just kept focusing on the next batch of three or four runners in front of me, and I'd pick them off, then I'd zero in on my next target. Soon I saw the finish line about 300 yards away, on top of a hill. I put it into high gear—or whatever my highest gear was at that point—and picked off several more runners before crossing the line. My fraternity brothers were there, cheering me on, going crazy. I had passed all but six runners, including two of my own teammates! I couldn't believe it, and neither could anyone else.

I should have left well enough alone. Next year, I ran in the same race, and this time I went out with the leaders, including the Big Ten cross country champion, figuring I could hang with them. I did manage to stick with them for about half the race. But I paid the price for going out too fast, and I faded badly, all the way to 68th place.

Those two races taught me a valuable lesson, though. Even when I didn't know what I was doing, as in the first race, but just got the most out of my talent, I did quite well and I could surprise a lot of people. When I got in over my head, went beyond where my expertise should have led me, as in the second race, I—and my team—suffered.

∽

My parents and Sandra came to the US in late October 1945. My dad entered a real estate development partnership with a couple of other Italian businessmen, building houses on Long Island. He also convinced his partners to buy half a city block on what is now known as the Avenue of the Americas, between 57th and 58th Streets. At that time 6th Avenue, as it was then known, was nothing special; in fact it was a bit rundown. But my father saw potential in the area that his partners didn't. A few years later they broke up the partnership and, in doing so, sold the property for a small profit. Had they held on to it, they would have made a small fortune, but my father didn't have the money to keep it by himself.

Meanwhile, Sandra met Giorgio Sonnino in New York; Giorgio was a fellow Italian refugee. He proposed to Sandra in early 1946 and they were married a few months later.

A month after Sandra's wedding, my mother and father returned to Italy to pick up some of the pieces of their lives that they had left behind. Except for my Nonno Vittorio and Nonna Alice, all my relatives were alive and well. My parents built a house over the ruins of the old villa in Bosco, which the Nazis had destroyed a few years earlier, and Bepi Rosini came to work for Dad. My parents' home base was to remain in New York, but they would return to Italy for about three months each year.

Whenever my dad was in Italy he carried a riding crop, which he called *Il Foscarino*, intended for use on Ludovico Foscari, the Fascist leader in Venice who had ordered my father beaten and imprisoned. Unfortunately, Dad never ran into Foscari again. Or perhaps it *was* fortunate, because Dad might have justly wound up in jail for what he would have done to Foscari.

&

I returned to Italy in 1946 as well. I was eager to return to see what had become of my country. It seemed ages since I had been there—indeed, so much had happened in my life since leaving Italy that my memories of it seemed to be from another lifetime. I could find no other passage, so I took a Liberty Ship, one of the cargo ships that helped win the war. It had six cabins and a grand total of 12 passengers. It wasn't quite the Ship from Hell that transported me to Ecuador, but it was not a luxury liner, either. At least this time I knew going in it would be something I would simply endure. All I needed was a way to get across the Atlantic. I ended up playing bridge every night with the captain and two other passengers, and won enough money to pay for about half my trip, which took 15 days.

The first person I wanted to see when I got back to Italy was Bepi Rosini. I had written that I was coming and when he pulled open his door one early evening in Bosco, he grinned and pulled me in, hugging me and then slapping me on the back. His wife, Nella, came to greet me as well.

"Paolo! Look at you! You're all grown up!" Bepi said.

"I don't know about that, but it's great to be back."

"Tell us all about your time in Ecuador. You're on holiday now from school in America?"

"I'm off until September. I couldn't wait to get back and see everyone."

And so he brought me in, and Nella fed me while I told them stories of Ecuador and of returning to America, and what school was like, and how hard it was at first without knowing the language but how I had caught on—at this Bepi winked at Nella, as if to say, "I knew Paolo could do it"— and I told them all about Sandra's wedding and how my parents were doing.

"Over here, things are much better," Bepi said. "It will take some time to recover, but we will recover. Justice won out in the end." He told me how Italians had celebrated the deaths of Mussolini and Hitler, how the Germans destroyed the villa in Bosco and had taken over so many other villas and used them for their operations. The Germans had also stolen many horses, but Pasquina and Vespa were safe and well with their new owners.

"Justice on a large scale won out," I agreed. "But on a small scale, there are still scores that could be settled."

Bepi raised an eyebrow. "Such as?"

"I was thinking of the *fattore*. Ghirardelli."

A slow smile came across Bepi's face, but his eyes were glistening and hard. "Yes, Ghirardelli, the Judas who tried to sell your father to the Fascists."

"Bepi!" Nella admonished. She was a Roman Catholic; for her the reference was not appropriate.

"Better that I call him a cowardly ass, then?" Bepi asked. He shrugged. "It fits as well."

The next day Bepi and I returned to *Prati Nuovi,* the old farmstead, riding a motorcycle on war-ravaged roads. Adrenaline flowed through my body as we walked on the land that my father had worked and had been forced to give up. I was not big, but I was no longer a kid, and I intended, plain and simple, to beat the daylights out of the *fattore*. Bepi intended to get his licks in as well. He was as wiry and supple and strong as ever. Ghirardelli, on the other hand, was probably plumper than ever. A fatted calf.

"There he is!" I said, pointing to a man in the distance who was walking toward one of the barns.

"Hey! Ghirardelli!" Bepi boomed. The man stopped and turned toward us. We quickened our pace as he watched us approach. I could see him looking warily first at Bepi, then at me.

I walked up and said, "My name is Oreffice." He cringed when he heard the name, and I hit him, knocking him back a few steps.

"No, no, it's my brother you want!" he said, putting a finger to his split lip.

Bepi eyed the man, perhaps considering whether it would be fair enough to beat up Ghirardelli's brother instead of the *fattore* himself. Evidently he decided against it. "Come on," he said to me. "I know where he lives."

I could feel the wrong Ghirardelli staring at us as we walked off. We climbed back onto Bepi's motorcycle and headed for Ghirardelli's house.

Even as we got off the motorcycle, several men came out on the long porch of the house. His brother must have forewarned him. Finally, Ghirardelli himself came out.

"Come down and fight like a man," Bepi called out. "One on one. Without your goons."

"There's no need to fight," Ghirardelli said, trying to find courage in the numbers around him.

"You have a debt to repay to the Oreffice family. This is Paolo. You remember Paolo, I'm sure, the son of Max, whom you betrayed with scandalous lies?"

One thing about Bepi; in his simple country ways he was not hard to understand.

"I have no idea what you're talking about."

"That's okay. I didn't come to talk. Come down off that porch, if your shaking legs can carry you. One on one, if you're man enough."

"I already told you, I don't want to fight you."

"Me?" Bepi put his hand on his chest in mock surprise. "Not me. I am not an Oreffice. As much as I would delight in whipping your sorry ass, I am leaving that pleasure to Paolo."

Ghirardelli looked at me, then back at Bepi.

"He comes down off that porch, we all come down," one of the men said.

"Strength in numbers. Just like during the trial, when you went with what you thought was the stronger side—the Fascists. But you turned out to be wrong, didn't you, Ghirardelli?"

Ghirardelli started to fume; he wasn't used to what he considered a farm hand talking to him in such a manner. And he *did*, after all, have strength in numbers.

"Get off my land!" he shouted, walking down the steps, making sure that his men were following him.

"Not so fast," Bepi said. He put his right hand in his coat pocket and pointed something directly at Ghirardelli's belly. The *fattore* stopped.

"Let it be understood that the traitor is also a coward, one who refuses to fight a teenager one on one, because he knows what that teenager would do to him. Let it be understood that the traitor is doing what he does best: hiding behind people. Let it also be understood," and Bepi said this last part very slowly, "that the traitor better think very hard before coming any closer."

Ghirardelli looked at Bepi's coat pocket. He couldn't tell what Bepi was pointing at him, but he wasn't going to take a chance.

Bepi stared long and hard at Ghirardelli. Though the day was pleasant, I could see beads of sweat on Ghirardelli's face. "You haven't seen the last of us, Ghirardelli," Bepi growled, and then we turned and began walking back to his motorcycle. I was shaking, not from fright but from anger and impatience. I wanted badly to tear into Ghirardelli, but I knew now was not the time.

As we got back to the motorcycle, I turned and shouted, "You're dead meat! Dead! Do you hear me, Ghirardelli? Deader than all these lamebrains you surround yourself with! I'll find you someday when you can't hide behind your pals! I'll get you, Ghirardelli! You don't mess with my father, you don't mess with my family, the way you did, you scumbag!" Anger flowed out of me that I didn't know I had. Seven years of pent-up emotion at the injustices done came roiling out. I think in the next moment I would have rather foolishly rushed Ghirardelli, but Bepi grabbed my shoulder while training whatever he had in his pocket on one of the men coming my way.

"That's enough for now, Paolo," Bepi said. "Let's go."

As we rode off, I said, "I didn't know you were carrying a gun."

He smiled at me and pulled off the road for a moment, stopping his motorcycle to fish in his pocket for what I assumed was his gun. Finally he produced his weapon: a fountain pen.

For many years, Bepi would write an annual letter to Ghirardelli. It would vary only slightly in its wording. *Paolo Oreffice is coming back for you,* he'd write. *Paolo is going to find you alone, and he is going to wipe the ground with your plump, useless body. And then he will apologize to the ground for defiling it with your body.* Bepi's entire literary efforts were poured into these short, descriptive missives. I pictured him writing them with a look of glee on his face. *This will keep him in fear for another year,* he would think to himself. *And maybe Paolo can really return and take care of business so I can stop writing these letters.* But then he would pause, considering. The letters were so delicious. They brought joy to Bepi. They brought fear to Ghirardelli. And that, in the end, was good enough for me.

❧

Though I was not officially an American citizen yet, I felt like an American visiting Italy in the summer of 1946. My father's abuse at the hands of the Fascists had something to do with this. So did Italy's role in the Rome-Berlin-Tokyo Axis. Being away for six years had eased the pain of separation. Having to flee your native country for fear of your own safety at the hands of your own government had something to do with this feeling, too. I still loved Italy, and loved my family and friends back there, but from now on, I would only return to visit, not to settle. My old life was in Italy, my new life was in America.

When I returned to Purdue in the fall of 1946 for my sophomore year, I felt much more comfortable. I knew the language now, I knew the campus, I joined the fraternity, I knew how *not* to drop a course, and I proceeded to do well in my remaining two-and-a-half years at Purdue, graduating early because of the 20 credits I had been given upon entrance. I won the all-campus ping pong championship once and finished second twice, and was part of the doubles championship team three years in a row (my playing had not degenerated from when I had won the tournament years earlier on board the Manhattan on our initial trip to America). I continued on in chemical engineering, even though an aptitude test that I took in my sophomore year ranked chemical engineering as 64th out of 65 career possibilities for me. That simply made me all the more determined to become a chemical engineer. I had learned plenty about obstacles in early life to not be thrown by this; indeed, I was energized by it. I wanted to prove that the test was wrong.

Toward the end of my junior year, "Moose" Skowron, who would go on to be a five-time All-Star player with the New York Yankees, joined our fraternity. (The nickname, by the way, was a shortened version of his grandfather's joking pet name for him: "Mussolini." It would not have been a moniker I would have hung on anyone.) He was a multi-sport star in high school and starred in baseball and football at Purdue. In fact, he led the nation in punting one year and hit .500 in his sophomore year, a Big Ten season record that lasted for a decade. One time he was injured and couldn't go to football practice, so we begged him to play on our softball team, which was in the finals of the campus championship. He said he wouldn't do us any good; he couldn't run because of his injury. But we persuaded him to play, and he didn't have to worry about running, because he hit two home runs and walked around the bases.

Moose was the finest natural athlete I've ever been around, but he hadn't had to study hard in high school. So some athletic department officials instructed us to tutor him. He had to pass so he would remain eligible to play. Bob Groben tutored him in non-technical subjects and I tutored him in math and chemistry.

Moose was a great guy. We made a rule that he could only go out on Saturday nights, that he had to study the rest of the week, and he went along with it. He had a good attitude and was fun to work with. He wasn't dumb, either; he just hadn't been educated very well.

What I remember most about Moose is his south Chicago accent. If he hit a home run and two doubles, he'd say, "I got tree hits today." Bob worked with him on his diction, trying to get him to sound out the *th* in *three*. One day the three of us were walking across campus and Moose, who had been working hard on his diction, said he'd just seen his first cardinal of the spring. We didn't see it. He pointed to a tree and said, "Right there, in the top branch of that three." Bob and I burst out laughing, and Moose said, "What? What's so funny?"

I was hardly the athlete that Moose was, but I did manage to sustain a serious athletic injury, one that would have even slowed Moose down. I was playing in a touch football game and ran head-on into a blocker weighing about 250 pounds. No need to tell you who won that battle. I took the brunt of the blow on my right shoulder, and when I went to the infirmary the next day, I was told I had a separated shoulder. They wrapped it and gave me some medication, because it was quite painful. I went on to class, but it was hard to write, because I'm right-handed. It was hard to do anything: dress myself, brush my teeth, take a shower, you name it.

This happened in early November, and I was due to graduate on February 6. I ended up missing some of my classes because I was in too much pain, it was too difficult to get around, and I couldn't write anyway. By early December my condition had not really improved. My parents encouraged me to fly to New York to see a specialist. So, I flew to New York and was seen by a specialist, who told me, "You have not only a separated shoulder, but a broken collarbone and scapula as well. We'll have to put you in a splint."

And so I was fitted up with what the doctor called an airplane splint, where my arm was lifted over my shoulder. I kept that splint on for a month.

I went back to Purdue in early January, with barely a month to go before graduation. I had two months of work to catch up. I went from professor to professor, telling them I was willing to do whatever I had to do to make up the work and graduate on time. They were all willing to work with me except for a chemical literature professor. She stuck her nose up in the air and said, "It's impossible. You can't catch up." Then she simply turned away, dismissing me.

I had to petition the dean to make sure this chemical literature professor would at least give me a chance. In the meantime, a betting line had sprouted at the fraternity house, and the odds were 5-1 against my graduating on time.

I had no intention of sticking around West Lafayette longer than I had to. I could smell the finish line, and my airplane splint and my awkward left hand was not going to keep me from getting there by February 6.

I not only graduated on time—disappointing many of my fraternity brothers who had bet against me, and delighting the few who had bet on me—I graduated, for the first time, as an honor student. I got the best grades of my college career that semester. I did nothing but study that final month; I made up for lost time with a vengeance. In my Chemical Engineering Thermodynamics class, the average score on the final exam was usually about 40 out of 150 points. That semester, as a class we did slightly better; the professor told us our average was about 55. He went on to say that three people scored higher than 100, and then looked squarely at me and said, "What the hell happened to you, Oreffice?" My heart sank. My first thought was, *All that work for nothing!* I figured I would be sticking around West Lafayette another semester, trying to pass Chemical Engineering Thermodynamics.

But the professor said, in mock offense, "You scored 145 out of 150. No one scores that high on my final. Maybe my test is too easy." We all assured him that wasn't the case.

I floated out of that classroom like I was walking on air. I had aced one of the toughest finals on campus. I had graduated on time. I had come through under pressure, doing things that normally I would not have been moved to do. That taught me a valuable lesson about my ability to perform under pressure. It was a lesson I was to use many times later on in life. It was one more obstacle overcome.

∞

My collegiate career ended on a high note, but it didn't last long. Companies weren't on the lookout for graduates in February as they would be in May and June. The going was slow, and I was graduating with a lot of war veterans, older guys with more moxie and experience than me, many of whom had been in the working world already. Pickings were slim, to say the least. I interviewed with a handful of companies, but the only job offer I received was from Seagram's, located in Lawrenceburg, Indiana, a tiny town on the banks of the Ohio River, a stone's throw from both Kentucky and Ohio. So I tossed my few belongings in my new Plymouth and headed for Lawrenceburg.

I worked for Seagram's for almost two years. At first I worked in the lab, then I ran sections of plants, and in my second year I became supervisor of a bottling plant. It was at the plant that I got my first taste—or should I say *dis*taste—for unions. Twice I was hauled in front of the personnel committee because I had violated union rules. It was the nature of the violations that set me off, and educated me about the folly of unions.

My first violation occurred when I saw three defective bottles sitting near the end of a bottling line. Twice I asked someone to take them to the dump tank. No one did, so after awhile I grabbed the bottles and took them myself to the tank.

Big mistake! This was the work of a union person, not management. I was there to tell union people what to do, not to do it myself. It didn't matter that I'd told union people twice to do the work and it hadn't been done. And my management agreed: I had committed a violation. I walked out of that meeting fuming.

But that was nothing compared to my second violation. A couple of months later, following the usual practice, an employee at the beginning of the bottling line took the cases and emptied them, putting the bottles on the line. This person then put the case in an overhead conveyor so it could be transported to the end of the line, where it would come down and meet up with the filled bottles.

The conveyor jammed, and cases began falling dangerously close to a couple of female operators sitting under the conveyor. As I was passing by, I shouted at someone to shut down the line and started grabbing the cases so they wouldn't fall on these women.

Once again I was hauled in front of the board, as if my hand had been caught in the company till. The personnel director said, "One more time, Oreffice, and you're gone." Again, my superiors were siding with the union. Apparently I was supposed to let the cases fall on the women; that was within the realm of my responsibilities. I was disgusted with the union leaders and even more disgusted with the management officials for cowing to the union.

The only positive thing I took from my time in Lawrenceburg was something that happened outside of work. Still battling shyness and with a distinct aversion to public speaking, I joined a Toastmasters Club. I knew I had to improve my ability to speak to others, to overcome my shyness, and those one-and-a-half minute and five-minute speeches that I was forced to give helped me more than anything else to be more at ease in front of groups and to say what I had to say.

Many years later, in 1977, I gave the commencement address at Texas A&M. On the flight down to College Station I wrote my speech, and delivered it several hours later on a stage at the basketball arena to about 12,000 graduates and their relatives. I shared with the graduates 10 tips on how to succeed:

1. Do the common thing uncommonly well.
2. Know how to use your education. You might not be sure of what you want to do now. Your education gives you options; consider them and use them.
3. Experiment early in your career to see what you are best at.
4. Always stand up for what is right. You can fight City Hall, but be graceful if you lose. You must live to fight another day.
5. Learn how to communicate. Be clear and concise, and learn how to listen.
6. Beat the boss at anything. There's no such thing as "customer golf." A winner is a winner is a winner.
7. Make others around you look good. Make your boss look good and let him take your ideas. It will pay off in the long run. I call this the "Godfather Principle."
8. Have fun in whatever you do. People who enjoy their job are the most productive.
9. Be kind and understanding.
10. Behind every problem is an opportunity. See solutions, not problems. Be positive.

I closed with this: "You will find a lot of people that tell you that the world is full of problems. So, what's new? Has there ever been a world without problems? Behind every problem is an opportunity. You education will give you the tools to take advantage of the many opportunities our free enterprise system makes possible. Following the tips I have given you, and honest, hard, dedicated work, at whatever you're most suited for, will help you take advantage of these opportunities. With your optimism, your enthusiasm, your effort, your brains, and your dedication, we can keep this the greatest country in the world, as it has been for 200 years."

The address was a huge success, notable in that it was delivered in a post-Vietnam War era that left many college students at odds with anything they saw as establishment, be it government or corporate America. Numerous parents came up and thanked me for delivering the message to their sons and daughters, and one Texan drawled, "That's the best speech I heard since Winston Churchill!" For months I received letters of thanks from parents, and, because the speech proved so successful, I used it as the basis for all my talks with student groups over the years.

My advice to students going into the workplace always started with "do the common thing uncommonly well." This simple principle can help young people more than anything else I can think of. If you do everything well, regardless of how menial the task appears compared to your education, you will be noticed by management. I used this principle throughout my career and it helped me immensely.

∞

It was a different war, the Korean War, that allowed me to leave Seagram's not long after I had been upbraided a second time by union officials. I had been classified 1A and was only too happy to serve my adopted country. I took a brief vacation in the Catskill Mountains in New York before I had to report for my physical in New York City. I had an appendicitis attack one night and was rushed to St. Luke's Cornwall Hospital in Cornwall-on-Hudson, a small town south of Poughkeepsie. My appendix had burst and I had peritonitis, caused by the rupture. I was operated on that night; the next morning, the surgeon, a tiny Austrian doctor from Vienna, visited me.

"You are very lucky," he said. "A few years ago, I would have had no recourse but to let you die, because the antibiotics I needed were not yet available." He was speaking of penicillin, which had only been in civilian use for a few years.

I was happy to be alive and happy to be gone from Seagram's. After recovering from surgery, my father drove with me to Lawrenceburg to get my belongings. This was around Thanksgiving, 1950, and on our way back we drove through one of the worst snowstorms on record; more than two feet of snow was dumped from Ohio to New York. There were no interstates back then, of course, and the roads were clogged with holiday traffic that was sliding into ditches, slowing to a crawl, or completely stopped by accidents and snarls.

One such snarl occurred in Pittsburgh—during those days you had to drive through cities, not around them—and after we sat for a few minutes in stopped traffic, I said, "You take the wheel. I'm going to see what's holding things up."

I slid out from behind the wheel, trudged forward a few blocks, snow whipping into my face, and came to an intersection with cars stopped in all directions. I went into my best traffic cop imitation, directing the flow first one way, then another, holding up my left hand while using my right to motion a line to snake through. I made sure our side got through quickly, and when my dad approached in my car, I hopped in and we continued on our way.

"Not bad," my father said, nodding at me in appreciation.

I had to admit it was pretty amazing. I didn't really think I'd be able to do anything with that traffic jam. It told me that if you exhibited some leadership ability, people would listen. It was a lesson I would remember and put into practice many times over the years.

∞

I was inducted into the Army on January 11, 1951, and reported, along with 650 other souls, to Fort Devens, Massachusetts. Of the 650, all but four were assigned to the 319th Infantry in various regiment companies. The remaining four were assigned to Fort Dix, New Jersey. I was one of those four. It turned out that the army had requested four recruits for special services, and they selected the four who had tested the highest on IQ tests. I consider myself extremely fortunate, in this and many other ways, because the 319th Infantry suffered heavy casualties—two-thirds of those in the 319th were either wounded or killed in Korea.

I spent my time teaching math to recruits in the Signal Corps in Camp Gordon, Georgia, and then was transferred to the Chemical Corps at the Army Chemical Center in Edgewood, Maryland. Of the 1,800 enlisted men there, 1,600 were chemists or chemical engineers. I worked with Alvin Weiss, another private; Alvin later became a chemistry professor at Tufts University. Alvin and I worked on many projects together, and we were given complete charge of our projects, so that even lieutenants had to report to us. Of course, outside the office, we had to salute them.

It was in my stint in the Army that I first experienced, and quickly developed my dislike for, the Civil Service. Alvin and I were asked to solve an efficiency problem in the Diamond Alkali plant. Diamond Alkali was one of the biggest companies in inorganics in those days, and they had a big chlorine-caustic soda plant at the Army Chemical Center. Alvin and I licked our chops at being able to work on a practical, real-life problem. We were so excited we asked for permission not to go to reveille, but to have two cots put in the plant, where we could work all night long if needed. And many days we did work nearly around the clock.

The work paid off, because in two weeks we had the problem solved. Exhausted and happy, we marched into the office of the civilian project manager and told him of our success.

"What do you mean you've 'solved the problem'?" the manager growled, growing red in the face, either from anger or from embarrassment. We explained what we had done and how we had done it.

"Impossible!" he barked.

"But it's not impossible," I countered. "We did it. Come on over to the plant and we'll show you."

"I already told you, it's impossible! We've allotted two months for this project, and only two weeks have gone by."

Alvin and I exchanged looks of disbelief.

"Look," Alvin said. "We'll write a report explaining what we did. If we write the report, will you read it so we can be on our way?"

"If you want," he said, dismissing us with a wave of his hand. I had never seen anyone so angry at having their problem solved early.

We wrote our report and turned it in. Not long after, Alvin and I were called in to speak with the project manager again.

"Your report looks fine," he said.

I breathed a sigh of relief, because I had figured he was going to give us more trouble. "Good," I said. "Then we can return to our other duties?"

"Not until your two months are up."

Alvin and I argued for about ten minutes with this guy. Our problem in arguing with him was we were applying logic. Our logic bounced harmlessly off the barriers he had erected around his mind—a prerequisite, it seemed, in entering the Civil Service. The upshot is, we spent the next six weeks doing nothing, as opposed to returning to our office and actually working. And this made the Civil Service happy. The records show that we took two months to solve that problem at the Diamond Alkali plant—just as the Civil Service had predicted.

The records *don't* show that I was sent to the brig at the Army Chemical Center, because I never was. But I came close. I was bored one afternoon, so I left my office early and went to play golf at the base course. As I approached the first tee I saw, to my horror, my commanding officer coming off the 9th green and headed straight for me. I had about 10 seconds to think before he reached me.

"What are you doing here, Oreffice?" the captain said. I snapped my best salute and said, "The same thing you are, sir, only I am nine holes behind!"

He looked at me a moment before letting out a laugh. Then he walked off to his car. I took a deep breath and continued golfing.

⚬

When I was drafted I had a permanent resident's permit. It was during my time in the Army that I became a citizen of the United States. I was given leave to return to Lawrenceburg in February of 1951 to complete the process. I had all my papers in order, was interviewed by an immigration and naturalization service official, and took the English and civics tests. The next day I entered the courtroom and soon they called my name. I rose, wearing my Army uniform, and the INS official began to report my test scores.

The judge stopped him, calling out loudly, "Hold on a minute! The uniform is good enough for me." I took the naturalization oath and became a citizen of the United States.

Just so you know: I did pass my tests. But I was impressed that the judge respected the uniform enough to expedite the process. If a man was willing to defend a country in battle, the judge didn't need a test score to tell him whether that man should be called a citizen of that country.

I was proud, to say the least, to have become an American.

⚬

I had been drafted for two years. After six months, I was offered a commission to first lieutenant, but I turned it down, because I would have had to sign up for three more years. I was happier remaining a private and getting out sooner.

So, a private I remained, and at the end of my term I was making $96 a month and biding my time until I got out. Not long before I was due to be released I got lucky again. I had to have some work done on my teeth, and hooked up with a base dentist, a reserve major who took a liking to me. He began scheduling me for two hours instead of half an hour, so we'd have more time to chat. He talked about the stock market, about various companies, and about a certain company called Dow Chemical. It turned out that Dow was one of his major stockholdings. He gave me a spiel about how great Dow was. I learned more about Dow from this dentist than I did in my coursework at Purdue.

By the way, it was this same dentist who invited me to play golf in a foursome with him, General William M. Creasy, who was the head of the camp, and a colonel. I played as part of this foursome a few times, inciting great jealousy among the young officers on the base, who were livid that a private was allowed to play with a general.

It was fun playing golf with a general, but my big break came when the president of the American Institute of Chemical Engineers came to our camp to make a speech. This man happened to be a retired DuPont executive. Each of our detachments named one person to escort this man around and have dinner with him. I was named from my detachment.

I was a little nervous, because I couldn't think of anything useful to talk to this man about, so I asked the advice of my friends.

A guy by the name of Bill Turner came up with an idea that helped steer the course of my life. "You know, there are a ton of chemical engineers who are going to be getting out of here in the next few months. Why don't we ask him if DuPont would be interested in interviewing us?" Bill said.

We all thought that was a great idea. The former DuPont executive thought it was a great idea as well; from his perspective, there were many good candidates at the camp.

"Do you think other companies would be interested as well?" I asked him as we strolled along the grounds.

"I can't speak for them, but I will talk to some of my colleagues."

That got the ball rolling. I worked with both the retired DuPont executive and with General Creasy to get the interviews set up. We had more than fifty companies come out to Edgewood. General Creasy set up a suite of offices and assigned a couple of people fulltime to work with the companies who came out to interview the privates and corporals who were about to enter the corporate world.

It so happened that Dow Chemical was one of those companies that sent a representative—Gordon Clack—to interview candidates. My interview with Gordon went very well.

∞

I interviewed not only with Dow, but with DuPont, Monsanto, Pepsi Cola, Sherwin Williams, and Diamond Alkali. I got second interviews out of each company, and started flying around the country to meet with them. I got job offers immediately from everyone except Dow. I did go to New York to interview with the Dow International office there, and learned later that the report from New York was to pass me over; I couldn't make it. But Gordon Clack believed in me. Gordon persuaded Midland—Dow's headquarters are in Midland, Michigan—to interview me. So Dow flew me out to Midland.

I was relaxed; it was my last interviewing trip and I already had five other offers. DuPont had made a very good offer, and I figured I would go with them if Dow fell through, even though Pepsi Cola had offered the most money. So I was calm and poised for my interview with Steve Starks, who was the head of the technical training program.

I showed up at Starks' office and Elaina Shaefer, his secretary, asked me to have a seat and then called Mr. Starks to let him know I was there. Five, ten, fifteen minutes went by. Elaina was typing away, occasionally glancing up at me, and I wondered if I was ever going to get in to see this guy. Finally Starks buzzed Elaina's desk and she smiled at me and said, "Mr. Starks will see you now."

I walked into his office and he didn't even look up. He was busy writing something. He kept writing and I just stood there, watching him write. He even paused to think a little, then wrote some more. Finally he deigned to look at me.

"Sit down," he ordered. "I'm the guy who sets the rate."

I had to bite my tongue from saying, "Just pay for my trip home then. I'm not going to work for you." But I had come a long way for the interview, and I figured I might as well go through with it. I merely endured the interview with Starks, but I was very impressed with the other people I interviewed with that day, and even more impressed knowing that Dow had just made a momentous decision to convert from a North American company to a global one. "The world is going to become one market," they said. This was a remarkable statement in 1952, especially when made by people who had lived in the Midwest all of their lives. I figured that my background played in my favor, as I knew five languages and had lived in Europe and South America. I seemed a natural fit for their international business, and expressed great interest in it.

Imagine my shock, then, when I got a letter from Starks offering me a job in the general sales training program of the company, with no mention of international. Their offer was $256 a month. DuPont, Monsanto, and others had been in the $320 to $340 range, and Pepsi Cola had offered $400 a month.

I was staying with my folks in New York at the time. I ripped off a letter to Starks, saying, in part, *You offer me this lousy salary to come work in your general sales training program when my talents and interests are in the international end. Unless your job offer can lead me to the international end, I have absolutely no interest.*

I showed the letter to my father, asking him how he would respond if he were to receive it. He read it, raised an eyebrow at me, and said, "I'd tell you to go to hell."

"Good."

"You want them to tell you to go to hell?"

"I want to go in with the understanding that I need to be headed toward the international end, or I don't go in at all. I think this letter will get that point across."

"Oh, it'll get the point across," my father said, handing me the letter. "Good thing you have some other offers to fall back on."

So I sent the letter off to Midland. If Dow told me to take a hike, I'd go to DuPont.

The letter was addressed to Starks, but, his secretary, Elaina received it and read it. Her first thought, she told me later, was, "Oh, an applicant who's telling us to go to hell! That'll go over great!" She knew how Steve Starks would respond. She had liked me from my initial visit; she thought I had some spunk. So she held the letter for a couple of days, until Starks went on a trip to Lansing. Then she took the letter and my resume to Bill Dixon, who was general sales manager for Dow US, and asked if Bill would respond in Starks' absence. She put my letter in proper context, explaining, in respectful terms, her own boss's rudeness. She went to bat for me without being disloyal to her boss. Dixon smiled, thanked her, and assured her he'd take care of it.

I got the most amazing two-page letter back from Bill Dixon. It was a masterpiece, because he was able to justify why the offer was made as it was without directly slamming Starks, yet making it clear that Dow would be remiss not to steer me toward international. Bill explained that the general sales training program was a necessary step to international, and said, "You know, it would be foolish if we didn't put you where your talents will serve you and us best, and that's obviously international." He ended his letter by saying, "We want you."

I had rolled the dice, and I had won. It was a calculated roll, but there was a bit of luck involved. Had Elaina taken that letter to Starks on the day she received it, I wouldn't be writing this book, at least not in this fashion. (And I wouldn't have ended up dating her for awhile once I moved to Midland, either.) Had Bill Dixon not responded as he had, I would have been headed toward Seaview, Delaware, and DuPont. And you know, here again I was very fortunate, because I don't think I would have survived in DuPont's structured environment.

Bill Dixon was a brilliant man, a great speaker, someone who truly knew how to deal with people. If not for a drinking problem, he would have become Dow's CEO. Fast-forward many years later to his retirement party, a black-tie affair for men only at the Midland Country Club. After dinner, Bill went around the table, using his orator skills to tell warm, poignant, and often funny tales about each man at the table. When he came to me, he put his hand on my shoulder and told the story of how I was hired, including, of course, my letter and his response. As he talked about his response, I whipped out Bill's original letter from my breast pocket. "Here's the proof," I said. Bill looked at me, and then at the letter, and his face softened, and he began crying. Tears flowed down my cheeks as well. I framed the letter for him, and he displayed it over his desk at home until the day he died.

Sometimes things work out. In this case, the Army dentist, Gordon Clack, Elaina Shaefer, and Bill Dixon each played a part in my decision to go to work for Dow Chemical. And I'm grateful to each one of them.

I called Midland and accepted the job. The starting salary was low, but the opportunities were there. I agreed with the Army dentist: Dow would be a great place to work. So on February 12, 1953, I loaded my Plymouth in New York and headed west, toward Midland, Michigan.

CHAPTER TEN

∞

Early Dow Years

Midland is about 15 miles west of Saginaw Bay, at the confluence of the Tittabawassee and Chippewa rivers. When it was incorporated in the 1890s, it was a fishing, fur-trading, and logging community. Just a few years before it was incorporated, though, a young man by the name of Herbert H. Dow arrived and began a business that became known as the Dow Chemical Company. As Dow expanded, Midland became Dow's national, and later, international headquarters. When I rolled up in my Plymouth in 1953, it was a town of 16,000 souls, about 12,000 of whom worked for Dow. Many of the Dow employees lived in nearby towns and farms.

As one of the newest employees, I was put under the tutelage of Fred Dow, no relation to the founder. Fred ran the Dow sales training program, affectionately and unofficially known as "Dow's School of Charm." I was one of six in Fred's class. "All right, boys," Fred told us that first day, "strap on your belts, because you're entering the real world now. No more coasting along in the world of academe." Funny he put it that way, because a few years later, Fred left Dow to head San Diego State University's business school.

Fred should have also warned us to strap on our welding face masks, because one of the first things we did was observe—and even work a little— in the welding shop. We visited the various plants, learned about the businesses, and were put through a battery of tests. I scored 50 out of 50 on the Wanderlich IQ test, the only time that had ever been done.

"You're a bright guy, Oreffice," said Joe McPherson, our head psychologist. "Maybe we'll use you as a light bulb if the electricity goes out."

I had an interesting experience during my sales training. Dow had come up with something they were calling Saran Film. They had been selling it as industrial film, but the head of that group, Carl Strosacker, had a vision: housewives, he said, would love the stuff. They could use it to wrap food and keep it fresh.

So Dow hired an expensive market research firm to determine whether housewives would buy Saran Wrap, the household version of Saran Film. The answer was a decisive *No*. Cellophane was cheaper, and so was newspaper. What housewife would spend more money to buy Saran Wrap?

Strosacker, one of Dr. Dow's originals, was undeterred. He commandeered the new recruits in the "School of Charm" and enlisted them in his own market research project. I and the five other guys in training were sent to knock on doors to determine what housewives thought of this new product. We targeted Cincinnati, Dayton, and Toledo, because Saran Wrap had been advertised in those cities.

We were as unfinished, in terms of our sales polish, as was the product, which was still in its experimental stages. We went into both well-to-do and poor neighborhoods. We were better received in the poorer sections of the cities. One of the guys, Roger Zoccolillo, whom I had known in the Army and who came into the program just a few days after I did, reported that the housewives weren't all that interested in the Saran Wrap, but they couldn't keep their hands off of him. In fact, according to Roger, essentially every woman he came into contact with threw herself at him. It was just something he'd had to deal with his whole life, he said. Roger had a wonderful imagination.

The result of that survey, though, was that women loved Saran Wrap. The expensive market research group advised Dow to confine Saran Wrap to the industrial market. Carl Strosacker's hodgepodge group of neophyte salesmen refuted these findings—and, to Dow's credit, the company launched Saran Wrap in the retail market. It was the first plastic wrap on the market, and it has done exceedingly well for Dow. Here again is an example of someone—Strosacker in this case—sticking to his guns and risking something because of his beliefs. Many people would have accepted the market research group's findings and not been willing to risk their own reputation. I learned again, this time from Carl Strosacker, that sometimes you need to take risks.

I have to say that I considered myself then, and still consider myself, very fortunate. Midland was a typical conservative Midwestern community. All the people there were WASPs—White Anglo-Saxon Protestants. I only qualified on the "W." But I was accepted there, as everywhere else in America, despite my accent, and the fact that I didn't part my hair. I was not the Italian kid by way of Ecuador. I was just a new employee learning the ropes and also learning about the Midwest, where I was taken in as if I were returning home after a long stay abroad.

∞

I found temporary housing in a farmhouse but soon moved into a house on Eastman Road. The house was two blocks from Dow International, which had just begun the previous year, in a converted grocery store.

The move into this house was fortuitous, because I moved quickly into the international side. In fact, I graduated in five weeks rather than the customary twelve from the sales training program, because the company was as anxious to get me into international as I was to get there myself. After all, I spoke five languages, I had significant international experience, and Dow needed people to help build up their international operations. I came into Dow at a perfect time. Steve Starks might not have cared about my interest in international, but Bill Dixon and others understood my potential there.

I was placed in a sales position under D.B. McCaskey, who ran the Latin American desk. We had an office in Montevideo, Uruguay; when Montevideo wanted to place orders or needed authorization for pricing or anything else, they contacted the Latin American desk in Midland.

Two days after I came to the Latin American desk, McCaskey told me, "I'm leaving on a trip for two weeks. Take care of things here." So much for my training, though in some respects I liked it that way. A few days later, when McCaskey was gone on another trip, Russ Zwick from our Montevideo office called. Russ needed a pricing authorization for polystyrene. "We have the business if we can meet a competitor's price," he said, "but I need an answer by early tomorrow morning at the latest."

With my immediate boss unavailable, I went to his superior, the sales manager for Dow International. He was at a meeting of the Dow Canada board and couldn't be bothered. So I asked for *his* boss: he was at the same meeting. Next I tried the pricing czar of Dow, Dave Baird. He's out of town.

I was running out of people to call. Finally, I tried Bill Dixon, figuring he'd been so nice to me that he could give me some good advice.

Maybe he could have, but he was out of town as well.

In desperation, I went to see Dow International's treasurer, a wonderful man by the name of Bill Clulo. Bill was very conservative. "You can't authorize the deal," he said with a kindly smile.

"But if we don't authorize it, we'll lose the business, and it makes sense to take it."

"You're asking my advice and I'm telling you I wouldn't do anything."

I went away frustrated. I'd spent a lot of time and energy on this, only to be told *No*. By the time I got back to my office, I decided to follow my instincts rather than the treasurer's advice. I called Russ Zwick and said, "Go ahead."

The next day everyone returned from the meeting in Canada. I went to see the sales manager, Howard Ball, and told him what I'd done. He became livid. "You ought to be fired!" he said. "Let's go see Clayton Shoemaker." Clayton was president of Dow International, and Howard no doubt saw him as my executioner. He marched me down to Clayton's office and told him that I had usurped powers, that I'd committed this grievous offense, and that I deserved to be fired. Before he could finish, though, Clayton put up a hand to stop the verbal onslaught.

"Hold on a minute," Clayton said. "Let me understand this. If Paul had done nothing, the business was going to be lost, right?"

"Well, yes," Howard admitted, not liking the direction that Clayton appeared to be taking the conversation.

"And, Paul, you went through all the proper channels, trying to get an answer?"

"I did," I replied.

"But the treasurer told him not to authorize it!" Howard said.

"It's not the treasurer's decision in the first place," Clayton said. "Paul had ascended the ladder all the way to the top, in the proper sequence, but no one was here to answer him, so he took it upon himself to make a decision."

"Exactly!" Howard said. "And it wasn't his decision to make. We can't have people. . . ."

"Paul," Clayton said, "I want you to know that, though I haven't analyzed the actual business decision, you did the right thing."

You could have knocked Howard Ball over with a feather. Here I was, steeled and ready to be fired, and the president was praising my action! I couldn't help but smile. It felt tremendous to know the big boss was squarely behind me. Had Clayton Shoemaker asked me at that moment—or at any other time in my career—to go swim the English Channel for him, I would have said, "Just let me get my swimming suit on." His response to stand behind this "young upstart," who was thinking for himself after finding no one else to guide him, taught me a lot about how to handle personnel once I got into management.

∽

I stayed in the Latin American desk for a little less than a year, then in late 1953 I was put in charge of the European desk. So I worked international from early on, but didn't live abroad while working for Dow until I went to Europe on January 2, 1955.

When Dow decided to go global in 1952, it was a major decision. Nowadays, everything is global, but not back in the early '50s. When I went to Europe, we had no real plan in place, no special orders other than to "get things going over there." There were four of us in Europe, and I spent four months in Zurich, living in a hotel, before going to Milan as Mediterranean Sales manager. This was a lofty title that really meant I was the only person covering France, Italy, Greece, and the Middle East. Suffice it to say I lived out of a suitcase. My "home office"—and the only Dow office in the Mediterranean—was my suite at the Hotel Duomo in Milan. The sitting room was the Dow Mediterranean office. After awhile I hired a secretary to work four hours in the morning. It was primitive, to say the least.

Primitive, perhaps, but life in Zurich was not uninteresting. My parents had met a nice Swiss couple on a liner from Europe to the US not long before I went to Zurich, and this couple had a 23-year-old daughter named Lise. She was, by both my parents' accounts, stunningly beautiful.

Seeing as I was a 27-year-old bachelor, I was not averse to stunningly beautiful single young women. I followed my parents' advice to call on Lise and ask her to dinner. I'm not certain how I had been described, but Lise, over the phone, was warm and receptive; she thought going out to dinner was a fine idea.

My parents had not exaggerated. As Lise greeted me at her door, I saw that she was indeed breathtakingly beautiful. I did my best not to stutter, stammer, or just flat-out stare at her elegant beauty. She invited me in and I met her mother. The three of us chatted for a few minutes before I suggested to Lise that we should probably go.

She smiled at her mother and said, "Ready, then?" Her mother smiled back, said she was, and called for her dog, which came scuttling in on the wood floor. I gazed questioningly at Lise; in response, she smiled at me, picked up her dog, and out we went—Lise, her dog, her mother, and me. A foursome. It was not exactly what I had in mind. Needless to say, Lise and I—and her mother and dog—never went out again.

It was also in Milan that I met Franca Ruffini. I dated Franca for a few months and on Christmas Day asked her to marry me. She said yes, and we began making arrangements for an apartment of our own in Milan, buying furniture and so forth. In the midst of this, Jack Stearns, executive vice president of Dow International, came to Milan, and said, "Paul, so far Dow has sold directly to customers only in the US and Canada. We want to do it in other countries, and Brazil is where we want to try it. We would like you to go set it up." It was a very attractive offer, a huge opportunity for a 28-year-old.

I was excited, but concerned, too, because I had just told my fiancé that we'd be in Europe for awhile, and we were getting our new apartment fixed up. But when I told Franca, she was thrilled. "It's been the dream of my life to go to either Brazil or Argentina," she said. "When are we going?"

That question, unfortunately, was harder to answer than it should have been. I immediately went to the US Consulate in Milan and asked the consul what I could do about getting my wife-to-be a visa.

"And you're going to get married in late May?" the consul asked.

"That's right."

The consul shrugged. "Then you can do nothing."

"But we're not leaving the country until mid-June. That's more than two months away."

"Yes, but we can't do anything about a permanent visa until after you're married, and from late May to mid June is not enough time to get a permanent visa."

"Well, then," I said, "how about a temporary visa?"

The consul shook his head and smiled, almost as if he were expecting this question and was holding a trump card. "I can't give her a temporary visa."

He sat there, making me ask the obvious. "Why not?"

"Because if we give people who are married to a US citizen a temporary visa, and they end up staying in the US, it costs a lot of money to deport them."

I calculated the response from Midland if I had to delay my trip to Brazil to serve a prison sentence for strangling a consul. Instead, I produced what I hoped to be a trump card of my own: a letter from Clayton Shoemaker, president of Dow International, stating that I was going to Brazil. Franca wouldn't have to be deported from the US.

The consul studied the letter as if it were written in code. Suddenly he broke out in a grin. "I have our solution!" he said, as if we'd teamed up on a terrifically difficult puzzle. "Just send your wife straight on to Brazil."

My answer came slowly and loudly, as if that would help his comprehension. "How would you like to go on your honeymoon without your wife?"

The consul shrugged again. "I'm divorcing my wife." I really felt like reaching over the desk and hitting him, but instead, I simply stared at him without speaking. After a long pause, he said, "All right, I'll give you a one-entry visa for three months." He acted as if he had done me a tremendous favor.

Franca and I were married on May 26, 1956, in a Catholic Church in Milan. Shortly after, we sailed to Midland for two months—she with her temporary visa—before heading to Brazil. I had done enough flying for Dow in the previous three years, but it was in Brazil that my career really took flight.

∞

When Franca and I moved to Sao Paulo, it was at the beginning of tremendous growth. There were 2.5 million inhabitants; now there are well over 20 million. It was, and is, the commercial and financial center of Brazil. More than a million Italian, Spanish, and other southern European immigrants came to Sao Paulo state, most of them settling in the city itself, drawn by the coffee boom of the late 19th and early 20th centuries.

Long before then, in the 1500s, Sao Paulo was known as the home of *bandeirantes*—adventurous explorers and frontiersmen who undertook expeditions into the continent's interior, searching for gold, diamonds, and other riches.

In a way, I felt like a modern-day *bandeirante*; Dow's foray into Brazil had been less than successful to this point. We were still exploring, seeking our own riches amidst the beautiful backdrop of this fast-moving cosmopolitan city, with its architectural landmarks, and the most imposing skyline outside of New York City. Although it sits on a high plain, San Paulo is not far from the ocean. Even in 1956, a modern highway allowed you to drive to the port city of Santos and the beautiful beaches of Guaruja. Sao Paulo was home to the very rich and the very poor; about 20 percent of the population lived in slum tenements or shantytowns, while the well-to-do merchants and coffee-growers lived in their mansions along Avenida Paulista. But the middle class was growing by leaps and bounds, presenting Dow a great market opportunity.

In economic terms, Dow Brazil was closer to Shantytown than to Avenida Paulista. Agricultural chemicals were about 90 percent of our sales, which totaled about $1 million a year, and nearly 90 percent of that was an ant killer. We had essentially no industrial business. This excited me tremendously. My father's son, I saw Dow's lack of success as an obstacle to overcome, an opportunity to take and run with. As I surveyed our situation in Sao Paulo, I had the fleeting image of my father surveying some marshland in northern Italy years before, envisioning the dikes, causeways, and levees that would transform the land into productive soil, seeing, in his mind's eye, bountiful crops of wheat or corn or white asparagus or grapes. I saw the same thing in Brazil; only the product was different.

I began with one salesman, a secretary, and an office boy. The latter was very important, because the mail and phone systems were not reliable. Inflation was extremely high in Brazil at the time, fluctuating between 25 and 80 percent per year. I knew, given the economy, the way we financed our business would be of critical importance. We couldn't just "do business as usual" in Brazil, because "usual" didn't have any buying power. I had to be creative in my approach to financing.

That became painfully clear two days after I arrived, when I went to see the Sao Paulo branch of City Bank of New York. The manager explained to me in a condescending tone, "Long-term money in Brazil is sixty days, and we don't have any to loan anyway." Dow's head office had made it clear that I was to work only with City Bank, but we couldn't do much business without money, so I would have to find other ways.

About nine months after I had landed in Brazil, Bill Groening, Dow International's general counsel, came to Sao Paulo to discuss a number of matters. We went out for dinner and as we began talking about Dow Brazil's financial situation, I said, "Bill, I have to fess up. I've been dealing with more than just City Bank."

"Oh? What other bank have you been dealing with?"

"Well, it's more than just one other bank." I drew in a sharp breath, knowing it might be one of my last as head of Dow Brazil. "It's twenty-four banks."

Bill stared at me for about five seconds, wide-eyed, a look of incredulity on his face. Bill was a somber man, not given to laughter, but he broke up laughing when he had fully digested this news.

"Twenty-four banks, eh? You've been quite busy down here."

"Money's hard to come by down here, Bill. In fact, I've created four more Dow companies so I could import more products, as there is a limit on how much any one company can import."

"So you're creating new companies without our legal department looking at them?"

"Yes, I am. But we do have good legal advice, and they're modeled after Dow Quimica do Brasil, which you were instrumental in setting up."

"So what do you call all these companies?"

"Dow Plastics, Dow Agricultural, Dow Alkali, and Dow Pharmaceutical."

Bill looked at me for several moments and shook his head. He laughed again. I had made Bill Groening laugh twice in the same meeting, almost as astonishing as my dealings with all the banks.

"I guess you'll need authorization for all these banks, won't you."

I grinned, relieved that he had taken the news so well. "Yes, that would be good."

Bill could have stormed out of that restaurant, flown back to Midland, and had me in very hot water within fifteen minutes of returning to his office. Instead, he got me official clearance to do what I had already been doing: financing Dow Brazil in whatever ways I could to grow the company from a tiny chemical company to the second-largest chemical company in Brazil in less than two years. Along the way, I could have lost my job several times for being a maverick, but Dow backed me all the way.

∞

The only way you could bring products into Brazil was to buy dollars, or other foreign currencies, at auction from the stock exchange on Tuesdays; on these days all the Brazilian stock exchanges sold currency instead of stocks. Once you had the currency you could apply for an import license. Once you had the license you could then place your order and import your goods. It was a long process, and money was tied up for five to six months before the goods arrived. Brazilian companies would pay a hefty premium to buy the goods delivered in Brazil rather than having to go through the process.

So I went to the stock market every Tuesday to bid on the right to buy "import dollars" with which to import goods. This surcharge we paid was called the "agio," and it was very steep. The official rate of exchange was 18.82 cruzeiros to the dollar. But the agio could be as much as 100 or 200 cruzeiros to the dollar. The fluctuations were very large, and so I would stand in a small booth with our broker, Luis Barrios, bidding in Sao Paulo but also working the phones with the markets in Rio, Recife, Porto Alegre, Curitiba, and other Brazilian markets. On the same day it was not uncommon to pay 20 percent less in one market than in another. It was a wild system, but being on the spot became my most important activity of the week.

"Luis," I said one day at the market after I'd been in Brazil for a little less than a year. "Doesn't the Banco do Brasil need dollars in the US?" This was the official government bank.

"Oh, they need dollars very badly," Luis said.

"What would happen if we loaned them dollars in the US, and they loaned us cruzeiros in Brazil for the same period of time?"

Luis considered this for a moment and shrugged. "It wouldn't hurt to ask."

And so the idea of a swap loan was created.

The bank was, indeed, interested. Luis and I visited with bank officials. "Give us a little time to think it over," they said. I didn't hear from them for a couple of weeks and thought they had given me the cold shoulder. I called Luis and he said, "Give them a couple more days."

So we gave them a couple more days—and two days later, they called. "We like it," they said. "Come in and let's talk."

I went in and negotiated with the Banco do Brasil and we settled on a deal. They were to loan us $400,000 worth of cruzeiros for $500,000 in US dollars. Of course, considering that US dollar interest rates were about 5 percent, while cruzeiros were going at about 36 percent, this was a good deal for us.

After making the agreement with the bank, I hopped a plane and flew back to Midland. The trip back was no piece of cake. We didn't have jets in those days; it was a 24-hour trip to New York, and then another flight to Midland. I arrived in Midland tired and a little nervous, because I had no authorization to make such a deal. I knew that I might have just written my ticket out of Dow.

Carl Gerstacker was treasurer of the company at the time. Over the years, Carl became like another father to me. He was Scottish and tight-fisted with his own money but he never minded acquiring debt for the company. Carl could be hard on me—he never let me off the hook—but I was never afraid of him, like most people were.

I met with the finance committee. Here I was, this 29-year-old upstart, swinging deals in Brazil with no authorization. The committee had been apprised of the basics before I entered the room. Believe me, the room seemed about twenty degrees chillier than the rest of the building. I was facing men who were twenty and thirty years older than me, who had been with the company a long time, and who didn't appreciate some maverick dealing his own cards down in South America. I received a few curt nods and several cold stares before the meeting began.

"Tell me again," a committee member said, "why we should give you half a million so you can get four hundred thousand worth of cruzeiros? Why don't we just give you four hundred thousand dollars?"

"I don't want dollars," I said, explaining that the Brazilian currency was devaluing at about 30 percent per year in relation to the dollar, so that when they repaid the dollars, they still had the same value, but we would repay devalued cruzeiros.

"But the rate is horrible," another committee member said. "Eighty cents on the dollar?"

"The devaluation of the cruzeiro will more than take care of that," I reminded the group, and gave them some actual numbers. At the end of five years, the $400,000 would be worth about $70,000 in terms of dollars at a 30 percent devaluation rate.

"What about the risk involved?" someone else said.

"They don't pay, we don't pay," I responded.

I continued to explain devaluation and inflation, but the committee either wasn't getting it, or they weren't buying it. We went round and round, getting nowhere. Finally, Carl Gerstacker broke in.

"Listen," he said to the group, "I don't completely understand this deal, but I think we owe it to Paul to have enough confidence in him to go ahead and let him do it."

The mood shifted immediately. If Carl trusted me on this, they would extend that trust as well. I received approval to make the swap loan. I flew back to Sao Paulo, relieved and elated. I finalized the deal with the Banco do Brasil and in a few weeks I returned to the bank to transact another swap loan, this one for $1 million for five years. We financed all our business in Brazil from 1957 to about 1969 through swap loans. We had the money, other companies didn't, and by the time they started using this financing tactic, we had captured the market.

Brazil was where I made my name with Dow. It was where Carl Gerstacker first took notice of me. Carl was once quoted as saying I had one of the most creative financial minds he had ever seen—high praise indeed from the man whose financial acumen had become legendary throughout Wall Street.

We set out to capture the caustic soda market in Brazil, a very important thing for Dow. When you produce a ton of chlorine, you also produce about a ton of caustic soda. The US market consumed a lot more chlorine than caustic soda, so disposing of the excess caustic was paramount for Dow US. And the Brazilians used a lot of caustic soda to manufacture soap, paper, and textiles. The big Dow plants that produced caustic soda were in Texas and Louisiana. That is where we shipped from, and while we later rented a warehouse in Sao Paulo to store thousands of drums and bags, our goal was to sell as much as we could while it was still in transit.

The freight rate to ship caustic soda in drums from the US Gulf Coast to the port of Sao Paulo was $16.90 a ton. The Europeans were shipping for $13.50—a pretty huge difference when you consider we were moving eight to ten thousand tons at a time, and selling it in Brazil for somewhere around $40 to $60 a ton. That shipping differential cut into our profits pretty significantly.

So I went to the shipping conference—a monopoly—and asked if the Gulf Coast shippers could lower their rates to match the Europeans. This apparently outraged them; they raised their rates to $18. When I heard this, I said, "If you do that, I'm pulling Dow out of the conference."

They laughed; I was a nobody to them. I pulled Dow out—much to the chagrin of our shipping office in Freeport, Texas. "You can't do that!" the distribution manager said.

"I already did it," I replied. "Now help me find ships to charter."

And so we started chartering ships, with our base load being caustic soda. The freight rates were much better with these charters, and after about a year and a half of doing this, we had to slow down our orders from Brazil, because we were literally running our plants out of caustic soda. In addition, these better rates allowed us to expand our market for many other Dow products.

Indeed, in a short time we went from selling less than a thousand tons of caustic soda to selling 70,000 tons out of a 120,000 ton market against 35 competitors from all over the world. As I continued to go to the stock exchange each Tuesday, I became known as *O Rey da Soda Caustica,* the "King of Caustic Soda." A Syrian who was also at the exchange on Tuesdays would stop what he was doing when he'd see me walk in and he'd say, "All hail the King of Caustic Soda!"

So we continued our growth in Brazil. In 1958, Dow ordered all managers to cut staff by 10 percent; I had ten on board. I let one person go; I was going to release him anyway. But within two months I had built up my staff to twenty-one. We were growing by leaps and bounds.

If I was in Midland I wouldn't have been able to operate as I did in Brazil. Dow president Ted Doan used to say I had the most independent job in the company. It was very difficult to call Brazil in those days; the communications were lousy. In fact, it was a red-letter day when our office finally was able to buy two phone lines. Even as telephone service improved, I would say, "Whaaaaat? I can't hear you!" I would tell people in Midland that they had to make it short on the phone because if someone wanted to place an order, we needed an open line. Of course, you couldn't get by with that today.

❧

In 1959, Ben Branch became president of Dow International. Ben was six-foot-five, an imposing figure, and a lot of people were afraid of him. But he was the first one at Dow that recognized me as something special. He was an honest, hardworking Midwesterner, someone who hated paperwork and liked to manage by walking around. He'd pop into your office at any time, talk to you, find out what's going on. He treated people well, from upper management on down to secretaries and other people in the trenches. He was a big pussycat in many ways; he didn't like speaking in front of large audiences, though he was incisive and often brilliant in meetings of ten or fewer. In fact, once he asked me to make the acceptance speech for him when he received an award as CEO of the Year from *Financial World* in 1976. Of course I said, "Ben, you're getting the award. You've got to make the speech. There's no way out of it."

Anyway, Ben called me back to meet with him in Midland in the fall of 1959. I flew in, and we met for lunch, and we continued the meeting through the afternoon, through dinner, and into the evening. Ben spent ten hours picking my brain on my international dealings.

"You," he said, "have lived in many places and dealt with people on different continents. I need to learn from you."

We talked about the culture of different countries, how to do business in each, how different governments operated. In a nutshell, we talked about what we needed to do to have Dow grow internationally.

Here was the president of the company admitting that a 31-year-old maverick could help him learn.

Starting from that session, I learned a lot from Ben about how to manage and motivate people and how to surround myself with knowledgeable folks. I also learned not to be afraid to say "I don't know," and then figure out the best way to find the information. You can believe I went back to Brazil very pumped.

∽

My operations were aided in part by my ability to quickly become fluent in Portuguese. I went to Brazil even less ready, language-wise, than when I arrived on Purdue's campus knowing about 50 words of English. As I settled in Sao Paulo, I knew essentially *no* Portuguese. But I picked it up quickly. In fact, many years later I was at a luncheon at the State Department in Washington, seated next to the wife of the Brazilian president. We conversed about many things, entirely in Portuguese, and then she stopped and looked at me a moment.

"I have to ask you something," she said. "I was told you were an American, but it seems to me that you are a Brazilian after all."

I assured her that though I had lived for seven years in Brazil I was, indeed, American.

She looked astonished. "Impossible!" she said. "You must be from Sao Paulo! I would recognize that accent anywhere."

I was quickly accepted as a native in Brazil because of my fluency, and through the business relationships I developed through the Sao Paulo Golf Club and through playing bridge. I used to go every Wednesday to the club to have lunch. There was this one table where the top ten or twelve most important business people in Brazil regularly ate. One day they invited me to join them. This was a rare honor extended to a non-Brazilian. And I got to know what was going on through these people, who immediately accepted me as one of them. Often they grumbled good-naturedly about "those foreigners," and I always said, "I'm one of those foreigners"—to which they immediately replied, "No you're not! You're one of us." They let me know what was going on economically, politically, every which way—including what would transpire in the March 1964 coup against the government, which was drifting more and more toward becoming a Communist state. I had left Brazil by this time, but Ben Branch asked me to return to Sao Paulo to find out what was happening, because I had so many contacts there. It was at the country club that my group of Brazilian businessmen told me about the coup and the military opposition to the present government. I told Ben what was going to happen, and it took place just as these businessmen said it would. I never would have found that out, had I not been accepted as "one of them."

Brazil will always be a special place for me, not only because of its importance in my career, but because it's where my two children, Laura and Andy, were born.

∞

One of those Brazilian businessmen who took me into their inner circle at the country club was João Goncalves. João owned one of the largest paper manufacturing companies in Brazil, and he and I played poker one or two nights a week at the club, using cards his company had made.

João was an excellent businessman, but he was not so great at cards. He lost much more often than he won, but one evening he won about $150 off of me, and he was delighted with his victory.

"Do you want me to pay you in cash?" I asked.

"No, no! I want a check from you," João replied with a big smile on his face.

I thought this a rather odd request, but wrote him a check, congratulated him, told him it probably wouldn't happen again, so enjoy it, and went home.

Two weeks later, Joao threw a going-away party for me as I was about to leave for Spain. As I entered the country club, I noticed many people held a piece of paper in their hands. Many grinned as they noticed me.

"What's everyone holding?" I asked Humberto, a golfing buddy of mine.

"This?" he replied. "It's our ticket to get in. As guest of honor, you don't need one."

He showed me the "ticket." It was a photocopy of my canceled check to Joao Goncalves. A sheepish grin crossed my face as João came up to welcome me. A little later he told the crowd how delighted he had been to welcome me into the inner circle of influential Brazilians who met every week at the club, and complimented me on how well I fit in with that bunch.

"And I was also delighted," João continued, "to finally be able to savor a victory in seven-card stud over Paul Oreffice. When I beat Paul, I didn't want his cash. I wanted proof that I had beaten him! And here it is!" he said, waving the actual check above his head as the crowd roared its approval.

That didn't end it for João. A full ten years later, I walked into the restaurant of the Key Biscayne Hotel and Villas and saw Joao sitting there with his wife and another couple. He got up, gave me a big hug, introduced me to everyone, and proceeded to recount the story of the check. I cut in at one point saying, "And he even had the canceled check with him!"

"*Had?*" João said, giving me a mischievous look. He pulled out his wallet, and from that he produced a wrinkled, 10-year-old check, showing it to everyone as if it were a picture of a prize fish he had hooked. "I'm not letting this one go," he said.

So, I won some and lost some. But I don't think any loss gave more lasting pleasure to my opponent than this one did to João.

∞

In 2004, Andrew Liveris, the newly-appointed CEO of Dow, went on a trip to Brazil and attended a large reception for all of Dow's best customers. Shortly after his return, Andrew told me that he was amazed at how many said that they had become customers during my years in Brazil. Since I had left Brazil 41 years earlier, it was astonishing and very rewarding that they still remembered me.

∞

In late 1960, Dow bought half of a Spanish company by the name of Union Quimica Norte Espana. Ben Branch called me to Midland late that year and asked me to move to Spain and become the commercial director of the company. I wasn't thrilled on two accounts: first, I would be reporting to a Spaniard who was running the show, and I didn't really know what that would entail. I had gotten used to running the show in Brazil and wasn't so sure the move to Spain was a good one for me. Second, I would be going to a country with a Fascist-type dictatorship that had been in place since General Francisco Franco came to power when his Nationalist forces overthrew Spain's government in 1939. I had had my taste of Fascist regimes, and the taste was a bitter one.

"I don't know, Ben," I said one afternoon in Midland. "I don't think Spain is the place for me."

"Fine," Ben replied. "We have the two main Spaniards here, the managing directors, and we're having a cocktail party at Ted Doan's house tonight. If you accept the job, you're invited. If not, you can't come."

That was Ben Branch: you never had to wonder what he was thinking. I left Ben's office and returned later that afternoon. "I'm not thrilled, Ben, but if you think this is the right thing to do, then I'll go."

For a variety of reasons, including the company's difficulty in finding a suitable replacement for me in Brazil, I remained in Brazil until the spring of 1962. In the meantime, Ben was unhappy with how the new company in Spain was being run, and asked me again to go over. This time, instead of going over as commercial director, he told me I'd be going as general manager, meaning I had more control. That was fine, but I still had a problem living in a country with a Fascist dictator running things. At Ben's suggestion, Franca and I spent two weeks in Spain to see firsthand what it was like. And I found I was pleasantly surprised.

Franco had been as ruthless as any dictator, especially in the early years after the Spanish Civil War, which ended in 1939. But in the intervening years, his regime had softened. Unusual for a dictator, he surrounded himself with knowledgeable men who helped turn the country toward prosperity again. There was, in the early 1960s, a freedom under Franco's regime that was not evident in other dictatorial regimes. He gave his cabinet more power to do things than almost any other government I've seen. Yes, Franco was oppressive. But Spain in the 1960s was far different from Italy and Germany in the 1930s and '40s.

And so it was in the spring of 1963 that I moved my family to Spain and took the reins as general manager of Dow Spain.

∞

In December 1962, shortly before we moved to Spain, I went to Rome where my father was hospitalized with cancer. My mother and I went to see him; Sandra was still in the states but making plans to come back shortly.

"He's not well, Paolo," my mother said as we walked down the squeaky clean floors of the hospital. I nodded, grim. I couldn't imagine my father sick from a cold, much less a potentially fatal disease. I kept telling myself he would come out of this. It would be another family story: he had beaten the Fascists and he had beaten cancer too.

My mother's face looked pinched and troubled as we entered Dad's room. He looked pale and gaunt, and the fluorescent lighting did nothing for his coloring. He hadn't been able to eat much in the past few weeks. I tried to hide my shock at how poorly he looked as I walked up to his bedside. My mother kissed my father and he smiled, murmuring "Elena, my love," and then she drew back so that he and I could talk.

"Paolo." His eyes brightened upon seeing me, and he stirred a little in his bed, trying to sit up some.

"Papá. Stay as you are. You don't have to sit up for me." My eyes moistened as I could see how hard the cancer had hit him. I could see the pain that he tried to mask. His hair was grayer, and his cheeks had a gray-white stubble over them—very unusual for my father, who was always clean-shaven. His eyes were turned inward, forced so by his pain, even as he looked at me and smiled weakly.

"It's good of you to come."

"I came right over after I talked to Mamma."

"And so you will be in Spain soon?" I had told him about the upcoming move.

"Yes, probably in a month or two. And I'm glad of it, because I'll be better able to visit you."

My father closed his eyes for a moment, and they were crinkled in a slight smile, as if he were enjoying a private joke. Then he opened them again and looked kindly upon me. "Paolo, I'm not getting out of here except in a box."

The way he said it, I knew he was right. I found no words to reply.

"I'm only sorry," he said, "that I won't be able to see you when you're running Dow. Because you're going to, you know."

"I don't know about that."

"Look at what you did in Brazil. They reward you by giving you Spain, because they need you to do the same thing there. These are stepping stones, Paolo. They lead to the top."

I had never even considered running Dow one day until he said that. "It's hard to say, Papá." At that moment, my career path at Dow seemed trivial.

"I see it clearly, as clearly as I see you right now, right here." He took my hand, and he held it firmly. His grasp seemed frail and shaky, yet somehow firm. All I saw right now was my father, dying in a hospital room that smelled of starched sheets and antiseptic, the late afternoon light outside his window being drained out of the sky just like the color had been drained out of his face.

"Remember what your mother told you before we left Italy? I told you the same thing before you left Quito to go to America." My father paused, not so much for my answer as to regain some wind. I knew the answer but let him say it.

"'You are embarking on a great adventure,'" he said. "That was true then and it's true now. You're still on that great adventure."

"I think Spain will be a good move," I allowed.

"Spain is temporary. You will be running Dow someday," my father repeated, and then he closed his eyes to rest.

That conversation was a great gift to me. I had been running so hard I never had time to look too far down the road. Or maybe I didn't want to look too far down it; I don't know. All I know is, even as his own hopes and dreams were quickly fading, he gave life to a dream inside me, one that seemed at once outlandish and attainable, now that he had named it. I felt a little disoriented; at that moment, anything in the world seemed possible, except for the one thing I wanted most: for my father to be healthy again.

A few days after I returned to Brazil, my mother called to tell me he'd gotten worse, that I had better return quickly. I returned, and was by his bedside when he died on January 19, 1963. Two days later he was buried in the Jewish Cemetery in Lido of Venice.

He died of stomach cancer, brought on by the ulcers that began when the Fascists put him in jail nearly a quarter century earlier. From that perspective, you might say that the Fascists got him in the end. But that perspective hardly tells the whole story. He was 70 years old, and he had lived a rich, full life, one unsullied by fear. He stood up for what he believed, even when that belief brought him great harm. He lived his life earnestly and happily, unafraid of risks and challenges, undeterred by setbacks. When he left this world, he left it in peace, and even as I grieved his parting, I was renewed by his blessing.

∞

Franca and the kids and I settled in Bilbao, a seaport city in the Basque Country in northern Spain, in spring of 1963. My father was correct: Dow needed me to turn things around in Spain. When I arrived in Bilbao, Union Quimica Norte Espana, or Unquinesa, as it was known for short, was a company with about $8 million in sales, thirty-one hundred employees, and a serious case of corruption that ran through its entire infrastructure. In Brazil I began with nothing; in Spain I began with a peck of troubles, and those troubles originated in the spacious offices of the two managing directors, Federico Lipperhide and Rafael Guzman, whom I had met in Midland two years earlier when Ben Branch first persuaded me to go to Spain. They were the founders of the company and ran it like a private fiefdom.

These two directors had nearly 8,000 square feet of office space between them, including living rooms where they received people. There were twenty-eight Mercedes and twenty-seven chauffeurs at the disposal of management. The brother of one of the directors handled the company's insurance, and other relatives had a monopoly on shipping, and yet another relative supplied all office materials. We were losing money, but they had ways of hiding the loss: they didn't depreciate anything. I had brought in a young accountant from Dow by the name of Luis Cienfuegos, and he was the one to discover all these problems.

In the first meeting I attended, the directors were discussing what to do with the "profits" from the previous year. The three main questions they pondered were, "How much do we want to pay in dividends?" That was first. Then, "How much should we distribute to the directors?" Finally, "How much should we give the government?" They paid essentially no taxes. Only if there was something left over did they put it into depreciation.

The chairman of the board of the company was also the chairman and CEO of the Banco de Vizcaya, our largest shareholder outside of Dow. He was Pedro Basabe, the Count of Cadagua. He was about 30 years older than me, a wonderful gentleman, and we became good friends.

I called the Count one day and said, "Major changes must occur in this company. I'd like to sit down and talk with you."

"Certainly. Why don't you come to my home. That way, we'll have more time to talk."

So I showed up at his house around seven o'clock the next evening, and he greeted me at the door. He was an imposing figure: tall, erect, baldheaded, and always perfectly groomed. We sat in large leather chairs in his home office, and we talked for three hours before I went home to dinner. I told the Count about the financial problems, about the accounting practices, about the corruption, and he listened intently to this young

American guy who had just come into his country to clean up a Spanish company.

"We are decapitalizing by paying dividends we don't earn," I said. "We have to cut the dividend to zero and shut down several inefficient plants. And we need to fire the two managing directors. They're the cause of all this, and the problems aren't going to stop until they're gone."

As the Count was considering this, I added, "And I need your help to do all of this."

Then it was the Count's turn. He asked me question after question about the operations, about the directors, about the plants and accounting practices. At the end of the three hours, he said, "Senor Oreffice, I have three roles. I am the chairman of the board of the company. I am chairman of the board of the Banco de Vizcaya, the largest single shareholder outside of Dow, and I am the largest individual shareholder. Now, as a large individual share-holder, I am all for your program. However, in my other two capacities, I need to investigate further, to ask you more questions, before I can say I am ready to support your program. Do you understand?"

I understood. I returned each of the next two nights, and we had long talks. At the end of the third night, the Count said, "I am now ready to back you up in all three of my capacities. As for the two managing directors, I will personally dispose of them. I will talk to them myself."

The Count had taken the toughest task. It was difficult for him person-ally because he had worked with these two directors, and they were longtime friends of his. But he had no qualms about firing them in light of their actions.

The Count lived in a beautiful mansion and often held dinners for distinguished guests. The dinners were served by very tall maids, all the same size and who all looked alike. There was always one maid for every two guests. So if we had fourteen at the table, there were seven maids, always serving us efficiently and pleasantly. The meals were outstanding, with the best wines. The Count loved food, and during my last meal with him, when he was 91, he ate a large, four-course dinner.

Every American remembers where he or she was on November 22, 1963, when John F. Kennedy was assassinated. I was in Bilbao, driving back home from dinner, when I heard the news on the radio. I was so shocked I almost went off the road.

There were not many Americans in Bilbao, and I was about the only American who was active at the Bilbao Country Club. The next day I went to the club's dining room for lunch. The moment I walked in, all conversation stopped, and after I sat down, every person in that room—more than 100 people—came by my table to give me their condolences. It was one of the most emotional moments of my life.

∽

When I came to Spain in 1963, we had, as I mentioned, thirty-one hundred people and $8 million in sales. When I left three years later, we had sixteen hundred people and $30 million in sales—and the 28 Mercedes were gone, and so were the chauffeurs.

By law we couldn't lay people off without just cause, so I went to see Leopoldo Lopez Bravo, the Minister of Industry, and proved to him that my choice was to fire a lot of people or shut down the whole company. He agreed to help us by placing people in other companies in the area. When one of those companies needed to hire, they would call us, and we would give our workers a severance of five months' pay, which wasn't much, and send them over to the other company.

About a year later, the government asked me to become an official advisor to them, regarding the chemical industry. For the Spaniards to ask the advice of a young foreigner about vinyl chloride and other industry issues was an extremely high compliment, and I knew it. In 1966, I was awarded the Encomienda del Merito Civil, Spain's highest civilian honor, for my contributions to the development of the petrochemical sector.

And I continued my bridge passion there: I became Spain's bridge champion in 1965. The tournament proved to be one of the most grueling six days of my life. It ran from 3 P.M. to about 3 A.M. every day, and I worked from 8 A.M. until lunchtime. I didn't get much sleep that week.

Spain was a wonderful place to live and to raise young children. We lived by the beach and had a nanny, a maid, and a cook. Laura was three years old and Andy was two when we moved to Spain. We felt totally safe there—so safe, in fact, that we never locked our doors. Crime was very low, because people feared Franco's militia—most people figured if they were caught committing a crime, they'd be thrown in jail and never get out.

In Spanish tradition, we had late dinners. The first time we were invited to dinner, we showed up at our friends' house, as requested, at 10:30 P.M.;

the butler was still adjusting his tie as he answered the door. We were the first ones to arrive; the rest of the guests didn't show up until 11:00 or 11:15.

Working hours were very different in Spain, too. Their workday began at 9:30 A.M. and was broken by a two-and-a-half hour break, during which time most people went home, ate lunch, and took a siesta. They worked longer into the evening and worked a half day on Saturdays as well. I suggested we go to the schedule most Americans are used to—a one-hour lunch and no Saturdays. I put it to employee vote, and it was turned down at first, because people didn't want to lose their siesta time. But more and more people liked the idea of having two days off on the weekends, and it was passed on a second vote.

∾

In Spain I continued my maverick ways. We were building a larger polystyrene plastic plant, and needed to build a new coloring plant with it. In the US, coloring was done by specialized companies, and Dow sold only clear plastic, but that was not the case in Spain. However, our request for authorization to build such a plant was denied.

About a year later, Bill Fletcher, head of our plastics business for international, arrived in Bilbao and told me that the authorization had finally been granted. I thanked him and took him to his hotel, and the next morning picked him up and drove him to the plant. On the way I explained that Spaniards were good in some disciplines but not in others.

"For whatever faults they might have, though," I said, "they are without a doubt the fastest builders in the world." And to demonstrate I pointed to a four-storey building housing the coloring plant authorized only the night before.

Spain was a very different experience from Brazil, but it was good for me as well. However, Midland had other ideas for me. I guess my father was right: Spain was to be a stepping stone, with the next step being back to the US.

∾

In June 1966 we packed up once again and moved from Bilbao to Coral Gables, Florida, where I became president of Dow Latin America. Dow was dismantling Dow International and dividing the world into five profit centers: the US, Europe, Latin America, Canada, and the Far East. It was a major change in our global approach.

In Midland, they had pretty well decided to set up the Latin American headquarters in Lima, Peru, but I thought that was an awful choice, so I devised a study that used a point system to select the area headquarters. I placed heavy emphasis on communications, transportation, and availability of bilingual help. As a result of this study, Coral Gables, a suburb of Miami, won out over Lima, Mexico City, Sao Paulo, San Juan, and other Latin American cities. The communication by phone and cable was much better in Miami (in fact, in those days, if you made a call from Santiago, Chile, to Lima, Peru, the call went through Miami). It was easiest to fly directly from Miami to Latin American cities. And Miami was ideal in terms of bilingual help. Add to that that the Brazilians and the Chileans and the Argentineans couldn't get mad if we chose Miami, because we had not chosen one Latin American country over the others as our hub, and Coral Gables was the ideal choice.

It was another hard sell to the Dow board, since they thought of Coral Gables as simply a place to vacation in the winter. After a long meeting, Carl Gerstacker, by then chairman of the board, asked me, "How are you going to keep the Midland people from invading you in the winter?"

To which I replied, "From May through October, you're free to come, but from November through April, even you need Oreffice's visa."

That resolved it, and the word quickly spread to everyone in Dow Midland. "Oreffice's Visa" became the law.

The point system that I devised to select the headquarters, by the way, was adopted by Coral Gables and Miami to attract other international corporate headquarters to locate their international corporate headquarters in either Coral Gables or Miami. They attracted nearly 40 other companies in just over two years using this point system. As a result, when *The Miami Herald* came out in 1993 with its list of the 100 most influential people in the history of south Florida, I was on that list—along with Chris Evert, Claude Pepper, Don Shula, and a host of others, including Christopher Columbus and Ponce de Leon!

We set about really capturing the market in Latin America, especially in Argentina, Brazil, and Chile—I called them the ABCs of Latin America. We also did very well in Columbia. I worked with an outstanding group of people in Coral Gables.

∞

I also kept up my bridge-playing, hooking up with John Scanlan, who was a noted player in Canada, to play in some tournaments together. John was an accountant for Deloitte, which was Dow's auditor; he had asked to play with me.

I had never met John before, and when I first saw him, I have to say I wasn't very impressed. He looked like the average milk-toast accountant. But he could make the cards sing, and we won the first tournament going away. We formed a great partnership, and we soon met the Dallas Aces, who had represented the US in the world championships, in the finals of the Southeastern US Championships. John and I were to play Jim Jacoby and Bobby Wolff, two of the Aces, and two of the best players in the world. As we were about to play them for the championship, Jacoby sized us up and said, "How come we haven't seen you guys around?"

"Who, us?" I said innocently. "We just started playing bridge last week."

The very first hand, John made a spectacular play, and they were clearly shaken. We beat them easily to win the championship.

John later left Deloitte and ran a snowmobile company for about four years before he had a breakdown in 1973 and wound up in a mental institution in Canada. His wife wrote me a letter saying in John's talks with a psychiatrist at the institution, all the psychiatrist could get out of him was about "how great it was playing bridge with Paul Oreffice." John either said nothing or he talked about bridge. "All he talks about is you," his wife wrote me. "I think it would really help him if you wrote him a letter."

I immediately wrote John, focusing mainly on our bridge escapades of the past. We really were quite the duo; we could read each other's minds. John wrote a long, glowing letter back to me. He let me know there was a national tournament coming up in St. Louis and asked me to enter it with him.

Interestingly, the guy I won the Spanish Open with a few years earlier had been in an institution for awhile. It gave me pause to think I might be the common denominator here. Now here was John, with his only happy memories, seemingly, of playing bridge with me.

So we hooked up again in St. Louis for the tournament. I have to admit I was a little leery about entering a tournament with John, given his condition—but we played well and finished fourth in the nation. John was delighted, as was I.

I'm a competitive guy. I like to play, and I like to win. Bridge was probably what I was best at. As it was, I won national championships, and I believe I could have been in the top handful in the world if that's what I had focused on. I was also good at other card games—poker and gin rummy especially. In 1968, when I was running Latin America, I was invited to Midland to a meeting of the top 40 in the company. That first night, a pretty high-stakes poker game broke out. I did all right that night, and did the same the next night. The vice president of marketing was drinking liquor and was trying to push me out of most hands while making loud remarks in the process. I was drinking Coke, and cutting him to ribbons while smiling and being gracious. I ended up winning $3,500 in those two nights—a huge sum for me in those days.

A little later, Ben Branch took me aside and said, "Kid, you're the most elegant winner I've seen. The way you cut up that stupid SOB was beautiful. But the way you handled yourself in winning was even more beautiful. It's not easy to be a good winner—especially around guys like that."

I received another lesson in winning and losing from Carl Gerstacker, the fiery Scot. Carl thought he was one of the best table tennis players in the world and *the* best gin player. So, in Midland, Carl and I played ping pong, and I beat him six games in a row, though all the games were close. He *was* good. He got mad because he thought I was toying with him, but I wasn't. "You got me at ping pong, but you won't get me at gin," Gerstacker groused at the end.

At that time, Dow was run by the troika of Gerstacker, Branch, and Ted Doan. They decided that each one of them would "godfather" a different section of the world. Branch had Europe, Doan had the Pacific, and Gerstacker had Latin America. So Carl and I took many trips together.

Our next trip, we flew from Miami to Sao Paulo to Montevideo and to other locales on the east coast of South America, and then to Santiago, Chile, on the west coast, and finally back to Miami. On all these flights I'm playing gin with Carl. Well, by the time we got to Santiago, he was far behind. On our return trip to Miami, which was from 8 P.M. to 8 A.M., Carl wouldn't even allow me to eat on my own time. "Where do you think you're going?" Carl would growl when I'd get up to answer the call of nature.

Carl didn't allow me to sleep on the way back to Miami, but he couldn't catch me, either. We weren't playing for big money, and money wasn't really the issue, though Carl, true to his Scottish ways, didn't like to part with his own money. Carl's pride was the problem. It was difficult for the man who was my boss—and much more importantly, for the man who considered himself the best gin player in the world—to lose to me. But, lose he did, and by the time we landed in Miami, he owed me $85.

He didn't pay me. He flew back to Midland, and I figured he just didn't plan to pay me. But a few days later I got a letter from him, conceding I was the better table tennis player *and* the better gin player, along with a check for $85. "Show me a good loser and I'll show you a loser," he wrote, I guess by way of explaining why he was late in paying.

We did very well in Latin America. The late '60s were crucial years for building solid foundations down there, for expanding what we had already been doing. We went from opportunistic business to really capturing the market in Brazil, Columbia, and some other Latin American countries.

∞

I faced one of my toughest decisions during my Latin American days, and it had nothing to do with business. I was holding a management meeting in the Bahamas, and at 6:30 A.M. on the second morning, I got a call that Bob Kincaid, our vice president for commercial operations, and a good friend of mine, had just suffered what appeared to be a heart attack. Ed Coon, the caller, told me an ambulance had been called.

I rushed downstairs as Bob was being carried out on a stretcher. The ambulance was parked at the side door of the hotel where we were meeting. A couple of teenagers watched as Bob, whose eyes were closed, was loaded into the back of the ambulance.

"You think he's dead?" one of the kids said.

"Yeah, he dead, man," the other said solemnly, as though he had seen a lot of dead men carried out on stretchers.

As the second teen pronounced Bob dead, Bob opened one eye and winked at the kid, whose own eyes became huge. Both kids took off running.

I rode in the ambulance and soon was appalled at the conditions of the hospital emergency room. I remember one man sitting in the room with blood flowing from a large cut on his cheek. They didn't have time to treat him right away, so they gave him a bedpan to catch the blood.

It wasn't much better for Bob. We had to wait for an EKG machine to be brought from a doctor's office because the EKG machines at the hospital weren't working.

As I waited, I called Dorothy Garrett, my tremendous assistant in Coral Gables. She already had a Lear jet on standby in Ft. Lauderdale. She had also talked to her boyfriend, Ernie, a cardiologist who was the family doctor for many Dow people. It was Ernie's day off, and I asked Dorothy to have Ernie hop the Lear and come over.

Ernie did, and after he examined Bob, he took me outside the room and said, "Paul, we have a real dilemma here. Bob has had a major heart attack and if we leave him here he might die because they don't have the facilities. On the other hand, if we fly him to Florida he might die on the way. But if he makes it we can take care of him back there."

We tried to contact Bob's wife, but couldn't. Someone had to make the decision.

"Let's fly him back," I said.

I had made a lot of business decisions, but this one was much tougher, because it was literally a life-and-death issue, and it involved a good friend.

We flew Bob back to Florida. He survived the trip, received the treatment he needed, and is doing fine, I am happy to say, nearly 40 years later.

∞

One day in late 1969, Carl called me to Midland and laid out a plan. At that time he was chairman of the board and chief financial officer. Carl liked what I had done in Latin America, especially in Brazil. He wanted to create a new position for me, in Midland; he wanted me to return to Midland and become director of financial services. "I want you to look into setting up a worldwide banking institution and be part of the financial group," he said. "Then, after awhile, we'll make you head of all finance."

"You must be nuts!" I replied. "I'm a chemical engineer, and my background is in sales. I don't know the lingo."

Carl grinned. "You pick up languages fast enough; I'm not worried about that. I know what you did in Brazil, the financing you arranged, the swap loans, working with all the banks down there. You have a real touch for finance. You're my man."

"You are willing to take a chance on me?"

Carl, ever the gamesman, narrowed his eyes and said, "I don't see any chance involved here."

And so I moved back to Midland, the place where it all began for me.

∞

CHAPTER ELEVEN

Climbing the Ladder

Coming back to Midland didn't prove to be the easiest of transitions. Carl Gerstacker had brought me back to become head of finance, but Carl wanted me to tread water for a bit before that happened. That treading became quite tiresome, because Bob Bennett, the treasurer of Dow, knew why I had been called back and that his position was in jeopardy. Carl was unhappy with the whole setup in finance, and specifically with Bob's performance. Bob simply wasn't cut out to be the treasurer, but he was the son of Earl Bennett, one of the great men in Dow's history. Earl Bennett had been Dow's chief financial officer and Carl's mentor, and that complicated matters.

Bob proceeded to shut me out in a number of ways. He spread this message to the Dow Treasury people: "Don't talk to Oreffice. He's not our friend." I went through about six months of being left out of finance meetings and being undermined in other ways before I finally met with Carl.

"Carl, I was a very happy man down in Coral Gables," I said. "Down there I ran my own show. Up here, I not only don't run the show, I'm not even *at* the show." Carl sighed and nodded as I gave him several examples of being shut out of meetings and not being given a voice at the meetings I did attend. "If you're not ready to make the move you told me you were going to make," I said, "then that's fine, and I understand. But if that's the case, give me a different job. I can't stand the situation as it is. Every day I have to fight against the system, against the people who should be working with me."

"I've been very unfair to you," Carl replied. "I've put you in an impossible situation. And I'm going to solve it."

Within one week—in October 1970—I was named chief financial officer. Bob Bennett began reporting to me as treasurer. Bob took early retirement not long after that.

As I mentioned earlier, Carl held tightly onto his own money but didn't flinch at acquiring debt for Dow. While I agreed in principle, I was not quite as aggressive. This amused Carl so much that at one point he described me, in an interview with *Forbes,* as "a little old lady in tennis shoes." I shrugged and smiled and tucked that playful jab away for future reference. Many years later, at Carl's retirement party, I disappeared during the course of the black-tie dinner, emerging several minutes later wearing a dress and a gray wig and clutching a *Wall Street Journal* in my hand. As jaws dropped and fingers pointed, I made my way to the head of the table and stared directly at Carl. "I've come," I said in my best old-lady's voice, while brushing a wisp of wig hair out of my eyes, "to lecture my chairman about being such a wild man on capital spending." I shook my paper at Carl and glared at him in mock anger.

The whole room broke up laughing, but none enjoyed the joke as much as Carl. "You have a very long memory," he told me later, still laughing.

"Well, not many people have called me a little old lady in tennis shoes," I said. "Some things aren't so hard to remember."

As chief financial officer I developed a theory of inventorying money. This was an idea that Carl Gerstacker was totally behind. We didn't need a lot of money right then, but knew that with Ben Branch at the helm we would build a lot of new plants. I figured if lenders were willing to give us 30-year money at around 7 percent, why not take it? So every few months we issued 30-year debentures, usually in pieces of $150 million or $200 million. Since we didn't need the money right then, we loaned some of it out on a short-term basis to recover most of the interest cost. We didn't always recover all of the interest, but we assumed a very small expense to have money available for the future. And when interest rates went to double digits during the late '70s, it was really nice for Dow to have an average cost of money of less than 8 percent when everyone else was paying 12, 13, 14 percent for their money.

That's one of the things that stamped my early years as CFO, and I was lucky that I was in a company like Dow that encouraged innovation, creativity, and the willingness to take calculated risks. Most companies thought of finance as a cost center; we thought of it as a *profit* center. That was a very unusual idea at the time, one that made Carl beam almost like a doting father.

This made Carl beam, too: on August 31, 1973, Dow Chemical was the largest lender to the banking system in the US. How did it happen that an industrial corporation became the nation's largest lender for a day? Well, in 1973, the US had some regulations that required banks to have certain balances between their domestic and foreign branches, and August 31 was the key date. We got a call from Citibank that they were willing to pay 40 percent annual rate of interest for overnight money. They had to raise the money to stay within the regulations. We were hardly off the phone with them before another major bank called and said they'd pay us 60 percent. Then another bank and another called. Soon the rate was 100 percent.

We ended up loaning several billion dollars to Bank of America, Chase Manhattan, Citibank, and a few other banks for that one night. We raised all the money in commercial paper and we made a few million dollars that night by using our credit.

One other brief anecdote about my time as CFO. The Dow Bank, headquartered in Zurich, Switzerland, started loaning money in the US. As part of a bank syndicate, it had loaned $10 million to Mattel, which was a very large Dow customer. We supplied them with various plastics, and in the mid-1970s there were tremendous shortages of plastics.

Well, Mattel couldn't repay the loan on time. Citibank and Bank of America were the syndicate leaders, and executives from these two institutions came to Midland to talk to me. They asked me to participate in a new loan to Mattel.

"That's unreasonable," I said. "We already give Mattel preference on receiving material that is scarce right now and that we could provide to other customers. We will continue to do that for Mattel. We'll continue to keep them afloat by giving them credit, but we can't participate in a new loan. They need to repay their current loan to us first."

The bankers agreed in person. But two days later I got a phone call from these two bankers, and they said they had run up against resistance and again wanted Dow Bank to maintain its position as lender. Wilson Gay, our treasurer at the time, was in my office. I saw his eyes grow big when he heard my reply: "I did not know I was dealing with people who welsh on their commitments. You made a commitment to me. You are now welshing and I will not go along with that. We are calling our loan right now."

Wilson wrote me a note that said, "You hear that noise? That's somebody passing out on the other side of the phone." I had just told the two largest banks in the country that they were welshers.

Not long after this, the bankers called me from a meeting they were having with Mattel in California. Again they insisted we had to stay in the loan.

"If that's what you want," I said, "we'll cut off credit to Mattel and put them in bankruptcy and that's your problem."

The Mattel CEO called me a little later. He was grateful to Dow because we were extending them credit and supplying them with hard-to-come-by materials. "They called you a son of a bitch and a whole lot of other things, some of which I'd never heard of, but you're going to win."

He was right: the banks finally acquiesced, because they couldn't afford to have Mattel go bankrupt. We continued supplying materials to Mattel, and they eventually recovered. Mattel was forever grateful to Dow, and I enjoyed the whole thing tremendously, because for once I had defeated the big banks and knocked a little of the arrogant wind out of their sails.

∞

So while the move to Midland in the spring of 1970 didn't start out so well, once I was named CFO, things went very well for me. I was in this position for five years, and the confidence Carl Gerstacker invested me was paid back tenfold. I was put on the board of directors in January 1971 at age 43, which is pretty early in the game. Not long after that appointment, Ben Branch stopped me in a hallway.

"I wish you weren't so damned young, kid," he said.

"What do you mean?"

"I want you on the Dow executive committee, but some people think you are too young. I'm going to get you on that committee."

And so I was placed on the company's executive committee as well. This began a very long period of being on the board and the executive committee. And during my 22-year tenure on the board, I never missed a single meeting, setting an all-time company record by attending 252 board meetings in a row. That record will never be broken, because they have fewer meetings now.

Ben Branch may have been a big, imposing figure, and he was part of the troika that ran Dow, but he didn't like controversy. Ben had a protégé, Elmer Stilbert, and Elmer was both devious and ineffective. In 1968, when I was in Coral Gables running Dow Latin America, Elmer was the coordinator for all associated companies outside the US. We were forming a joint company in Chile, and I kept getting reports from my people that Elmer was impossible to work with and very untrustworthy.

John Henske, who was executive vice president of Dow and who served on the Dow board, was Elmer's boss. I called Henske and said, "John, be careful, this guy is bad news. He's setting people up against each other. He is accusing my people of dishonesty when he is the one twisting the facts."

John replied that he would look into it. A few days later, he called me back. "Paul, I think you've got the wrong take on Elmer. He's doing a fine job. I fully support him."

I was stunned. "John, what you're saying is that my organization is dishonest and stupid, and by implication that makes me dishonest and stupid. I am not going to accept that. You are wrong, dead wrong, in supporting this guy. You have been warned."

Henske was livid. He said, "Screw you!" or words to that effect, and slammed down the phone. I had just stood up to the executive VP of the company; I was a nothing compared to him. Still, I wasn't going to let my guys down, and I wasn't going to let Midland intimidate my organization.

So I decided to attack rather than wait. I went to Midland to talk with Ben Branch.

"Ben," I said, "I've got a very serious problem here. It's very serious principally because one guy, a guy I know you like, Elmer Stilbert, has really screwed up our organization and John Henske is backing him and by implication, John Henske is calling me and my organization dishonest, and I will not tolerate that. Period. Next chapter."

"Well, I've heard some of the other side as well. It's important that we get together. I'll tell you what," Ben said, "John Henske and I will come down to Coral Gables and we'll talk this out."

So I picked Ben and John up at the Miami airport when they came down. As I took them to my office, Ben, in typical fashion, said, "Okay, kiddies, you work this out, and I'll go talk to some of the other guys around here."

"Hold on a minute, Ben," I said. "You sit right there."

Ben sighed and said, "Okay, let's hear what's going on."

As we all sat, I said to Henske, "Well, John, since you are the one making the accusations of my organization, why don't you tell us where we've been wrong."

Henske started in. He talked about what Stilbert had supposedly done and said, and he talked about the surrounding issues, and every time he brought something out, I'd pull up a paper proving him wrong. I had a stack of papers seven inches high on my desk, all proving my point. This scenario happened over and over again. Henske would say something about our operations, and I'd refute him with evidence that proved otherwise.

Ben was nonplussed. It was obvious to him that I was right and Henske was wrong, but he didn't want to arbitrate. At the end of the discussion, he said, "Let me think about it."

He thought about it out loud with Carl Gerstacker and Ted Doan back in Midland. "Guys," he said, "I've never seen a situation like this. Usually someone is 60 percent right and the other guy is 40 percent, or fifty-fifty. But Paul is 100 percent right and John Henske has made a fool of himself."

This actually led to Henske leaving the company. At the time this happened, Ben Branch was chief operating officer. The day before he was to become CEO, he and I were standing in the hall that showcased the pictures of the former directors. Henske's picture was up there, but by this time he had left to become CEO of Olin.

"When I become CEO," Ben said, "that SOB's picture comes down from the wall."

"What's the big deal?" I said. "He's gone."

"I don't like what he tried to do to one of my guys," Branch growled, staring at Henske's picture.

And I said, "Who's that?"

Ben turned to face me. "What do you mean, who—you! I'll never excuse him for what he did. He was dead wrong, and I want his picture off the wall."

I had never realized until that moment that John Henske had actually wanted me fired. Later on, John and I got along quite well when he was at Olin. I didn't harbor a grudge. There was no reason to; I had won.

∽

The confrontation with John Henske was just a skirmish compared to what I would go through with Zoltan Merszei, who succeeded Ben Branch as

CEO in 1976. Zoltan had run Europe for Dow, and Ben liked him. I had just been named president of Dow US; a number of upper management moves were being made as Ben was stepping down as CEO.

Zoltan had been a good friend of mine for a long time. He was instrumental in building up Europe for Dow, and when I was in Spain I worked for him. But while there, I stayed as independent as possible from Zoltan, because he liked to dictate and he liked to yell. I knew firsthand his strong points and his shortcomings.

Zoltan was not named CEO without some controversy. Ben favored him, but Ted Doan favored Earle Barnes. Earl was president of Dow US at the time. Carl Gerstacker was on the fence. Carl finally sided with Ben, and they chose Zoltan. The troika flew out to Jackson Hole, Wyoming, to Earle Barnes' vacation home, to break the news to Earl. Earl made it clear he would not work for Zoltan Merszei, and said, "Look, you've got the guy. Why don't you make Paul Oreffice the CEO? You know he's going to be it. Why don't you go ahead and do it now?"

Though it was the consensus that probably someday I would be CEO, it was too soon. So they named Zoltan Merszei CEO, and Earl Barnes announced his retirement from any executive capacity.

Things changed quickly. Carl Gerstacker stayed on the board, but gave up his job as chairman, Ben Branch became non-executive chairman, and I became president of Dow US.

Zoltan was a much different type of CEO than his predecessors. The open-door policy that had long been in effect was terminated, and Zoltan ran the company like a dictator. He disrespected his immediate predecessor, Ben Branch, warning people not to listen to him because he was over the hill. This was the same Ben Branch who had been Zoltan's most ardent supporter, as well as his mentor. Zoltan started issuing orders, a method we weren't used to. We didn't discuss matters; he just issued his decrees from on high.

For example, one day he called me in to his office. Zoltan was perusing a report on our consumer product business, a business anchored by Ziploc bags, Saran Wrap, and Scrubbing Bubbles.

"This business is no good," he mused. "Let's get rid of it. Why don't you sell it off."

I resented that he phrased that as a statement, a command really, rather than a question. "I think the consumer product business has a real future," I replied, and I proceeded to outline that future, how I was going to build it up.

Zoltan dismissed my plans with a wave of his hand. "Just get rid of it." End of conversation; he had said all he wanted to say.

"Let's think about it," I said as I left his office, though I knew he'd finished his thinking on it.

A month or two later, he cornered me in a hallway. "Have you gotten rid of that consumer product business yet?"

"I don't really think we have to sell it."

Zoltan's eyes flashed. "I told you to get rid of it! Why haven't you gotten rid of it?"

"I think we're making a hasty decision here." I again proceeded to tell him why I thought we should hang onto the business.

"I'm not asking you your opinion," he bristled. "I'm telling you what to do: sell it."

I thought selling the business was a horrible decision, so I went underground. I avoided Zoltan as much as possible, and when he inquired into the matter, I told him I was still looking into it, trying to sell it, though I wasn't, and had no intentions of doing so.

The same thing happened with the pharmaceutical business: Zoltan ordered me to sell that, too. Again I disagreed, again Zoltan wouldn't listen and put some trust in his management team, and again I refused to sell.

Zoltan had some numbers to back his decisions to sell these businesses that neither I nor anyone else in the company had seen before. It turns out he had a spy in the controller's department. A subversive atmosphere began to permeate the corporate office. Zoltan set people up against each other, put people on edge, made them suspicious of the people around them, guys they had teamed up with for years.

Zoltan ran things differently in other ways as well. He brought his valet from Europe with him; this man would run errands, serve dinner, and drive for him and his family. Nobody else had a driver. It's safe to say that Zoltan Merszei was not your typical Dow executive.

⌘

For my part, I had a fabulous job as president of Dow US. This was by far the largest operating job within the company. I loved all aspects of the job. Though I had a lot of experience at Dow by this time, I had never been part of the US staff; I had always been on either the international side or the financial end. The sentiment with many in Dow US was that the international stuff was monkey business, that we were wasting the resources we had earned in the US to build up an international presence. So I really couldn't have had any other job in Dow US except for that of president, with that being pushed from Ben Branch and others at the top.

One of the first things I did after becoming president of Dow US, then, was to hold a meeting with the top 50 people. I gave my "Paul Oreffice from A to Z" speech, telling them how I thought, what I liked, what I didn't like, trying to give people an insight into who I was and how I operated. I won't share all 26 points here, but here are some of the highlights of that speech:

- Stand up for what you think is right, but make sure the facts are on your side. I am usually well documented in an argument.
- I am an intuitive manager and will sometimes jump at something before it's completely ironed out. I might make some wrong decisions, but will lose fewer opportunities because of a lack of decision.
- I am willing to take risks. A manager is always in danger of failure but greater danger exists when fear dominates thought and action.
- I believe strongly in delegating responsibilities.
- I trust people—until they cross me.
- I hate the word *impossible*. Most "impossible" things are just a little more difficult to achieve.
- If you want to make me mad, just try one of these:
    1. Treat me as though I were stupid by humoring me.
    2. Doubt my word when I make a positive statement.
    3. Say, "You're the boss," instead of arguing with me.
    4. Try to get something done by going around me when you know I'm against an idea.
- Once I make a decision I will stand by it, and if I tell you it's your decision to make, I won't second-guess you.
- I do not tolerate drunks. Booze is one of the worst problems in the business world.
- If you want to impress me, keep it short. I will not read anything over two pages, unless specifically requested by one of you. Monthly reports are to be on one sheet of paper.
- Too much talk is one of the greatest problems in the business world.
- Too much paper is an even greater problem in the business world.
- I believe in timing. The best idea is no good at the wrong time.
- I am a gambler, and if the odds are right I like to play.
- I am a low-pressure salesman. This builds long-term relationships.

- Flexibility is a very important word in the English language. I like to think I'm a flexible person.
- It isn't too difficult to sell me a bill of goods *once*, but that once can cost you later.
- I believe in working hard and playing hard. That means total dedication to hobbies.
- I am a very good friend but a lousy enemy. I become an enemy only to those people who are dishonest with me.
- I am a competitor. I don't believe in the Olympic motto that the important thing is to participate. *I always play to win.*

Many people told me later that they appreciated the speech, as it helped them to get to know me.

I wanted all Dow US employees to get to know me. I set a goal of meeting with at least 5,000 of our people a year at a minimum (at that time there were about 30,000 people in Dow US). I actually reached over 10,000 every single year. I was not some guy they didn't know just sitting up in the main office.

My biggest problem at first was to get managers to understand that I wanted to meet with all Dow employees, not just the top levels. I wanted to communicate with them directly, to eliminate the filters. At all sessions, whether with the whole staff of the sales office or a cafeteria full of people at a manufacturing division, I spoke for a few minutes and then answered questions. It was very well received.

∞

Zoltan's reign became untenable for me and for many others. Earl Barnes and I took a flight together, during which we discussed our concerns. Unbeknownst to me, Earl went back and talked to Ben, Ted, and Carl, who were still very influential in the company. "I think Paul Oreffice is so unhappy that he's going to leave the company," Earl said.

I never considered leaving Dow, but it's true I was quite unhappy. Carl met with me and prodded me on how things were and how I felt about how the company was being run.

"Do you want me to tell the truth or do you want me to smile?" I asked.

"I want the truth," Carl said. So I gave it to him.

Ted and Ben did the same with other people. Merszei's leadership methods were called into question by most people, and our former troika visited with Zoltan to discuss those issues. They told him a lot of people were unhappy and that he had to change his ways. He waved them off. It was clear that Zoltan considered the troika old men who no longer knew what they were talking about. They were wrapped up in the history of the company; he was, he figured, the key player in the company's future. But Zoltan agreed to have a survey done of the top 40 or so people at Dow, to see how they felt things were going.

The survey's results were devastating, but Zoltan dismissed them, calling them picky and inconsequential.

The board of directors didn't see it as inconsequential. What followed was an intense, emotionally-charged series of meetings that drained everyone involved. Near the end of it, the board voted overwhelmingly against Zoltan remaining as CEO. Zoltan got up and left the room as soon as he heard the results.

The board's work wasn't finished. They had deposed one CEO, and they had to name another. So each of the board members was interviewed as to who should be running the show. Two people's names kept coming up most often: mine and Clyde Boyd's. Interestingly, Zoltan had set Clyde and me against each other not long before this, but Clyde and I had seen what was happening and worked things out.

I had by far the most support, and Clyde was second. Based on that, the board was about to name me, but I put a halt to the informality. "No," I said. "I won't do it unless the vote is unanimous."

So another vote was taken, and it was unanimous. After the vote, I was congratulated by the board. People were exhausted, relieved, and happy. A celebratory feel replaced the intense mood that had prevailed for the previous seven days. Although it happened in April 1978, we came to call it "the 7 days in May" after a well-known movie of a few years earlier. As I was being congratulated, I thought back to the words my father spoke to me 15 years earlier, shortly before he passed away: *I'm only sorry that I won't be able to see you when you're running Dow. I see it clearly, as clearly as I see you right now, right here.*

And, for a moment, I saw my father clearly as well. I nodded, far away now from those around me, and had to fight back tears as I silently said, "I made it, Papá. I really made it." Carl Gerstacker and Ben Branch had shown great confidence in me over the years, but the first man to do so was my father, and I had gained much of my confidence from him.

Unfortunately, there was some fallout from those "seven days in May." In a big mistake, Ben Branch, who felt responsible for bringing in Zoltan in the first place, gave up his chairman of the board position so that Zoltan could remain with the company as a non-executive chairman, without portfolio. I wasn't particularly happy with that setup, but went along with it, because Dow didn't normally wash its dirty linen in public. Ben should have remained chairman, and we should have ousted Zoltan. As it was, Zoltan kept trying to run things, and Carl Gerstacker and I had a couple of talks with him, reminding him that he had no executive capacity and that he would have to leave if he kept trying to give orders. Zoltan claimed to understand, but he never stopped. Within a few months, Armand Hammer, the head of Occidental Petroleum, hired Zoltan, and the Zoltan Merszei chapter in The Dow Chemical Company was over.

※

Carl Gerstacker, Ted Doan, and I had tried to talk Ben out of giving up his position as chairman. But he refused, saying that was the only way to do it.

The day after Ben had resigned his position, he came to my office in tears. "Well, everybody gets something out of this but old Benjie," he said.

"But Ben, we tried to talk you out of resigning."

"It's too late. It's over now."

Although it was his idea, Ben felt alienated about how it had ended. That made me sad. He had been my role model, my teacher, and a friend for me. He had played a tremendously important role in the company, fueling its growth with his insight and vision, and I had great respect and admiration for him, but he had tied my hands. And when he walked out the door, he never returned. He didn't come back for stockholder meetings, he didn't return to the office at all, except for, at great coaxing on my part, Ted Doan's retirement party. He left Dow feeling resentful and unappreciated, in a manner most unfitting for one of his stature.

※

As CEO, I soon learned that setting priorities was essential. Everyone wants your time, and if you don't prioritize, you wind up spending a lot of time on less important matters. To do it properly, you need a top administrative assistant, and starting in 1966, I had three terrific ladies working with me. Dorothy Garrett was my right hand in Coral Gables, and Dorothy Bolenbaugh and Pat Sibbald played those roles in Midland. "Little Pat"—all five-foot-zero of her—was with me for most of my time as CEO, and she had to be tougher than nails with those in and out of the company that wanted my time. These three ladies all became friends and confidantes. The day Pat started with me I said, "Pat, if we are to work together, there can be no secrets between us. You will have very sensitive information in your possession and you will know all about me as a person. If I ever have a girlfriend, you will know about it." When, many years later, I met JoAnn Pepper, my current wife, Pat was the first to know.

∞

Even though I had become CEO, I was still a salesman at heart. I thoroughly enjoyed making sales calls when I was CEO, and often was called in if there was a problem. I particularly recall visiting one of our biggest plastics customers near Chicago. Their CEO was a crusty old guy who greeted me with, "I am about to tell Dow to go to hell." I let him vent for about 20 minutes about how we had missed some delivery, we had some quality problems, and so on. At the end of his tirade, I said, "We will take care of all that. But tell me, what other problems does your company have?" He explained how environmentalists had given them some specific problems and I interjected, "We have a real specialist in the field. Can we help you?" I then asked to use his phone and called our expert to come down the next morning. I followed the same routine to solve some of their personnel problems.

This CEO and I parted on good terms, and ten days later he called me and said, "Your two experts have solved our two most vexing problems. I love Dow!" Calls like that gave me more satisfaction than a big pay raise.

∞

One thing that I worked hard to change at Dow was a problem that it, like many other large companies, faced: it had become too bureaucratic and centralized. I went about breaking the company into smaller pieces. The geographic organizations were all profit centers, and each country had its own balance sheet. The same was true of product groups. The trick was to keep everyone headed in the same direction while giving them a feeling of owning the particular piece of the company they were associated with.

This, after all, had been my own MO as a young maverick in Europe, South America, and Coral Gables. It had worked for me. Why not for others?

Most multinational companies of whatever nationality are run from a central headquarters, with mostly indigenous people in the top management jobs. We made sure to promote people of all nationalities, and we placed a lot of management abroad. At one time, in fact, Dow's executive committee consisted of two Cuban-born members, one from Bulgaria, a Brit, an Italian, and only two native-born Americans. If you're going to operate throughout the world, you better have people who understand the way of thinking, the mores, and the ways of doing business in the countries you operate in.

⚬⚬

I reinstituted the open-door policy and maintained a managing group of three to five people to run the company. I spent considerable time visiting Dow facilities all over the world and talking with the employees, letting them know my agenda. Because I was fluent in six languages, I could talk directly with them, rather than speak through an interpreter.

When I was named CEO in spring of 1978, I told Carl Gerstacker, "The Dow Chemical Company has repeatedly given me jobs for which I was not totally qualified. They put me in way over my head when they sent me to Brazil as a 28-year-old to start a new company. Then you gave me the Chief Financial Officer's job and I really had no preparation except for a B.S. in chemical engineering. I felt I was out of my depth. Several times you just threw me in the water and said, 'Swim, Paul, swim!' Now, for the first time in my career, I feel I am totally ready for a job." I felt completely qualified and ready to be CEO of The Dow Chemical Company. All the experience I had gained in those other positions prepared me to lead the company.

The first thing I did as CEO was to bring Earl Barnes out of his short retirement to head up all technical aspects of the company. I then asked Bob Lundeen to join us in a three-man management group. Not long after, I worked on bringing Bob Keil back on board. Bob had a checkered history at Dow; he was a tremendous intellect, a fine businessman, and a very talented salesman, but sometimes his ego got in the way. At other times he was too smart for his bosses. I gave him increasingly bigger jobs and soon named him chief financial officer. Bob didn't have experience in finance, but neither had I when Carl named me CFO. Later, Bob became executive vice president, and really my right hand man.

Bob Keil was a challenge. He had his quirks, but he was very smart, he worked hard, and he contributed a great deal to the company. The greatest thing I did, personnel-wise, was to put Bob Keil in a position to succeed, give him room to operate, and manage him according to his needs.

I faced much larger challenges than handling Bob Keil.

It was the late 1970s, and the country had been through one recession a handful of years earlier and was about to enter another, courtesy of the energy crisis. The price of oil had increased threefold, reaching more than $30 a barrel, and all the experts "knew" that it would soon reach $60 to $80 a barrel.

Well, as CEO I had inherited a new major petrochemical project ready to go in Yugoslavia, with similar major projects ready to go in Saudi Arabia, Australia, Canada, and California. Each project required an investment of more than $1 billion.

I knew we couldn't do all those projects. But I also knew that the price of oil wasn't going to continue to go up exponentially, as the experts predicted. If it had, it would have broken the world economy. Something had to give. One day in 1980 I wrote a letter to all Dow managers in which I said, "I decree that the price of oil will not go over $30 a barrel on a regular basis."

I killed several of those projects, because I knew that once the oil prices dropped, we would have lost several billion dollars on them. As the recession hit in full swing in 1980, we entered a rough period for a few years. Contrary to my normal style, I found myself killing off projects rather than building more plants. That approach was dictated by the recession—which was actually more like a depression in the chemical business. Our debt load was higher and our profits were lower.

✂

While shrinking some parts, I needed to expand others. But the next move was another shrinking. In 1980 the part of Dow that made the most money was Dowell, a division servicing oil and gas wells in the US and Canada. We had an international company that we owned jointly with the Schlumberger Company, called Dowell Schlumberger, and Schlumberger had expressed interest in buying half of Dowell, so that Dowell Schlumberger could cover the whole world.

Nobody in Dow wanted to sell half of Dowell. But I knew that Jean Ribaud, the CEO of Schlumberger, wanted this deal very badly. So we initiated a negotiation to sell Schlumberger half of Dowell. It was to be my finest negotiation as CEO.

Schlumberger said half the company was worth somewhere between $200 and $225 million. I sat down with most of my management team—Bob Keil, Hunter Henry, David Rooke, and Keith McKennon. "Guys," I said, "Schlumberger wants to buy half of Dowell for $200 to $225 million. I think we ought to consider it."

To a man they all felt selling Dowell was a lousy idea. It was late in the day and we were making no progress, so I finally said, "Just go home, wash your brain with soap, and come back tomorrow morning at 7:30. Let's sit down then and revisit whether this is a good idea or not."

After sleeping on it, they came back and were not averse to the idea. David Rooke was the lone holdout, but even he said, "If we could get $300 million, we ought to take it." I could have invoked my 51% of the vote, but I preferred to arrive at a consensus rather than dictating what to do. So I was quite pleased that they were open to the idea.

I called Jean Ribaud and said, "Let's talk about it, but you are totally off on the price. I think there are many angles to this that need to be discussed before we can even begin to talk price."

Bob Keil talked with Schlumberger in New York, and as they were reaching agreement on personnel and other details, they brought up the price and told Bob, "Maybe it's worth a little more than we had said before. Maybe $250 million. Why don't you try that on Paul Oreffice?"

Bob came back to Midland and told me what they'd said. I told Bob, "Go back and tell them I kicked you out of my office, that the price is an insult. That I wouldn't even consider it. Just tell them that."

So he did. Bob and I kept playing good guy/bad guy. By coincidence, we found out that our two boards were meeting on the same day, so Jean Ribaud and I agreed that it would be desirable to have an agreement on price that we could take to our boards. I had already talked with the Dow board, and everyone felt that $300 million was a great price for half of Dowell, that we should leap at that amount if it was offered.

Well, a week before the board meetings, Ribaud came up to $300 million. To his astonishment, I refused. "Jean, we can't go for less than $450 million," I said. Two days before the board meetings, Ribaud called back.

"I think $300 million is the most we can pay," he said.

"Jean, I already told you, we can't accept less than $450 million, not one penny less. That's the approval I have from my board, and I can't do anything about it."

We talked awhile and he finally said, "Okay, how about $330 million?"

"Jean, you don't understand. I said $450 million."

"Well, why don't you think about it and call me back?"

"Jean, if I hang up this phone, the whole deal is off."

Bob Keil and Wayne Hancock, our general counsel, who were sitting in my office during this conversation, were completely stunned. Jean and I went through this routine seven or eight times, and each time he crept up in his price, to $350 million, $370 million, $400 million, $420 million. I kept refusing. Keil and Hancock kept passing me notes: *Take it. Are you crazy? Just take it.*

Finally, Ribaud went up to $430 million.

"You know what I said, Jean."

Keil wrote me a note that said, *Why don't you split the difference?* I wrote back: *I want him to suggest that.*

After some more conversation—which seemed to take an eternity—Ribaud said, "Why don't we split the difference?"

"My board is going to kick me out," I replied, "but, okay, let's do $440 million. You've got a deal. Let's take it to our boards on Thursday."

My shirt was soaked through when I finished that conversation. My board had been happy with $300 million, and Ribaud had offered that amount, and here we had $440 million—though with each passing moment, I was running the risk of having the whole deal fall through.

After I hung up, Wayne Hancock said, "I felt sorry for Mr. Ribaud. It must be difficult to negotiate with a sphinx." Shortly after the deal, oil and gas prices came down, oil field exploration dried up, and Schlumberger had to shrink Dowell and take a substantial writeoff.

∞

I might have gotten the upper hand in that deal, but that didn't mean anything when it came to dealing with the media. In 1985, *The Wall Street Journal* wrote a story about successful executives and their daughters, and Laura and I were featured in the article. About six months later, an editor from *Glamour* magazine asked me to be only the second man—the first being Henry Kissinger—to write an op-ed piece. The subject was a follow-up to the *WSJ* article on how a busy executive related to his daughter.

I spent a whole Thanksgiving weekend writing and rewriting a piece that I wanted to be just right. I sent the piece in, and a few days later the assistant editor called and said the piece was great and that they had only made some minor changes to conform to their style. I was pleased to hear that—until I saw their edited version.

One of the things I had written was, "After living with a father and a brother who are sports nuts, Laura knows almost as much as her brother and me about sports." Well, one of the "minor" changes was they took the word "almost" out. I told the editor this was wrong, but she insisted it had to be their way or they wouldn't print it. I wouldn't bend, and neither would they, so they scrapped the piece. It was the first time I ran into censorship with an American publication, and it was greatly disappointing.

∞

I mentioned Keith McKennon a bit earlier as part of my management team. When I moved Keith over to run our Government and Public Affairs department, it was one of the greatest personnel moves I ever made. Keith has more common sense than any person I know. We needed a common-sense approach, one that combated the insularity that sometimes seeped into our operations in Midland. Keith brought a new meaning to our relationships with the outside world, particularly with Washington, with the Environmental Protection Agency, and with the outfits and organizations that we needed to work with.

Keith filled another role as well. Because of his extraordinary common sense, I regularly batted ideas around with Keith. He sharpened my ideas and I sharpened his. I used his brain whenever I could, and Keith McKennon quickly became an integral part of my team. Eventually, Keith became the president of Dow US.

Just as things were really clicking professionally for Keith, he underwent a terrible personal period. He attended the Indy 500 in the spring of 1984, and when he returned, he said, "I have a sore back." The Midland doctors gave him some exercises, but they didn't help. In August, he went with me to the Greenbrier Clinic at the Greenbrier resort in the Allegheny Mountains in West Virginia. There, doctors discovered a major lymphoma on the spine. It was inoperable, though doctors operated unsuccessfully on him in Midland. He then went to the Mayo Clinic and underwent severe chemotherapy. There were times when Keith wouldn't sleep for four or five nights in a row because of the treatments and the medicine he was taking. But that didn't stop him from working, from always being in good humor, always smiling, picking up his hairpiece and twirling it around. As he twirled the hairpiece on his fingers, he'd smile and say, "My wife made me get this. Doesn't it look ridiculous?" Keith's spirit, optimism, and ability to sing through his problems were the greatest inspiration I have ever seen within a company.

If it hadn't been for his illness, Keith McKennon would probably have succeeded me as CEO. That didn't work out, but the better news is, he's still alive 20 years after his bout with cancer began. He's not just alive; he's healthy and living life the way he wants to.

∽

One of Dow's greatest strengths was its ability to design, build, and operate large chemical plants better than anybody else. We had a tremendous manufacturing tradition and many superb people helped to generate and maintain that tradition. Three of these stood out especially for me; they were my "technical gurus."

Levi Leathers was a genius chemical engineer from Texas who was recognized worldwide as the best of his era at process technology. He was so passionate about his work that he spent many of his vacations designing improvements at our plants.

David Rooke and Hunter Henry also started in our Texas division and eventually became key members of my management team. They were bright businessmen, honest and sharp, unafraid to voice their opinions. They were my colleagues, my friends, and my confidantes for many years. I never had to worry about "yes men" with either of those two around.

All of these men came out of our Texas division, which encompasses Dow's largest plants in the world. And what a crew they were: tough, hard working, and with a great sense of humor. It was mostly our Texans who went around the world building our manufacturing presence, and they did so magnificently. They were known as the "Dow Texas Mafia" and usually stuck together. I was privileged to work with them and to become an honorary member of the Dow Texas Mafia.

∽

In my tenure as CEO—which lasted from 1978 through 1987—I felt it was vital for Dow to expand from being strictly a chemical and plastics company. We had a base in pharmaceuticals, but that was one area that I felt we needed to expand in a major way. As a first step, we acquired Merrell, the pharmaceutical division of Richardson-Merrell, and Merrell Dow became the fastest-growing part of the company. It was the beginning of making Dow into a major pharmaceutical player.

I pushed product diversification throughout my years as CEO, diversification that didn't take away from our mainstay in chemicals and plastics, but that supplemented and augmented it. Product diversification was the primary stamp of my time as CEO. There were pressures and temptations to get out of basic chemicals and plastics, as Monsanto and DuPont did, but I'm glad we didn't, because they have remained very strong, the company's staples.

When we bought Merrell, the auction closed at 5 P.M. on a Friday. I sent our bid in at 4:45 P.M., $260 million, which was considerably lower than the executive committee thought we should offer. Perry Ruddick of Smith Barney, our investment banker, called at 10 P.M. to let me know we got it. Someone else had offered $260 million as well, but Richardson had decided to go with us. "Great," I said. "Let's close tomorrow."

"But tomorrow's Saturday. no offices are open on Saturday."

"Find one that will open, get some lawyers there, and let's close. I'll be there tomorrow morning. Call me back as soon as you make the arrangements."

So they opened up some offices at the Chase Manhattan Bank in downtown New York, and lawyers were there for both sides, and we signed the final agreement. At one point I said, "Folks, I've got to hurry because I've got to get back to Midland. Ronald Reagan is going to make a speech at the Dow hangar, and I have to be back for that by 2 P.M." Reagan, of course, was a presidential candidate at the time.

I flew into Midland with just moments to spare, and as the Dow plane approached the hangar, the crowd surged, because they thought it was Reagan's plane. They were a bit disappointed to see it was only me—but I was glad to be back on time.

∞

Another thing I'm proud of is the human element: during my tenure, we went from 63,000 employees to 52,000 without a single layoff. We accomplished this mainly through attrition. I think it's scandalous today how companies lay so many people off. How can you expect allegiance from your employees when you don't show them any yourself? It's no wonder that so many people jump ship nowadays.

I rewarded employees based on their performances, and made sure we didn't just reward the managers. I changed the whole compensation package to tie it more to the performance of the company overall and to the group, and tied many more people into the rewards. Before I began as CEO, about 150 to 200 people received stock options in the company. More than 2,200 received options every year when I was CEO.

I learned from Ben Branch to manage by "walking around." I popped into people's offices, I talked to the secretaries, and I had lunch in the company's cafeteria every day. More often than not, I took my tray to a table with three, four, or five employees. It's amazing how much you learn from the rumor mill this way.

I didn't do things by the numbers. I could be soft, but I could also be the worst SOB that you could imagine if you crossed me, if you weren't truthful with me. I did what I thought was best for the company, for the employees, for the shareholders. I used to run shareholders meetings, attended by a couple of thousand shareholders, by showing charts and talking about results for five minutes, and then I'd step out from behind the podium and talk off the cuff about new products and company developments. I wouldn't use a teleprompter; I'd just walk around the stage and talk. When CEOs from other companies would hear about this they'd say in amazement, "And your lawyers let you do that?" They were just as astonished when I told them, "I never asked our lawyers."

∞

Like every executive, I had my share of controversies, and I never shied away from them, or from talking about them, when appropriate. I learned from my father that you don't run from confrontation; you face it. You don't stop speaking the truth when doing so might get you in trouble.

Jane Fonda spoke in the fall of 1977 to students at Central Michigan University, an address for which she was paid $3,500. Her lecture was on "Politics in Film," but during it she made a number of critical remarks about Dow: we were, according to her, exploiting people, polluting the earth, and what have you. This is the same Fonda, of course, who told students at the University of Miami, "I would think that if you understood what communism was you would hope, you would pray on bended knees, that communism would someday become our form of government." And this is the same Fonda who, not long after those comments, was photographed in

North Vietnam, posing behind a gun that was used to down American planes.

I was livid. Dow had contributed $73,000 to Central Michigan the previous year. I wrote a private letter to Central Michigan University president Harold Abel:

> While inviting Ms. Fonda to your campus is your prerogative, I consider it our prerogative and obligation to make certain our funds are never again used to support people intent upon destruction of freedom. Therefore, effective immediately, support of any kind from the Dow Chemical Company . . . has been stopped, and will not resume until we are convinced our dollars are not expended in supporting those who would destroy us.

The very funds that Dow contributed to Central Michigan were a result of the free enterprise system that Fonda saw as so evil. I ended the letter by saying that if Central Michigan really believed in freedom of speech, they should even out the scales by allowing me to speak to the student body and paying me the same honorarium that Jane Fonda received. I would contribute the honorarium to an organization that existed to support free enterprise.

Nothing happened for a few days. Then my letter somehow got to the press. The incident received national attention. And I began to take a lot of heat, because people thought I wanted to curb free speech. The media didn't seem to care that Jane Fonda was a communist sympathizer, or to understand my point in that context.

Zoltan Merszei was still CEO at the time; I was president of Dow US. Zoltan backed me at first, but as the uproar started, he backed down and chastised me for writing the letter and putting Dow in a bad light.

Well, I got about 2,000 letters from all over the country, and all but about 80 supported my stance. I had spoken for a lot of people.

Central Michigan did give me a chance to speak to their students about a year later. I arrived to a jam-packed auditorium. They had to hold up the start for awhile to put loudspeakers outside the auditorium so people could hear out there. As I waited to go on, it was obvious that the students had an organized leftist group occupying the middle of the auditorium, and as I was introduced the reception was decidedly cool.

I took my coat and tie off, rolled up my sleeves, and began talking. I talked about the free enterprise system and the good that it did for this country, and I contrasted that to how communism would reduce the freedoms that we had fought to earn and now enjoyed. I talked for about 20 minutes, and then I fielded questions for about an hour and a half, most of them from hecklers shouting accusations about Agent Orange and free speech. Agent Orange was the US government's name for an herbicide that was normally used to clear pastures. Our military used it as a defoliant in the Vietnam War. It was manufactured by Dow and other companies under orders from the government.

An amazing thing happened during that Q&A session. As I kept my cool and answered the hecklers evenly and reasonably, the heckling began to die down. When the evening was over, I got one of the biggest standing ovations I've ever had in my life. There were still a core of hecklers that were going to be against me, no matter what, but the majority of the auditorium was packed with people who were willing to listen. And once my side was heard, once the facts on both sides were revealed, the audience turned in my favor.

By the end of the evening I was drained, but I was happy that I had done it. It had not been an easy night. I was proud of myself, proud of standing up for my principles and for the company. I didn't really care what timid people thought, because I knew I had done the right thing, and I knew I had done it well.

In the ensuing years, I received several hundred copies of letters written by alumni to their universities. These letters were written to withhold support because their universities had paid Jane Fonda to speak there. Evidently I had hit a nerve with the "silent majority."

⨯

That was not my first run-in with college students. In 1969, with the antiwar protests still going strong on college campuses, I was invited to speak to about 1,000 business students at the University of Miami. Two days before I was to speak, the president of the university called and said students were threatening to demonstrate against me because Dow made napalm, which was being used in the Vietnam War. He gave me an out if I wanted one. I told him that nothing was going to stop me from speaking, but that I would like to meet with a delegation of the demonstrators after the speech to fully discuss the issue.

When I arrived at the auditorium, it was full, and I noticed a lot of students standing in the back. I also noticed that they all looked very big.

After my speech I learned that those guys in back were all football players brought in to help quell any troubles.

Two days later, at my office, I received a delegation composed of four students and three professors. I listened to their accusations and countered every argument. They thought that Dow had invented napalm; I showed them data that napalm was first used by the Germans in World War I. To their accusation that we were warmongers and profiteers, I proved to them that we made almost no profit but were operating under a mandatory order from the Department of Defense. I added, "Even if we didn't have a mandatory order, as long as we have American kids fighting a war we will do our best to supply them with what they need, whether that's pharmaceuticals or napalm."

At the end of the meeting the professors were unconvinced, but the students were downright mad at the misinformation they had been supplied by their teachers!

∞

I didn't believe in misinformation or in being dishonest, and I didn't have any qualms about stating my opinion. These traits developed as a result of growing up in a dictatorial regime, where misinformation and dishonesty abounded and where you could get into serious trouble for expressing an opinion that ran contrary to the state's views.

In 1986, Ralph Nader interviewed me for a book he wrote with William Taylor titled *The Big Boys: Power & Position in American Business*. In the Winter 1986 issue of *Best of Business* magazine, he was asked how I was as an interviewee. He said, "He was the toughest interview. You couldn't break through his response strategy, which was to lay bare his ideology. Oreffice went directly to declaring, 'This is what I believe.' Where do you go after that? And he was disarming. Just when you thought you had him typecast on foreign policy, he'd say something like, 'Yes, the United States did exploit Latin America.'"

∞

In late 1987, we had a bit of a run-in with General Electric. Jack Welch, widely—and rightfully—recognized as one of America's best CEOs of the last half century, was chairman of GE at the time, and earlier in his career he had been the head of GE Plastics. Jack and I had become good friends and business associates.

Dow is the world's largest producer of plastic resins, but when it came to polycarbonates we were a start-up competitor to GE, the dominant producer. In October 1987 an internal GE Plastics publication had an insulting piece about Dow that finished with "We will be harsh with them. What do you do when you see a cockroach? I do the same." It was signed by Uwe, their sales manager.

Keith McKennon, then president of Dow US, wrote Jack Welch saying, in part, "It is difficult for me for me to believe the enclosed garbage represents the legacy Jack Welch intended to leave at GE Plastics."

The response from Jack was immediate. "The first thing I want to do is apologize for our bad manners," he wrote. "Dow is a longtime friend of GE, and while you and I haven't had a chance to meet, I have been an unabashed fan of Paul Oreffice for many years. As I have told everyone, he represents the best of what an American CEO is all about, and our company and I would do nothing to in any way denigrate Paul or Dow."

∽

I was very lucky throughout my career at Dow. I came into a company founded by a great man, Herbert H. Dow, a company that had the courage and foresight to go international at a time when that was uncommon, a company that offered me many opportunities for growth and advancement. I had the good fortune to work in many countries for Dow, to begin and oversee many businesses for it, and to eventually rise to the top, as my father had said I would. With another company, my early maverick ways would have landed me in trouble. With another company, I wouldn't have been given the jobs I was given, because I didn't have the "proper schooling."

I was fortunate to come in at a time when Dow was, due to the efforts of many fine people, on the rise. During my years at Dow, we went from the fifth-largest chemical company in the world to the largest. This expansion began before my time, and I continued the efforts.

Bob Keil, the supposedly hard-to-get-along-with and hard-to-manage brain, the one who had gotten himself almost fired from Dow before I brought him back for many more fruitful years, retired in 1991. I planned his retirement party, and afterward he wrote me a glowing letter thanking me for everything—including the last 15 years that we had worked together. At the end, Bob said, *For me, it was a great time to stop. I wouldn't have had it any other way. It sure was a helluva trip while it lasted. I can't think of anyone I would rather have taken it with.*

Those are my sentiments precisely—not just about Bob Keil, but about working at The Dow Chemical Company. As my parents had told me many years before, I had embarked on a great adventure. And what an adventure it was.

∞

CHAPTER TWELVE

Only in America

On December 1, 1992, having just turned 65 years young, I retired from The Dow Chemical Company. Other than my stint in the Army and my brief stay at Seagram's, I spent my whole career with Dow. My final board meeting took place a few weeks before I retired. I opened my remarks to the board this way:

> *So the day has come and I'm ready for it. Believe it or not, I'm ready to retire from this great company that has been my life for almost 40 years. But, I must admit, it's a very emotional moment. And, it's possible that on the second Thursday in January I'll be fidgety thinking of you meeting here without me. It's also possible that I won't think of you at all as I bask in the Arizona sun.*

∞

As I approached retirement I tried to encapsulate the factors that had allowed me to succeed well beyond my wildest dreams. I came up with 10 such factors, and I mention them in hopes that they will help others.

1. It happened in America. Only in America could an immigrant be given the opportunity to become the CEO of one of the country's leading corporations.
2. It happened at Dow. I was lucky to work for a company that believed in entrepreneurship and tolerated my maverick ways. I took a lot of

risks that could have ended my career but I always thought that they were worthwhile risks. Intelligent risk-taking always involves a potential reward that is worth the risk

3. I believed in people. A large company has a lot of "hidden" human resources. Making sure that we discovered talented people early and gave them the proper assignments became a passion with me. That's why I called myself "The Phantom Personnel Director."

4. I believed in motivation. You cannot overestimate the importance of highly motivated people creating a better whole. While management gets all the glory, I was and am convinced that the real strength comes from the guts of the organization. Keeping employees motivated is the key to success and I acted accordingly.

5. I believed in technology. Discovering and making the best products was a great motivator. "We are in business to make products that the people of the world need and to do so better and cheaper than anybody else" became my motto.

6. I believed in numbers. Numbers don't lie. I became very good with numbers and they in turn became my friends.

7. I believed in listening. Communication experts talk of oral and written communication and forget the important third leg of this stool: *listening*. As my longtime colleague Bob Kincaid used to say, "You never learn anything with your mouth open." I kept mine shut at the appropriate times and did a lot of listening.

8. I believed in second chances. The only way to make no mistakes is to do nothing. I made sure our people knew that there was nothing wrong with making a mistake as long as you learned from it and didn't repeat it.

9. I believed in the American system. I learned early on that free enterprise is much better than government edict. I have spent the rest of my life living it and defending it.

10. I believed in learning from others. The foundation of what success I had was created by taking from some extraordinary role models:
    - From my father's independence of spirit, fearless idealism, and dedication to a cause.
    - From my mother's indomitable will to fight and overcome long odds to get things done.
    - From the *prefetto* of Venice, who risked his life to save my father's.
    - From Ben Branch's optimism, inspirational management style, and moral rectitude.
    - From Carl Gerstacker's brilliant innovativeness, willingness to take a risk, and total dedication to Dow.

❧

It had been, as Bob Keil had put it, a helluva trip. While working for Dow, I had lived in Zurich and Milan, in Sao Paulo and Bilbao, in Coral Gables and finally back in Midland. Dr. Herbert H. Dow founded The Dow Chemical Company in Midland because of the abundance of underground saltwater in the area, from which he extracted chlorides, iodine, magnesium, and bromides. Midland was the perfect place for the company to be headquartered, and the perfect place for me to be. The company took on the ethical standards of a small Midwestern town, and that had a lot to do with our success. We lived right next to our plants, and that shaped our growth as leaders in health, safety, and environmental matters. If there was pollution, it wasn't affecting *those guys*; it was affecting *our families.*

And I want to speak about my own family for a few moments. As I mentioned earlier, I married Franca Ruffini on May 26, 1956. Franca had many good qualities, but she had trouble trusting people's motives. For example, my parents came to see us off at Genoa where we boarded the Andria Doria, bound for the United States. They gave Franca some heirloom jewelry shortly before we got on board. Later, when we were alone on the ship, she said, "Why do they hate me?"

"What do you mean?"

"They wouldn't give me such expensive jewelry if they didn't want to buy me off."

Franca's mistrust of people didn't end with that incident. After we had been in Midland for a couple of weeks, and had been warmly received by many people, Franca said to me, "These people are false."

"What do you mean?"

"Well, why would anyone be that nice to me? They must have some kind of hidden agenda."

I don't blame her. She was a product of parents who split up before she was born, and was raised by two competing families.

Franca gave me two wonderful children. And to the outside world, we had a perfect marriage. This was important, in part because I felt I was a role model at Dow. My three predecessors as CEO had had pretty messy divorces, and I wanted to show you could run a company and have a good family life too. Family has always been of utmost importance to me, and it always will be.

∞

My two kids, Laura and Andy, are now in their forties. I can truly say that from the time they were born in Sao Paulo until now they have never given me cause to worry. They were a joy as children and they are intelligent and caring adults now. We are very good friends.

Laura is 16 months older and when they were kids she was the leader. On trips, Andy would only eat what Laura recommended. It was also on trips that I started giving them arithmetical problems to solve in their head, much as my father had given me. Although Laura was and is a whiz with numbers and was two grades ahead, the competition was pretty even. They both now tell me that they didn't necessarily enjoy it then but that it has been useful as life progressed.

I appeared a number of years ago on CNN's *Pinnacle* on a segment featuring CEOs. I was asked, "Name your greatest achievement in the last year." I spontaneously answered, "That my kids who are in their upper teens still like to go on vacation with me."

Not much has changed. I still enjoy seeing my kids and their families as often as possible.

∞

A year after we moved to Michigan, Andy announced that he was going out for Little League baseball. He had just turned 10 and was big and klutzy for his age. I took him to a sporting goods store and bought him a first baseman's mitt. He had not played much before, and his first season was a disaster. He couldn't hit and his fielding wasn't much better. At season's end he was despondent, so I said, "Things don't come easily in life, you know. You have to work at it. If you want me to, I will work with you every day that I am here, but you have to ask me." I got a backstop and 100 tennis balls and every afternoon when I came home we worked on his hitting and fielding.

The next season Andy was one of the leading hitters in the league and was a superb fielder. It was a great lesson for him. It showed him what hard work can accomplish.

∞

Andy and I have always been close. We lived in Coral Gables when the Miami Dolphins were formed, and I started taking Andy to the games when he was six years old. In those days he was embarrassed by his father jumping up and down and screaming for the team. Over the years, we've gone to Dolphin games all over the country—and while he's normally reserved and shy, he's worse than I am at games. In fact, the only time he really goes wild is at sporting events.

Another bonding experience for Andy and me was tennis. Andy became a very good tennis player, and he continues to improve, even in his 40s. When he was 17, he asked me to partner with him in a tournament in Saginaw, Michigan. I was floored, because it wasn't a father-son tournament. But he still wanted to play with me. And we did all right.

Andy has always been shy. He might have been shyer as a kid than I was, though that's a tossup. He rarely dated in high school. He followed in my footsteps to Purdue, and as he started dating around, I was given the opportunity to meet most of his girlfriends—some of whom I didn't think a great deal of. A few years after he graduated, he moved to North Carolina and started dating a young woman named Jamie Sciarrino. As soon as I met Jamie, I told Andy, "*This* is the girl for you." And I was right. They have a wonderful marriage and two great kids.

✂

As I started to do better in life, I wanted to put something back into society. So I took some of my Dow shares and created a foundation to support medical research and patient care. Through this I became active in the National Parkinson Foundation, of which I am now chairman of the board.

I met JoAnn Pepper, the niece of former Florida Senator Claude Pepper, at a pre-gala dinner for the National Parkinson Foundation in February 1989. I had been giving the foundation money and served on the foundation's Board of Governors, along with folks like Dick Clark and Bob Hope. Claude Pepper was on the board as well, and he introduced me to his niece JoAnn. As she and I shook hands, a bolt of electricity went through me. It was something I had never felt before, and it seemed like the current lit up my smile and charged my body. I was smitten.

The next night, at the gala dinner, I sat at the head table and was having a nice conversation with Delores Hope, Bob Hope's wife, but I kept glancing at the table where JoAnn was sitting. When the dancing started, I walked over to her and asked her to dance. After the dinner, we went out to Tobacco Road, the oldest bar in Miami, she in her resplendent evening gown and me in my tuxedo, and we had a beer, sitting amidst kids in tee-shirts and jeans. But I didn't feel out of place; I was with JoAnn.

JoAnn awoke in me feelings that I didn't know existed. I had never been unfaithful in my 33 years of marriage, and I never imagined I would be. But I had never been in love like this, and after awhile I told Franca about JoAnn. Franca was stunned, but she accepted the news fairly well. In August 1995, Franca and I were divorced, and two months later, JoAnn and I were married.

And I have never been happier. The electricity that was there that first night is still running strong. She is a giving, loving person, a wonderful mate, very unselfish. We go everywhere together; we travel extensively and we've only been apart five nights in the first nine years of our marriage. She loves my family and they all love her.

In fact, when I first told Laura that I was getting divorced and remarried, she said, "Dad, why did you wait so long? You deserve to be happy." Those were magical words for me to hear. JoAnn gets along wonderfully with Laura and her husband, Jon Jennison, and their twins, Alexander and Andrew, and with Andy and his wife, Jamie, and their son, Kyle and daughter, Jillian. Kyle was born less than two weeks after JoAnn and I were married. We love getting together, and do so as often as we can.

∞

If I was nervous telling Laura about my wedding plans, she had been just as nervous in telling me about some plans of her own several years earlier. She came to our home in Scottsdale and asked Franca and me to sit down. Laura is normally a very headstrong woman, but at this moment she was hesitant and anxious.

"Mom, Dad, I need to tell you something," she said, and she cleared her throat as we waited. "Jon and I intend on getting married someday, but for now, we are going to live together."

I glanced at Franca and saw she didn't look pleased. I immediately swung my attention to my daughter and gave her a warm smile. "Good. Good for you, for both of you!" I said. Laura let out a big sigh of relief.

"I wasn't sure how you'd respond," she said. "I thought you might be mad, or shocked."

"Mad? I'm ecstatic!" I said, hugging her. To be honest, the biggest surprise was that Laura planned to get married at all. She was a businesswoman; she was working for Citibank in Arizona at the time, and she had let it be known that she likely would never get married, and if she did, she would *never* have—in her words—any brats running around the house.

Well, she was half right. She did get married, but her twin sons are not brats.

∽

One day in 1999, when Laura and Jon were living in Portland, Oregon, Jon had a seizure. Laura called 911, and Jon was rushed off to a local hospital, where doctors discovered he had a tumor on his brain. Jon was told the tumor was inoperable because of its location.

Laura called Vic Sonnino, my nephew, who is a neurosurgeon, and subsequently sent him the scans. Vic immediately said, "The best brain surgeon in the world is Dr. Ray Sawaya at MD Anderson Cancer Center in Houston. Dr. Sawaya examined Jon and said, "Of course we can operate on him." A large tumor was removed on December 3, 1999, and Jon has been fine ever since.

∽

So what do I do in retirement? I stay active. JoAnn and I travel a lot, as I said. We maintain homes in Saratoga Springs, New York, Paradise Valley, Arizona, and Lake Tahoe, Nevada. We go to Florida to visit her family and friends. I'm active physically, too. I do 200 sit-ups and 100 pushups a day, and I play a lot of tennis.

I have a land development company with a great partner, Lowell Williamson. His wife is Dorothy McGuire of the famous McGuire sisters singing group. They have become dear and wonderful friends. Their son, David, runs the company, and we're busy with some very interesting projects.

And I have served, and still serve, on several boards. Besides chairing the National Parkinson Foundation board, I am on the visiting board of the MD Anderson Cancer Center, as I was quite impressed with how the center responded to Jon's situation, and I serve on several for-profit company boards as well.

Throughout my Dow career I was very selective in accepting outside board positions. In 1979 I joined the board of Connecticut General Insurance and remained on it through the merger with INA to create CIGNA. In all I spent 19 years on this board and learned a lot about insurance. In 1987 I joined the board of Morgan Stanley and in the eight years I served on it I got a real education about investment banking from the inside, rather than just as a client.

In 1983 I joined Nortel's board and served on it for 15 years. Their communications technology really opened my mind to the infinite possibilities in the field. When I retired, I put two conditions on Nortel's having a retirement dinner for me. First, there would be no cigars. Cigar smoke usually made me leave dinners early. Second, I wanted Louise Smith sitting next to me. Louise was a very nice lady who took care of all the directors' needs, from hotels to transportation to secretarial work, but when a dinner was in progress she was expected to sit outside the dining room twiddling her thumbs while we ate. Nortel complied, and I enjoyed a cigar-free dinner with Louise at my side.

In December 1980 I was invited to Washington with other business executives to meet some of the people that were expected to be in the administration of newly-elected President Ronald Reagan. At the first coffee break I rose from my seat and someone tapped me on the shoulder. I turned and this man said, "Do you know you are my role model?" Before I could express my surprise, he stuck his hand out and while shaking mine said, "I am Roberto Goizueta of The Coca Cola Company. You were born under a dictatorship and so was I; you had to run away from your country, Italy, and so did I, from Cuba; you studied chemical engineering and so did I; you went to work for a large American company and so did I; you've made it to the top of your company and I will one of these days."

Of course, Roberto became the legendary CEO of Coke about a year later, and shortly after that he asked me to serve on his board. I was on the Coca Cola board for 18 years and it was a great experience. My only real regret is that I couldn't talk Roberto into quitting his smoking habit; he died of lung cancer at an early age.

Coke and Pepsi were mortal enemies and didn't talk to each other. Through tennis I got friendly with Pepsi's CEO, Wayne Callaway, and, after checking with both Roberto and Wayne, I introduced them to each other at a meeting of the Business Council, which was comprised of CEOs of major companies across the country. It was the first time ever that the CEOs of the two companies had spoken.

Membership in the Business Council was by invitation only, and it had always galled me that Dow's insularity had kept us out while DuPont, Carbide, and Monsanto had several generations of CEOs who were members.

Another national organization that Dow was active in was the MCA, the Manufacturing Chemists Association. The MCA was not much more than a good old boy's club when I was asked to join the board by Jim Affleck, the CEO of American Cyanamide. I told Jim, "I will only if we can reform the association and make it more useful for our industry."

"Why, God bless you, that's exactly what I want to do," Jim replied. Together with a group of like-thinking people, we transformed the MCA into the CMA—the Chemical Manufacturer's Association—and converted it into a powerful lobbying arm for the industry. And a few years later I became chairman of the CMA, an event that gave rise to one of the most serious and at the same time most laughable moments of my life.

Congress was discussing enactment of the Superfund, a federal fund financed by government and industry to clean up and monitor hazardous waste sites. Superfund was a good idea that went astray and became one of the largest boondoggles in American history. I received a call from Doug Costle, the head of the Environmental Protection Agency at the time, and he said, "Paul, you are single-handedly standing in the way of the US Congress passing Superfund. I need your help." The thought that I was single-handedly controlling 535 Senators and Congressmen was ludicrous, but it at least made me laugh. If what he said was true I would have been the most powerful man in the US.

When I would not give in to the EPA's demands, they found a friend in our industry in Irving Shapiro, CEO of DuPont, who helped pass the bill despite his own people's objections.

The CMA, the Business Roundtable, and the Business Council were forums for business discussion and for contact with the government. I always considered these associations as important for Dow and took them very seriously. I learned much from all my board activities and applied what I learned to my Dow life.

❧

Another organization I have spent a lot of time with is The American Enterprise Institute, the Washington think tank that promotes free enterprise and democratic capitalism. AEI has more brains per capita than any organization I have ever known and it was a privilege to serve as the chairman of its board of trustees for many years. While I was chairman the board not only consisted of high-powered CEOs but also of such luminaries as Dick Cheney, later to become Vice President and one of the smartest men I have ever known; Paul O'Neil, later to become Secretary of the Treasury; and his successor at the Treasury, John Snow, among others. That an immigrant like me could lead such a powerful and distinguished group is yet another demonstration of why this is the greatest country in the world.

∞

When my son-in-law Jon was being operated on at the MD Anderson Cancer Center for his brain tumor, I flew down to Houston to be with Laura at the center. While there, I received an urgent call from the secretary of the Coca Cola board that we had to have an immediate phone meeting of the board, because Doug Ivester had just resigned as CEO. After several hours of discussion we had the announcement ready to go before the stock market opened on Monday. At that point Jimmy Williams, the CEO of Sun Trust Bank, asked Warren Buffet how he thought the stock market would react.

"It will be a nonevent," the legendary investor said.

"Maybe I shouldn't disagree with the Oracle of Omaha," I interjected, "but I think that the stock will take a big hit tomorrow."

Unfortunately I proved to be right as the stock declined about 10%. Warren, to his credit, chased me down in Washington the next day to say, "I'm sorry, I was wrong and you were right. You are the new oracle!"

At the next finance committee meeting, when the Coca Cola CFO asked him a complicated financial question, Warren responded by saying, "I don't know, you better ask Paul!"

∞

A lot of times, if people want to talk with me, they need to track me down at a racetrack. I never lost my interest in horses. When I came to the US, I didn't have the money to continue my activity. Later, when I had the means, it was too late to start riding again, so I decided to get into racing. After some aborted attempts, I met Cot Campbell in 1989. Cot invented the concept of syndicating horses, and partnerships in racing are now very popular. We have had a marvelous partnership ever since. Cot owns and runs Dogwood Stables, and I own one-quarter of each of the 60 to 70 thorough-bred horses we have at any one time.

One of my first horses was Summer Squall, and I was hooked. In 1990, "Squall" won the Preakness in record time and finished second in the Kentucky Derby to Unbridled, whom Squall beat four out of six races over his career. Pat Day, one of the best jockeys ever to ride, said Summer Squall was the most courageous horse he'd ever ridden. At the 1989 Hopeful Stakes in Saratoga, Pat was riding Summer Squall, and they were behind four other horses when they came out of the final turn. Summer Squall saw a bit of an opening and shot through it just before it closed. In fact, Summer Squall got banged around as it was closing, but he had a nose for the finish line and out-sprinted the others. "I didn't push him through the hole, he just went on his own," Pat told me.

Summer Squall retired with earnings of almost $2 million, and sired more than 30 stakes winners, including Charismatic, who won the Kentucky Derby and the Preakness in 1999. In fact, Summer Squall's offspring have bankrolled about $25 million.

I also co-owned Storm Song, the daughter of Summer Squall, who in 1996 was voted the Champion Two-Year-Old Filly after winning the Breeder's Cup. I have co-owned six other Kentucky Derby participants, and we have finished second, third, and fourth. One of these days we will win that race too.

Horse racing is a tough business. The majority of horses win seldom, if ever. I have had my share of losses, but the bottom line is that there is nothing more exciting in sports than watching your horse thunder down the stretch toward victory. And the closer the race, the better . . . as long as we win!

∝

Through racing I have met an enormous number of wonderful people. Cot Campbell and his wife Anne are two of the nicest and most upbeat people one can ever imagine and I prize my partnership with people like Margaret Smith, Jim Wilson, and Jim Pippo. The other owners, the trainers, and the jockeys dedicated to our sport form an interesting and diverse group.

Among the jockeys, Jerry Bailey stands out as the best of the last 20 years. As we go to press, his mounts have earned $296,000,000 and he is poised to break the all time mark of $297,912,019 set by another great jockey and wonderful gentleman by the name of Pat Day. Jerry Bailey used to be my tennis partner but when he discovered golf he was hooked.

Among the trainers two names stand out. D Wayne Lukas, whose horses have earned nearly $250,000,000, is the standard of the industry. In addition to horses, he has trained about a dozen young men and women who have gone on to be successful trainers on their own. The most outstanding is Todd Pletcher, who went on his own at age 29 and now, at age 38, is simply the best. In 2005 his horses earned a record $20.9 million. He is the main trainer for our stable and a great part of our success.

The owners are a wonderful group. They come from a varied background but share a great love for horses. They are people like Robert Clay, Tracy Farmer, Arthur Hancock, Robert Lewis, Jack Oxley, Ogden "Dinny" Phipps, Mack Robinson, Barry Schwartz, Jerry Shields, Mary Lou

Whitney, and many others too numerous to mention. They and their spouses are all fierce competitors, but at the same time we are all friends and pull for each other to come up with the "Big Horse." I feel privileged to call them friends and to share with them the inevitable highs and lows of our sport. The summers in Saratoga are fun and exhausting, with races six days a week and more parties than I can handle.

∞

Every once in awhile my mind drifts back to when I was nine years old and breaking Vespa, the cantankerous horse that no one else could ride. I can still see my mother running out of our house at Chirignago, shouting at my father, *Stop! You're going to kill my boy!* as Vespa tossed me time and again onto the soft grass.

After my father died in 1963, my mother lived in Italy for the rest of her life, though she often visited us in Michigan. She organized a 25th wedding anniversary party for Franca and me in May 1981; most of my cousins came to Venice to celebrate with us. In October of that year, she suffered a stroke and passed away. She was still living alone at the time, not far from Sandra and her husband.

My mother was always a perfect lady, very intelligent and aware of what was going on in the world. A savvy investor, she looked after her own stock-holdings until the day she died. In today's world, she would probably be a business executive.

To the outside world, she looked like a good housewife and mother—which she was. No one would have thought her capable of gaining an audience with Galeazzo Ciano, Mussolini's son-in-law, and successfully demanding the release of her husband. Likewise, she was sweet with Sandra and me, but we knew who was boss. She taught me, among many other things, that you *can* be a nice person and still exert your authority. She was liked and respected, a status I think I achieved in business.

Her health wasn't always the greatest, but she never complained and made the best of whatever life dealt her, just as she did when playing bridge with a weak hand. When she passed away on that October day in 1981, she did so as gracefully as she lived her life.

∞

As for Sandra, she and her husband, Giorgio Sonnino, spent the '60s and '70s in Italy before returning in 1981 to the US, settling in Bloomfield Hills,

Michigan. Sandra late in life found religion; she went through bat mitzvah at the tender age of 67. Sandra and I remained close throughout the years. Though we both understood that I was our mother's favorite, we developed a great friendship and respect for each other. The only argument we ever had was over how to divide the proceeds after my mother passed away. According to the will, we were supposed to split the proceeds in half, but I insisted that she take it all, as I had no need for it. Finally Sandra relented, and we placed the money that she got from the proceeds in an account that I managed for her until the day she died. She passed away in 1996 of congenital heart failure, just two weeks after celebrating her 50th wedding anniversary.

Sandra and JoAnn hit it off wonderfully. Though they knew each other for only half a year or so, Sandra thanked me many times for giving her the sister that she never had.

∽

When JoAnn and I got married, she made me promise that I'd take her to Italy at least once a year, and I've followed through on that. I still have a lot of cousins in Italy, and we enjoy going over and visiting them.

A few years back, on one of our trips to Italy, I went to Bampa, the Venice hat shop from which I knew that my father had bought his hats. I walked into the store, and two elderly gentlemen were there, running it. I greeted the two gentlemen and said, "I think my father used to buy his hats here, but that was a long time ago."

"And what was your father's name?" one of the men asked.

"Max Oreffice."

Both men immediately smiled warmly at me. "Oh, Max Oreffice!" said one. "I remember Max very well. He was a wonderful man."

"Yes, he was," the other agreed. "And elegant. Always impeccably dressed."

I told them how he was better-dressed when he rode his horses than most grooms were at the altar. They chuckled and nodded.

"He always bought his hats from us," the first man said. "We can't tell you how happy we were to see him when he returned after the war was over."

The second man's eyes moistened. "He was the greatest man I've ever known," he said.

"A lot of class went out of Venice the day he died," his partner agreed.

⌘

My father wrote me a letter that he began in June of 1947 and continued in 1949. He was 55 years old when he began it; I was attending Purdue. He never finished or delivered the letter; I ran across it for the first time just a few years ago while I was sorting through some papers. It gave me some insight into what had shaped him and how he responded to things both good and bad in his life. I'm going to reprint a portion of it here.

My dear Paolo,

This is not a letter, this is not a will, this is just a chat that I want to have with you so that it may help you understand the mindset that guided certain actions and attitudes of my life. . . . I don't know if these lines will ever be completed and I don't know for sure that you will ever get them. Maybe I am writing to spend a long spell of time with you during a period of moral depression and, therefore, physical depression.

This is a period of time during which you represent the greatest joy in my life and in Elena's life.

Unfortunately, my youth was dominated by little desire to study; of, therefore, a cultural background that is not very deep, of a memory that is insufficient, of an intelligence that is neither superior nor inferior to normality. I always lived happily and I always came out looking pretty good, using that sprinkling of culture to face any problem superficially. I had a lot of gall, a lot of optimism, and a lot of good will.

The only thing that has been solid and very deep is my moral rectitude that often brought me financial damages but that always brought me a very deep personal satisfaction. . . . I owe this first of all to your grandfather Fausto and to the times in which my personality was formed. I started my independent life very early and so I was lucky to learn what a "free man" really is. . . .

I don't think I have ever hurt anybody, and if circumstances found me to act against lower level people, I did so reluctantly and in the kindest possible way. It was doing good and helping others that always gave me an unequaled internal satisfaction. I had no religious upbringing. My father was a free thinker and . . . free thinkers had their own religion based on rectitude, humanity, and love towards their neighbor, independently of various religions that were, as they are now, full of intransigence (and therefore compromise). These religions always had hidden agendas incompatible with the purity of their theoretical thinking. . . .

I was lucky to live a happy youth, without worries, with little money but lots of hope. . . . But the greatest wealth of the individual was to have the world open to them, without barriers or limitations. Then came the war [World War I], a war we fought feeling sure that once we stomped on the Germans we could go back to normalcy. [The letter at this point was broken off and resumed later.]

After nearly two years, on March 2, 1949, I start these lines again on a train from New York to Washington. My dear Paolo, you left yesterday for Cincinnati to start your fight for life. [I was heading off for my first job, with Seagram's.] *We had lived together for 40 days and I thank you for all the time you gave your old folks. You could not have given us a greater joy. But the separation for an undetermined period of time is, for me, a cruel wound and with the depression of the moment I restart this conversation interrupted so long ago.*

I was convinced that Italy would join with the Anglo-French to stomp forever on Germany's growing arrogance [referring to World War I]. . . . *With these ideals and the certainty that the triumph of our armed forces would bring the world freedom, tolerance, goodness, and prosperity, I fought the whole war with serene tranquility, a sporting spirit, and with extremely high morale, even when the sacrifices of the moment didn't really paint a rosy picture.*

In the disorder that followed the war, masses of malcontents all over, led by people with few scruples, used force at a time when governments were weak and it was difficult to form a parliamentary majority. And this led honest people to abstaining from public life, both in political and administrative positions.

And in the chaos of the period after the war I lived some of the most relaxed and wonderful times of my life. . . . They were years without worries, with little money but lots of dancing, lots of women, and lots of bridge playing. . . . I had found a job with the International Customs in China and I returned to Venice awaiting the departure for the unknown. Instead I found Elena and my life changed.

Yes, Papá, your life changed, and not long after, mine began. And when all is said and done, I was cut in your mold. Your moral rectitude became mine; I took on your distaste for bureaucracy and government intervention. Your optimism strongly influenced me, and as I saw you operate as an independent spirit, an entrepreneur, a maverick in the world of commerce, I operated in a like manner.

I share your distrust of formal religion and your love of bridge. Like you, I was unafraid of risk, undeterred by common opinion. Like you, I always stood up for what I believed was right, even at my own peril.

I held to your ideals of freedom, tolerance, goodness, and prosperity. Those ideals brought you through two wars, one that you fought on the front lines, one from afar. Armed with those ideals, you fought with, as you say, serene tranquility, a sporting spirit, and high morale. Those same principles and ideals are what have guided me through my life. I didn't learn them by chance; I learned them from you.

At the beginning of your letter, you called what you were writing not a letter, but a "chat." I beg to differ; I see it as you truly wrote it: a love letter to me, your son, who had left home and was beginning his own life.

Only now do I realize that this entire book, really, is a response to your letter. It is a love letter to you, Papá, and to Mamma also. The two of you forged in me a passion for life and for freedom, and a will to pursue that passion, that took me places I never dreamed of going, and doing things I never dreamed of doing.

It was your response to Fascism that turned me into a lover of freedom. It was your disgust for dictatorial regimes that made me an unflagging patriot of the United States. It was your willingness to take risks that shone a light on my path. As you were unafraid to venture into the unknown, so was I.

As you went through crises and came out stronger on the other side, I did not fear crises as most people do. Your crises did not break you; they forged you into the man that you became, one that was revered in Ecuador and Italy and America. I did not shy away from my own crises, but faced them with the same equanimity that you did.

It is only in America that an immigrant could come, knowing 50 words of English, and create a new life based on opportunities unheard of in other portions of the world.

It is only in America that an immigrant could take those opportunities, work hard, and rise as high as CEO of one of the top companies in the world.

It is only in America that an immigrant could find the freedom to grow, and take risks, and build a life that is blessed beyond belief.

I remember when you thanked Ludovico Foscari, the Fascist in Venice who forced you to drink castor oil and who threw you in prison. You thanked him because he had given you the idea to use castor oil for good purpose in Ecuador. As I reflect about my early days in Italy, about all that happened, about our escape to Ecuador and then to America, I realize that had it not been for a certain dictator, none of that would have happened.

While I am outraged at how Benito Mussolini ruined the lives of millions of people, he did not ruin ours, did he, Papá? I can honestly say that my life would not have been so wonderful had Mussolini not created the crisis from which we came through.

And so, in solemn remembrance of all the evil he perpetrated, and also with the knowledge that my life was forever changed—for the better—by what was meant for evil, I say this: Thank you, Mr. Mussolini.